A High Price
for Abundant Living

A High Price for Abundant Living

The Story of Capitalism

Henry Rempel

**Herald
Press**

Waterloo, Ontario
Scottdale, Pennsylvania

National Library of Canada Cataloguing in Publication
Rempel, Henry
    A high price for abundant living : the story of capitalism / by
Henry Rempel.
Includes bibliographical references.
ISBN 0-8361-9249-4
    1. Capitalism. 2. Consumption (Economics) 3. Capitalism—
Environmental aspects. 4. Globalization. I. Title.
HB501.R453 2003   337   C2003-903715-0

A HIGH PRICE FOR ABUNDANT LIVING
Copyright © 2003 by Herald Press, Waterloo, Ont. N2L 6H7
    Published simultaneously in USA by Herald Press,
    Scottdale, Pa. 15683. All rights reserved
Canadiana Entry Number: C2003-903715-0
Library of Congress Control Number: 2003108575
International Standard Book Number: 0-8361-9249-4
Book and cover Design by Merrill R. Miller
Printed in the United States of America

10 09 08 07 06 05 04 03 10 9 8 7 6 5 4 3 2 1

To order or request information, please call
1-800-759-4447 (individuals); 1-800-245-7894 (trade).
Website: www.heraldpress.com

To all men and women
who seek to find a balance between
pursuing profit and serving God.

Table of Contents

Foreword

Confused about the New Economy? Don't think you're alone.

Why do protestors shake their fists at the World Trade Organization? Why do local jobs vanish to sweatshops in Asia? What about globalization? Is it just a new buzzword for "the rich get richer"? Why do some companies freely befoul the air I breathe?

Can we make any moral sense of all this?

Here's help.

In a sense, this book was conceived in church. Gerhard Pries, chief financial officer for Mennonite Economic Development Associates (MEDA), was working on some church presentations dealing with economics. He kept getting signals that even many businesspeople who are key players in the capitalist economy do not always fully understand how it operates. He wished for a resource that would explain capitalism in lay terms, and would suggest how ordinary folk could relate to and perhaps even influence it. A book idea was born. He discussed it with MMA president Howard Brenneman, who generously arranged funding for research and writing.

The next step was to find an author, and Dr. Henry Rempel loomed as an ideal prospect. Not only has he taught economics for decades but he also has worked widely in development for organizations like MEDA, Mennonite Central Committee, and others. Few people have his rich blend of theoretical knowledge, a keen grasp of the issues, and grassroots experience.

During the writing, he met regularly with a small reference group representing faith, business, and development to ensure he interacted with diverse concerns and voices. The extruded result is a refreshing new look at the economic forces that drive us.

Rempel explains the system plainly, but that doesn't mean this is Capitalism for Dummies. Not by a long shot. He notes and illuminates the flashpoints where the system either intersects or collides with the realm of values. Besides offering a thoughtful critique of a system that saturates many with privilege he poses prickly questions: Do we worship our abundance? Does our economic system serve us, or dominate us? Then, most pressingly, "Could it be even better?"

Rempel suggests we test capitalism against a number of "shared values" that he draws from Christianity but which other faith traditions could also affirm. What would it take, for example, to ensure our economic system respected human dignity, helped build and maintain community, honored "work" as a form of creative participation, and promoted global peace?

He deals helpfully with two of the biggest economic changes of the twentieth century. One is the rise of powerful corporations that affect our lives far more than we think. Not only do they exert subtle control over us, they also choke competition, which in the mystery of capitalism is what keeps human selfishness in check so the system "works" to the benefit of many.

The other seismic change is the emergent voice of our natural environment that cries "enough" and has started to set limits to the pursuit of abundance. Enter here Rempel's call for a revamped incentive system and "ecolpreneurs" who will blend business ingenuity with environmental sustainability.

Rempel likens the capitalist system to a giant eighteen-wheeler barreling down the highway at breakneck speed. Do the brakes work? How about the steering? Who's driving this rig, anyhow? Does anyone know where it's going? Is it out of control? Since we're passengers, shouldn't we have some say in all this?

Read on.

—Wally Kroeker, editor, *The Marketplace*

Acknowledgments

The challenge to celebrate and to examine critically the comfortable way of life most of us enjoy is the product of a number of people. The initial stimulus came from Gerhard Pries. Howard Brenneman provided tangible encouragement by arranging financial support.

To guide a process of thinking about the way we work, consume, do business, and relate to others there was an initial reference group: Garry Loewen, Margaret Rempel, David Schroeder, James Alty, Karen Schlichting Enns, Albert Friesen, and Stuart Clark. The seven core values presented in the third chapter, which shaped the content of this book, were formed during discussions within this group. The use of Sabbath as a way of challenging our feverish work and our consuming without limit is one example of a value I would not have entered without the guidance of others.

Several members of this reference group also read individual chapters and provided valuable critiques on both content and writing style. Special mention needs to be made of Garry Loewen, who responded to a number of chapters, and David Schroeder, who has read at least one draft of all twelve chapters. Valuable comments also were received from Gerhard Pries and an anonymous reader, who read an earlier draft of the manuscript. Finally, my appreciation to Wally Kroeker who exercised much patience and understanding as he used his editing skills in a valiant effort to make me into a writer.

Where many aided the process of creating this book, I alone carry responsibility for the content selected, the observations presented, and the conclusions crafted in this book.

The behavior of the paparazzi in pursuit of Princess Diana was driven by the market.

1

Driven by the Market

Aahh, coffee! A mug of my favorite Kenyan blend sits before me. Its robust bouquet quickens my senses. Its bracing flavor dazzles my tongue and clarifies thought.

I paid a dollar for it.

It was a bargain when you consider all that was involved in its production. The dollar purchased a whole series of actions undertaken to ensure my personal satisfaction.

First, a farmer in Kenya was persuaded to give up the normal output from a prime piece of agricultural land. He chose not to grow something else, like corn or sorghum.

Second, this farmer decided to plant coffee bushes and tend them carefully for at least two years before they began to bear fruit. Growing coffee is more complicated than growing corn. The fruit is a red berry, which has to be picked and then processed carefully. The coffee beans are the seeds of that berry. It takes forty-eight hours of fermentation to separate a good-quality bean from the berry.

Then the beans had to be shipped five hundred kilometers from the middle of Kenya to the coast, where they were placed on a ship to North America. On arrival, the beans were unloaded and transported to a coffee-production plant. After some sorting, roasting, and packaging, they were shipped to a coffee shop located conveniently near my office. There they were ground to the right texture and the coffee was brewed.

In addition, my dollar paid staff to prepare the coffee, serve it, and wash the mug afterward.

If a customer uses sugar and cream, this story has to be expanded twice over. The sugar story starts with a farmer in the tropics being induced to grow cane, and it follows the journey of the sugar from the cane stalk to the coffee shop, where it is delivered in a highly refined form.

The cream story happens closer to my home. It starts at least three years before the customer's purchase with a farmer's decision to raise dairy cattle. These cows need careful attention and have to be milked twice daily. Before their milk enters the customer's cup in the form of cream, it has to be cooled, separated, pasteurized, and packaged.

A dollar bought all of this. It served to inform a coffee farmer in Kenya, a sugarcane producer in the tropics, and a dairy farmer in Manitoba of my particular tastes. In addition, it motivated a series of persons to coordinate their actions to ensure delivery of quality coffee beans, refined sugar, and fresh cream to my coffee shop in anticipation of the precise moment that I felt the need for my caffeine fix. Seeing this dollar at work is observing the market in action.

How Did All This Happen?

As I savor my coffee and marvel at the economic wonders that delivered it, I must admit that the market has told me nothing about the people who dedicated their labor to assure my pleasure.

- Was the market able to do so much for only a dollar because someone along the way was underpaid? If yes, how can a fair price for a product or a fair wage for labor be determined?
- Would we be able to bid against poor Kenyans, who need food, for the use of Kenya's land to grow coffee if

we did not have large corporations that are able to do business in a number of countries?

- Would I have been able to enjoy my fresh-brewed mug of tasty coffee at a convenient time and place without each business firm involved along the way giving careful attention to its own bottom line?
- If Kenyans can buy six tons of grain by trading one ton of coffee on the world market, are they better off using some of their land to grow coffee instead of food?
- Does my preference for good coffee harm or help other people, either nearby or in Kenya?

To address such questions we need to understand the economic system that governs our lives. This system is a modified form of capitalism sometimes referred to as the free enterprise system, and it serves our society in numerous ways. Many of us value the considerable personal freedom we enjoy within this system, and a number manage to profit from it and enjoy a high material standard of living. A minority, who are not served well, tend to question its value. Some feel that they are its slaves and it is their master.

We'll start our journey toward understanding our economic system with an expanded discussion of the market. Then in the next chapter I'll describe the ideal form of our free enterprise economic system. In chapter 3, I outline seven values that can help us to evaluate the system's performance.

In chapters 4 to 7, I focus on the main actors in the system: consumers, owners of capital and managers of productive resources, workers, and those who control our natural resources. In the final section, chapters 8 to 11, I look at such controversial issues as the government's role, poverty, globalization, and how our economic system affects people in low- and middle-income countries. In chapter 12, I ask where we can go from here and how we might get there.

The Market Provides Information for Decision Making

The market is wherever buying and selling takes place. It is not located in a particular building; nor is it limited to any one country.[1] The market is wherever producers and customers meet to exchange goods. The price they agree on is the market price for that commodity or service. The public and politicians alike need to grasp this reality. The market functions as the core, the nerve center of our capitalist economic system.

One of the market's important functions is to transmit information. The process of buying and selling informs potential customers of what is available, the particular qualities of each product, and the price for which each product can be purchased. It also guides the producer to provide what the customers are willing and able to buy.

A typical example of a thriving North American business firm is the Gibson Farm of Twin Brand Orchards, Inc. The market for the farm's apples used to be the nearby city of Toronto. Then an enterprising son of the owner used modern communications technology to expand the market to all of Canada and to other countries, such as Trinidad.

Filling the World's Basket

It's morning. It's raining. Migrant workers from Mexico are in the orchard, picking McIntoshes, Empires and Cortlands. In the packing plant, machines wash, wax and sort them, and women put them in bags. On the road, six trucks deliver the apples across greater Toronto.

And in the office, Mike Gibson is on the phone. The family has always known how to farm; the key to growth, Mike discovered, lay in marketing. "I don't think I have any kind of product to offer that's substantially better than anybody else's," he says. "I'd be lying to say I did. But since I joined the business four years ago, we've had huge increases in sales." The payroll hit 73 this fall. From $300,000 in sales in 1991, Twin Brand hopes to make $5 million this year. . . .

Three years ago, a farm worker from Trinidad told him, "We used to pay a lot of money for apples at home." That fall Mike loaded a container with Red Delicious apples and shipped them to the Caribbean island. "I went down with the first load I sent: Meet it there, try to sell it, make friends with the people, man," he explains. Now 8% to 10% of Twin Brand sales go to the Caribbean.

From Peter Kuitenbrouwer, "Filling the World's Basket," *The Financial Post* (October 11, 1997), 9. Material reprinted with the express permission of the National Post Company, a CanWest Partnership.

[handwritten margin note: in peoples minds 1. profit 2. religion]

It was information from a migrant worker that alerted Mike Gibson to a potential market for apples in Trinidad, and it was Gibson's act of taking a container of apples to Trinidad that allowed the market for Ontario apples to become established in the Caribbean country.

Major changes in our transport and communications industries have made this global expansion possible. Bargain airfares and easy flight connections enable workers in Trinidad to take temporary jobs in the apple orchards of Ontario. Fax machines, computer networks, the internet, and lower long-distance telephone rates allow information to move quickly and affordably over great distances. Finally, low-cost bulk shipping delivers Ontario apples to overseas consumers at a price they are willing to pay.

The Market at Work

a function of the market

Ultra-efficient communication and transport links are not themselves the market; they simply make it possible for the market to operate smoothly. These facilities relate to the market only if they are used to buy and sell goods and services. The buying and selling takes place according to information transmitted via these transport and communication links. The price set, the experience of the seller, and the ultimate satisfaction of the buyer all become additional information to inform future transactions. This is the market at work.

Sometimes people confuse the market with the free enterprise system; for example, people speak of a "market economy." The market is not a creation of capitalism. Markets existed long before capitalism. They were evident in communist countries like the former Soviet Union, and they still operate in China and Cuba. What is unique to capitalism, however, is a willingness to allow the market to serve as the primary means of communication throughout the economic system.

+ to interpret the communication in a way that is defined as GooD.

The market does not know to communicate certain things ?? externalities ?? long term consequences (the market is like a child, it wants what it wants now, ...

The Soviet Union tried to plan an economy, using computer technology to generate the information considered essential for sound business decision making and to transmit it to central planners. Given the limitations of the human element in accurate data entry, there is no computer system that can assemble as much information, transmit it as quickly, and adjust to changes as rapidly as a market. Hence the Soviet economy operated at a disadvantage, unable to keep up with the countries that allowed the market to direct their economic activities.

The Market Motivates People to Act

The market is more than an efficient communicator of essential information. It can also be a great motivator. For example, the photojournalists who pursued Princess Diana were described as "market driven." This means that the prices being offered for pictures of Diana were so high that the photographers were willing to risk life and limb to get "good" shots.

The more personal, the more intimate the pose of the princess, the higher the price for the photo. Indeed, the content of the picture was often more important than its quality, as evidenced by the grainy and out-of-focus images splashed across many tabloid covers.

Who is willing to pay such outrageous prices for photographs that photojournalists were willing to risk a dangerous, high-speed chase through the streets of Paris? Editors of particular types of newspapers and magazines. Why do these editors behave this way? Because such pictures boost sales. The more readers a publication has, the more it can charge for advertising space. The more ads, and the higher the prices for those ads, the more profits for the owners and shareholders. Newspapers and magazines do not sell in the market unless someone wants to buy them. Therefore, the readers of periodicals that carry such pictures are the real driving force in the market. The paparazzi are merely their willing servants.

You and I may want to deny our involvement in this process. Perhaps we make a point of avoiding such periodicals. But can we judge all those consumers who feel differently? Are they not the best able to decide how to spend their income to satisfy their personal needs and wants? *Short term?*

The photojournalists who pursued Princess Diana in Paris provide merely one illustration of how the market motivates people to behave in certain ways. We all seek to sell something in the market, and we want the best price possible. What most of us have to offer is some form of labor. Some of us sell this labor for a wage or salary. If our skills are specialized or our experience particularly valuable, we may be able to command a much higher wage or salary in the market. Others, who are self-employed, will use their labor to produce a product or a service to sell. Those of us who own capital likely produce goods and services at a particular cost and sell them for as high a price as the market will bear.

Similarly, we spend our money on products and services that we believe will satisfy us best. When we buy a

What Do You Want of Your Media?

Someone asked me a few days after the Paris car crash how I felt about the media's role in the sad affair and whether the media should share some level of guilt. The question really came down to whether the media's prying treatment of Diana, along with other celebrities, was invasive, inappropriate and unacceptable.

People sometimes seem to think that the media exists in a kind of vacuum, purveying information as a kind of public service. Well, a free press is a public service, but it is, and has always been, a business that follows fairly comprehensible laws of supply and demand. And the dynamics of market competition play as much of a role in news and analysis as they do in the sale of nuts and bolts. As a result, the audience is a key "gatekeeper" of what gets into the media. So that question about whether the media treated Diana right is really about the way the media treat anyone or anything; and it's best directed at the audience, because it hinges on what the audience wants and expects of the media.

From Wayne Gooding, "What Do You Want from Your Media?" *The Financial Post Magazine* (October 1997), 10. Material reprinted with the express permission of the National Post Company, a CanWest Partnership.

television set, kitchen appliances, or a car, chances are we seek out relevant market information to get the best model for the lowest price. If we put money away for retirement we likely search the market for where we can get the highest return with the lowest risk.

In all cases, we are market driven.

The Market Guides Us to Agree on Price

The activity of the market is buying and selling. One example is an auction, where the seller gives the auctioneer the right to decide when the price is right and a particular item should be sold. Rather than buying at a fixed price as if they were purchasing a box of corn flakes in a grocery store, the buyers bid against each other until the "right" price has been reached and the auctioneer declares the item sold. If two people both crave a certain item, the price keeps going up until one bidder stops bidding. Occasionally, great bargains can be had if no one else wants an item badly enough to bid the price up.

In a live auction the "right" price for an item—at least the right price on that particular day—becomes known in a very short time. And the rules of the market are clear because there is an auctioneer, a referee who guides the buying and selling process.

Most of the market's activity occurs without an auctioneer. Take, for example, a stock market in New York or Toronto, or a commodity exchange in Chicago or Winnipeg. These are like huge auction sales where agents, rather than the owners themselves, do the buying and selling, and the items being bought and sold aren't nearly as interesting. And there is no auctioneer to close the sale.

In the stock market the items being bought and sold are shares in corporations. The holder of a share is a part owner of the corporation that has issued it. On any given day there are persons who want to sell some of their shares and there

are others who want to buy. Agents, either stockbrokers or
managers of mutual and pension funds, usually do the buying and selling on the actual buyers' and sellers' behalf. As
shares are put up for sale, buying agents bid for them. If one
of them bids high enough to satisfy a seller, a sale occurs. It
really is like a giant auction sale, except here everyone, not
just an auctioneer, is yelling and gesticulating.

If more people want to buy shares than there are shares
available that day, the average price goes up. If more shares
are offered for sale than there are buyers, the price of those
shares will fall from the price set by the stock market the day
before. Changes in stock prices cause increases and decreases
in the indexes that include those stocks, such as the Dow
Jones Industrial Average or the Toronto Stock Exchange
(TSX) index.

In a commodity exchange, people bid on the future purchase or sale of a commodity such as wheat, corn, or pepper.
The purchase of a sixty-day futures contract is a commitment to take delivery of a certain quantity of wheat, at a
price set today, sixty days from now. The seller of the contract is agreeing to deliver wheat under those terms sixty
days hence. *gary — his corn*

Commodity markets allows buyers and sellers to determine a price today for a commodity that will be exchanged
at some future time. This specialized market is made possible because there are speculators who are prepared to buy or
sell today on the basis of what they think the market will be
in the future. This willingness to speculate allows others—
farmers and the processors of commodities—to reduce the
risk of doing business in the future. They can relax a little
knowing that the price of the grain being stored in their bins
will remain constant for at least a period of time. *But maybe less*

The other side of the coin is that, because their price is *then the*
locked in for the next sixty days, the farmers and the proces- *value.*
sors won't necessarily benefit if world prices skyrocket

during this time. The value of futures markets is that they soften the peaks and valleys, bringing a certain amount of stability to business firms that produce and process such commodities.

Commodity exchanges serve more than large farmers and corporations. For example, small farmers in southern India participate in an exchange in Kochi that has been established for pepper.[2] It handles contracts for as little as 2.5 tonnes and is serving six countries that produce pepper. Using futures contracts to reduce risk is important for pepper because it can be held in a warehouse for up to eight years. *farmers combis are expensive.*

The Market Does Not Discriminate

Each sale and each purchase—whether at an auction, garage sale, store, stock market, or commodity exchange—adds another tidbit to the flow of information going to all the other people who are current or potential sellers or buyers in the market.

Some of the information flows suddenly in unexpected places. Parents may recall the frantic rush for Tickle-Me-Elmo dolls some years ago. Just before Christmas, word got around that these furry toys with a built-in laugh mechanism were a must-have item. Stores could not keep them in stock. Prices on the informal market soared, with some people willing to pay just about any price to put one of these dolls under their Christmas tree. $300

Some time later the hot item was the Furby, another furry creature. In that year's pre-Christmas frenzy people were willing to pay up to ten times the retail value for one of these toys. In each case, the information about the toys traveled swiftly and efficiently between buyers and sellers.

Even though the actions of people form the core of the market, the market itself is impersonal. It makes no distinction between money earned honestly with a day's labor

True believer in Market (libertarian) believe no ethics, that ANY money should be allowed.

money obtained in a robbery, money obtained from selling *money inherited* an illegal drug, or money won by gambling. Each exchange of money in the process of buying and selling is merely another tidbit, another signal, that is sent by the market.

The market itself does not exclude anyone, though as a society we may try to limit access to the market. For exam- *yes it does.* ple, we have made it illegal to sell cocaine or child pornography. People who use the market for these purposes are punished if they are caught.

The paparazzi have been compared to sellers of cocaine, producers of child pornography, and murderers for hire. That makes them sound like people we would not want as friends. But in the eyes of the market itself they have just as much right to participate as you and me.

The market has only one method of control over its players—competition. For example, let's say a company discriminates against a certain ethnic group. If there is adequate competition, those discriminated against will be able to ignore this employer and find jobs elsewhere. But, where competition is limited—this firm is one of the few actually hiring at this time—those being discriminated against will suffer from its actions.

In a situation like this, the market itself cannot discipline the offending firm. The public might become sufficiently aroused to cause the government to create laws and regulations that limit the firm's ability to discriminate. Or those suf- *organize* fering from the discrimination might organize a boycott of *consumers* the firm. These actions may influence market performance to *& coalition* some extent. Without corrective actions of some sort, however, competition is the only real protection we have against attempts by others to manipulate the market in their favor.

But the market has few ways to maintain competition

Are Market Prices Fair?

The results produced by the market, a set of prices for various goods and services, are not etched in stone. They vary from person to person, depending on the circumstances. When we are selling, we tend to think the price is too low. When we are on the buying side, we constantly look for bargains.

In a free market, however, the price, over time, will have to be at least as high as the cost of production. Otherwise people will go bankrupt producing that particular good or service, and it will no longer be available. With that one exception, there is no such thing as the right price or a just or fair price. *The market is ethically neutral.*

Periodically throughout history people have resisted this fundamental tenet of the market system. In the thirteenth century, Thomas Aquinas tried to help craftspeople set a just price for their products. He said the price should provide enough income for the craftspeople and their families to maintain their place on the social ladder. The Catholic church at that time favored the status quo and did not want the emerging market to make waves and disrupt things.

Occasionally, we still think this way. In the 1970s U.S. Secretary of State Henry Kissinger condemned oil-price hikes by the Organization of the Petroleum Exporting Countries (OPEC), arguing that they were unjust. To him, a just price for oil was one low enough to allow the United States to maintain its dominant position in the global economy.

A similar logic is used by some people at the University of Manitoba, where I teach. When bargaining for salary increases, we compare ourselves to university professors in the province of Alberta: whatever they get determines what we feel is our just salary. However, the university administrators, who sign our paychecks, use a different yardstick: they argue that our salaries merely need to be a little higher than those of high school teachers in Manitoba. In both cases there is a feeling that we should maintain our place in today's social ladder. We merely disagree on which rung that should be.

An impersonal market also tempts us to behave in

unusual ways. There is tremendous pressure to conform. For example, if other farmers inject their livestock with growth hormones to boost the output of meat or milk, every farmer feels pressured to do the same so as not to be placed at a disadvantage. If our competitors successfully bend the truth in their advertising campaigns, we feel pressured to do the same. No doubt every farmer or person engaged in small business has experienced this kind of competition in the market. Similar ethical dilemmas exist in the professions.

The market is neither just nor fair; it is an impersonal taskmaster.

The Market Is Capitalism's Nervous System

The market's role in capitalism is like the nervous system in the human body. It reaches throughout the geographic, social, and economic space of a capitalist economy and carries signals back and forth through this space. On the basis of these signals the people who make up the economy are stimulated to act. The stimuli of capitalism's nervous system are activated whenever a dollar is paid to purchase a resource, a commodity, or a service. In the opening example, the purchase of a cup of coffee resulted in the sending of a whole series of stimuli that motivated people on three different continents.

The stimuli sent from the brain via the body's nervous system cause the limbs to coordinate their actions to enable the whole body to carry out the complex maneuvers of a sport or the rapid reflex action required to drive a car. In a similar manner, a coin placed in a coffee vending machine can transmit a set of signals via the market that causes totally unrelated persons in faraway places to coordinate their activities so as to deliver a hot cup of coffee with a dash of cream and a touch of sugar.

How these signals are transmitted is typically not visible to the human eye. We cannot observe the flow of electrons back and forth between an electric generating station and our computer. But we understand clearly that if someone pulls the plug and those electrons cease to flow, our emerging ideas will die instantly when the computer screen goes dark. Similarly, if the market breaks down for some reason, economic activity will be distorted and some activities may stop completely.

Market signals, like those resulting when millions of people join me in my morning coffee ritual, are real stimuli motivating decision makers to act. These decision makers act first to serve their own interests. As Adam Smith noted, the reason people have dinner on their table is not that the butcher, the brewer, and the baker are so generous. All three are in business to advance their own interests, the well-being of themselves and their families. But when their acts are coordinated via the market with the selfish acts of many other decision makers, the usual result is that significant material benefits are produced for large numbers of consumers. The market's ability to coordinate your and my selfishness into cooperation for mutual benefit is a wonder to behold.

Besides satisfying consumers, another major benefit of the market is that jobs are created along the way. In the process, though, some people may be short-changed. They may not have the kinds of work skills that the market is willing to pay for, so these new jobs don't benefit them. They may be part of a minority group against which employers discriminate. Or they may have been active as self-employed participants in the past but lost their money (and thus their ticket to play) in an ill-fated investment.

Market signals represent the will of those who spend the majority of dollars. Sometimes, perhaps often, this may seem unfair. If a rich minority of 10 percent of the people possesses more than half of the money spent in the market, they will disproportionately shape the kinds of items bought and sold,

Market is ruled by those w/ most dollars.

as well as the prices for those items. If you are an average consumer with only labor to sell, you may feel that the market does not properly represent your goals and aspirations. In that case you can throw up your hands and go along with the majority, or you can try to opt out of the system and barter for the things you want to buy but cannot produce yourself. The latter strategy seldom works for long. Alternatively, you may choose to become more active in the market and perhaps exert some influence on it. You can rally others to your cause by informing them of better alternatives, or you can become a more active player by devising a product or service that the buying public recognizes as superior to anything else of its kind available.

Ultimately, the control of the economic system by the market is of overwhelming consequence to the whole organization of society. It means no less than the running of society as an adjunct to the market system. The economy is no longer situated respectfully in the context of existing social relations. Indeed, the latter are compelled to change and fit into a powerful economic system.
—*Robert G. Simons*

2

The Capitalist Ideal

The ideal of a capitalist economic system has never been fully realized. Both England and the United States have tried, but the ideal was never implemented completely.

What we have now is a modified form of capitalism. The modifications in the United States are different from those in Canada, but our economic systems are similar in essence. As background for discussion of this current economic system, I first outline the basic elements of the capitalist ideal.

Our Productive Resources Are Limited

The basic economic ingredients every society has to work with are its natural resources (land), human resources (labor), and produced resources (capital). At any point in time, given the technology then in use, the supply of resources available is relatively fixed.

Natural resources include all the gifts of nature: land and its minerals and plant and animal life, water and all it contains, and the air that surrounds our earth. Human

Canadians Join U.S. Consolidation Game

A well-worn Wall Street joke contrasts the reaction of Americans and Canadians when a bank reports a $1-billion profit.

The Canadian audience is outraged at the size of the profit, and demands cuts in service charges and curbs on bank executives' salaries.

The U.S. audience is equally agitated and demands to know: why didn't the bank earn $2 billion?

From Richard Siklos, "Canadians Join U.S. Consolidation Game," *The Financial Post* (January 24, 1998), B5. Material reprinted with the express permission of the National Post Company, a CanWest Partnership.

resources come from people: their labor, thinking ability, organizing ability, willingness to take risks, and ability to care for others. Produced resources are goods made in society for the purpose of producing other goods and services. Some examples are the buildings we use for production, the machines in our factories, and the fertilizer that helps plants grow.

In economics the name for produced resources is capital, though people often mistakenly use the term *capital* to mean the money needed to buy ownership of produced resources. Improvement in human resources in the form of greater skill gained while working at a job or greater knowledge attained while attending a school, is development of human capital.

For a society to have capital it must decide to consume less than it is producing. When this happens, society is saving some of its income. When society saves, it frees up resources that then can be used to make additional productive goods, thus increasing capital. The use of savings to bring into existence producer goods is called investment; an act of saving can simultaneously be an act of investment. Some examples of such investing are clearing land, digging drainage ditches, building fences, and constructing roads, all activities that occurred when North America was first "settled" by Europeans.

Today, saving tends to take the form of putting money into a savings account, purchasing stocks and bonds, making mortgage payments, buying life insurance policies, and contributing to the Canada Pension Plan or the federal Social Security system in the United States. Banks, trust companies, and insurance companies then make these savings available to investors willing to pay the highest price in the form of interest. Taking out a consumer loan—for example, by using MasterCard or VISA—is not considered saving or investing. It merely represents the transfer of the savings of some people to other people so the latter can consume more than they could buy with their own income.

Our Capacity to Want Is Unlimited

Standing alongside these resources are people's many needs and wants. Economics exists as a subject of study because our resources in any year are limited, while our capacity to want is thought to be unlimited. At heart we are like children with the Sears Christmas wish catalogue. Because we want many more goods and services than we can produce, it is essential that we use our resources in a way that will satisfy as many of our needs and wants as possible. That is, we need to economize in the use of our scarce resources.

Economists' contribution to society is the measurement of the cost of wanting more of something in terms of the other things we would have to give up to get it. For example, the accounting cost of a university education includes tuition, fees, books, room and board, and the tax money the university receives for each student. The economic cost of the education includes all of this plus the income the student could have earned by working a job instead of going to school. For most students, getting good grades involves the additional economic cost of sacrificing a rich and varied social life.

A Means to Economize the Use of Resources

The way a society goes about economizing in the use of its scarce resources is its economic system. Three essential questions that every economic system must answer are:

- What goods and services will our society produce?
- How will we produce these goods and services?
- Who will receive the goods and services that are produced?

The method we use to answer these questions is our economic system, capitalism.

In our economic system the people who make up our society own the three types of resources: land, labor, and capital. Most of us own at least one of these, our own labor. Some of us also own land and capital. As participants in the economy we all behave in two ways: we attempt to buy goods and services to satisfy our needs and wants, and we sell or use the resources we own to obtain the income needed to make purchases.

The Consumer Drives the System

The first of the three considerations, what is to be produced, is answered by all of us as consumers. If we demand more of an item, we will bid up its price, thus sending a signal to business firms to produce more of it. Of course, our decision to buy more means we will have less income to spend elsewhere, so the prices of some other goods will likely fall, causing less production there. The resources left idle by this cutback in production can now be used to produce more of the first item, which is in greater demand. This up and down movement of prices in response to our changing demands is the market at work. It directs business firms and farmers to adjust their production decisions to meet consumer demands.

In the real world, though,

Agricultural Commodity Prices Fall Off a Cliff

Hog prices have fallen almost 50% in the past two months alone. Analysts say a record U.S. hog herd, with supply still exceeding slaughter capacity which has been running at a record pace, is prolonging a supply glut. . . .

Laurie Beekman, who helps run a 200-sow operation . . . with husband Gerrit, said their farm was losing $4,200 every week at current prices. The couple has cut spending and remortgaged their land, but Mrs. Beekman is not sure the business will stay afloat if conditions do not turn around quickly.

"We're optimistic that prices are going to go up and we'll grow. But if they don't, we won't be able to survive," she said. Like many consumers, Mrs. Beekman is unhappy with high pork prices in grocery stores. Her frustration is compounded by the knowledge that farmers are netting less than 10% of the retail price for their hard work.

From Ian McKinnon, "Agricultural Commodity Prices Fall Off a Cliff," *The Financial Post* (December 12, 1998), C1. Material reprinted with the express permission of the National Post Company, a CanWest Partnership.

these decisions, actions, and price changes do not occur in the same day. The process can be slow. Take, for example, the hog crisis of 1996. Many farmers, noticing that hogs had been getting high prices, decided to get in on the bonanza. They shifted their resources out of other commodities to invest in hog barns and breeding stock.

Two years later, when the mature hogs were ready for market, the price suddenly declined. Why? For one thing, too many farmers had gone into hogs. For another, an economic crisis in Asia caused a sudden drop in world demand. What appeared to be a sound business decision one day turned into a disaster and forced many family farms into bankruptcy. Their land, barns, and breeding stock were bought up at bankruptcy prices by other people, to produce hogs or something else. Others tried to hang on in spite of the losses, in the hope that hog prices would eventually climb back up. And they did, tripling only a year later.

Competition Eliminates Inefficient Producers

The second question, how things are to be produced, is resolved by competition among producers. Since consumers like low prices, the company that can produce an item more cheaply will generally enjoy better sales. Other companies will end up having to make the necessary changes in their production processes so they can compete. A producer using less efficient methods will have to change or risk going out of business.

The Economist lists a variety of approaches firms use to gain a competitive edge so they can survive.

- Innovate: Gillette has come out with the Mach 3 razor, which is intended to give a closer shave with less irritation, and the CrossAction toothbrush, designed to remove 25 percent more plaque than the average toothbrush.

- Offer extra services: McDonald's has spent $500 million on a new cooking system so staff can make burgers to the customer's order.
- Offer special services at a premium price: National Bicycle Industrial builds bicycles that match the customer's height and weight, and they make them in the customer's preferred color.
- Merge with other companies to gain economies of scale: Exxon merged with Mobil, and Daimler Benz with Chrysler.
- Keep inventory stocks low: Dell keeps its inventory of computers low to save money by reducing warehouse and handling costs.
- Reduce the amount of debt relative to the overall value of the company.[1]

Our Share of the Output Is Tied to What We Contribute

The answer to the third question, the distribution of the output, is determined by two things: the prices we obtain for our own resources, such as our labor, and the quantity of resources we own. For example, professional athletes and movie actors typically make much more money than nurses, teachers, and day care workers. Our willingness to pay high wages to athletes and movie stars gives them a much higher standard of living than the average worker. In other words, they are getting more of society's output than most of us are. Similarly, people who own many resources, such as land and capital as well as labor, also receive a much larger share than those of us who have only labor to offer.

This does not mean capitalism is value-free. Rather, the value prized most highly, above either equity or fairness, is individual freedom. The opportunity for all to act freely, voluntarily, without being compelled by the state or by society's customs is of prime importance.

This form of distribution of profit, based on such freedom of enterprise, contributes to the large disparity between the wealthy and the poor. The existence of profit, which is a reward for being entrepreneurial and willing to take risks, is not unique to capitalism. What is unique is that the profit flows to the owners of capital, the capitalists. In a socialist system, by contrast, the profit does not flow to individual owners, but is shared more widely.

The Origins of Capitalism

This ideal form of capitalism has never been applied completely anywhere. It came closest to full use in the middle of the nineteenth century in England and in the 1920s in the United States. As an approach to economizing society's scarce resources, it was first spelled out in 1776 by Adam Smith in his Inquiry into the Nature and Causes of the Wealth of Nations.[2] Smith had two major goals. First, for the "good of the nation" he wanted to reduce government interference and replace it with greater individual freedom. After all, he reasoned, if every individual had the freedom to achieve her or his potential the result would be the greatest possible good for the whole nation. Second, he wanted to see England enjoy the great increase in output that he felt would result from a division of labor.

Adam Smith's Visit to a Pin Factory

Smith uses his visit to a pin factory to illustrate the concept of the division of labor. At the factory he observed that a single person making a whole pin could produce about twenty pins a day. Ten people could make two hundred pins. But, he observed, if the pin-making process were divided into separate tasks in which one person would draw

> Business underlies everything in our national life, including our spiritual life. Witness the fact that in the Lord's Prayer the first petition is for daily bread. No one can worship God or love his neighbor on an empty stomach.
>
> —Woodrow Wilson (1912)

the wire, another straighten it, a third cut it, a fourth point it, and so on, ten persons working as a team could produce 48,000 pins a day. This form of specialization made each worker 2,400 times more productive than one person doing the whole job alone. This is what he called division of labor.

The way to reach these two goals of increased production and the good of all, according to Smith, was to set up an economic system in which persons seeking their own selfish ends would work for the good of everyone. This is basically what happens under capitalism, provided that everyone owns roughly the same amount of resources and there is enough competition to prevent any one buyer or seller taking advantage of others. These conditions were largely present in England during Smith's time, and they still prevail, in most cases, in the small towns and rural areas of North America. (where Big farmers are buying out smaller ones)

What Guided Adam Smith?

To understand why Smith proposed capitalism as the way to achieve these goals and why his ideas were received so well, we need to keep in mind the conditions of late-eighteenth-century England. First, God was understood as the one who had created everything and had provided everything the earth needed to operate well. No further interference was needed, not even from God. The various laws of nature that control physical behavior had just been discovered. The most obvious example was the law of gravity, which, according to Newton, is what causes an apple to fall down if it is detached from the tree.

Smith was convinced that the same God had provided us with additional natural laws, such as that of supply and demand, that would guide our social behavior. To him it was as natural as the law of gravity that producers would not continue to make (supply) a certain item if no one wanted it (demand). Therefore, Smith started a crusade to get rid of obstacles such as government, which kept interfering and making regulations that prevented the natural laws from working. His firm belief in the existence of these laws—he called them the invisible hand—led him to advocate a system in which each individual is allowed to pursue selfish ends as the means to achieving his two goals.

Smith also viewed nature as stingy. Up to that point, people had viewed nature as plentiful: all they had to do was apply some labor and they would be rewarded with gifts of nature. That didn't mean it would necessarily be easy, for even Adam and Eve had to get their daily bread by the "sweat of their brow," but nature provided enough for them to live. Smith believed this was no longer true. Nature did not provide enough to meet all human wants and people had to do more than apply labor to receive its gifts. They also had to build capital, which could be used with labor to squeeze more out of nature.

Finally, Smith had specific views on the nature of human beings. He believed that

- people are selfish;
- people are basically lazy and will work only if forced or paid to do so;
- people love to trade, and to bargain with each other while trading; and
- people take better care of that which is their own.

This last point is basic to capitalism and forms the rationale for the private ownership of resources. According to this view, resources will be handled best if their owners are also the managers of their use. Further, our dislike of work makes it important that we get paid only if we contribute to production. Then our selfishness, coupled with the fact that we find trading enjoyable, will ensure that the necessary goods are produced and distributed.

The market does not guarantee that we will receive quality products that are safe to use or consume, but there is a general assumption that quality will pay off eventually. The producer or seller who wants customers to keep coming back has a built-in incentive to pay attention to quality control. Smith was confident that as long as consumers could choose from a number of sources, competition would force producers to make sure their output was safe.

The Capitalist Drives the System

The need to produce capital justifies using some of our resources now to make producer goods so we will have a greater ability to produce in the future. Also, because having more capital goods is desirable, charging interest on loans is justified. A capitalist will borrow your and my savings from a bank where we have deposited them and will put them to work in, say, a factory. The capitalist intends to receive sufficient income from this factory to repay the loan to the bank, cover the interest being charged for the use of our savings, and still make a profit. Such an exchange of money is essential for the operation of capitalism.

The interest charged within this system is not the same kind of interest that was condemned by Jesus and by the church throughout history. That interest was on loans for consumption—as when a borrower takes out a loan to buy groceries—not for future production. Those loans might keep borrowers from starving but do not provide them with the means to repay the loans plus interest.

The key person in this investment process is the capitalist. The capitalist is willing to save or to persuade others to save by paying interest, then to put the savings to work in the high-risk business of earning more income. Capitalists are willing to live for the future rather than spending all of their income on the pleasures of today.

The Significance of Adam Smith's Ideas

Smith's ideas are significant for several reasons. First, they have worked, at least in selected countries and for certain time periods. What he wanted was greater individual freedom and an expanded capacity to produce material things. North America provides adequate testimony to capitalism's success in achieving these goals.[3]

Second, there is nothing just or moral about capitalism. The driving force of the system is human selfishness. The spoils go to the winner, provided that the winner has not been caught using illegal methods. Smith's expectation that there will be five hundred poor people for every rich person is hardly a way to build community.

> For one rich man, there must be at least five hundred poor, and the affluence of the few supposes the indigence of the many. The affluence of the rich excites the indignation of the poor, who are often both driven by want and prompted by envy, to invade his possessions. It is only under the shelter of the civil magistrate that the owner of that valuable property, which is acquired by the labour of many years, or perhaps of many successive generations, can sleep a single night in security.[4]

Third, Smith assumed that the ability of one person to take advantage of another person, either as an employer or as a seller of goods and services, is limited by competition. If each employee has numerous opportunities to work elsewhere, the employer's selfishness will be held in check. Similarly, if each consumer has a number of places at which to buy the same item, no one producer of that item will be able to exploit the consumer. This controlling device within capitalism is called competition.

The competition Smith envisioned is very different from some forms of competition we have today, like Ford's competition with General Motors, or the competition that America Online and Netscape together can pose to Microsoft. The competition Smith envisioned requires each producer and consumer to be too small, compared to the total size of the market, to have significant influence over the market as a whole. If any one person decides not to buy or sell, the effect on the market price will be negligible. In Smith's time almost all businesses were small, so this assumption was reasonably valid.

I concur with Adam Smith that without the control imposed by effective competition, the selfishness of some will enable them to exploit others. Even in his day collusion was a temptation. He observed that when people in the same line of business met, even just for lunch or socially, they soon ended up discussing how to advance their joint interests at the expense of the buying public.

Fourth, although Smith wanted to see government's role reduced so that individual freedom could be expanded, he did see several necessary functions for government. He thought that it was government's responsibility to set the rules by which the game of capitalism was to be played; government would draw up laws, especially property law and contract law. Government would also provide the referee in the form of the court system. Also, Smith believed that some vital services, like police and the military, simply would not be provided adequately if left solely to our demanding them individually. Since Smith's time we have expanded these necessary services to include road construction, education, mail delivery, fire protection, and garbage collection.

The Role of Money

We think of money as coins and pieces of paper. Actually, money is anything generally accepted within a community as a means of payment, including the payment of debt. Our forebears used beads and beaver skins. In prisoner of war camps cigarettes frequently serve as money. In certain African societies bride wealth is paid with cattle.

By serving as a kind of shorthand for units of exchange, money makes it possible for the capitalist system to operate. It is a great lubricant for the mechanism we call the market.

Let's look at Smith's visit to the pin factory. To take full advantage of the specialization Smith had in mind there has to be a market that will buy 48,000 pins every day. That's a lot of pins. A market that large requires a large geographic region with enough people who have sufficient income to buy that many pins. Selling to such a large market also requires money. Without money, the pin makers would have to find people who want pins and are willing to offer something desirable in trade. With money the pin makers can accept money for their pins and then use it to buy whatever they want.

Remember the cup of coffee at the beginning of this book? The market is able to coordinate the actions of a number of persons to deliver my cup of coffee for a dollar only because there are millions of coffee drinkers like myself. The existence of money around the world enables all these coffee drinkers to express their demand and facilitates the high degree of specialization evident in coffee production.

The Evolution of Money and Banking

Precious metals such as gold and silver were once common forms of money. Initially they were weighed out each time payment was made. Eventually rulers created coins bearing their own image. Each coin represented a certain weight of gold or silver. Some users could not resist chipping a tiny piece off of each coin they received. Once a coin was too chipped people refused to accept it as payment and the coin ceased to be money. It had to be melted down and recast once more as a coin.

The rich had some difficulty protecting all their coins, but neighborhood goldsmiths had vaults where coins could be stored safely. A goldsmith would issue a receipt for the gold deposited. Eventually people could not be bothered to go to the goldsmith every time they wanted to make a purchase, so they started passing the goldsmith's receipts around as money. That was the beginning of what we now know as paper money, such as a five- or ten-dollar bill.

Goldsmiths then began to observe that most of the gold remained on deposit most of the time. This led to the temptation to lend some of the gold through the back door to close friends in need of cash. As long as the borrowers did not tell anyone where the gold came from, the depositors all thought their gold was still safe in the goldsmith's vault.

These goldsmiths were the forerunners of modern-day banks. Today banks freely lend out deposits, counting on the fact that only a small percentage of the total depositors will show up on any given day to withdraw their money. So even though you think your money is sitting safely in the bank, the reality is that someone else likely has borrowed part of it and is using it to make an investment or to buy something they desire. This system enables the banks to create a multiple amount of money so that the value of checking account deposits in banks is many times larger that of the paper currency and coins in circulation. Indeed, we do most of our buying and selling by moving bank deposits around with checks and debit cards, rather than paying cash.

The advent of money greatly facilitated the operation of markets, and with improved, expanding markets, the opportunities for specialization and trade increased. The European Community's creation of a common currency, the euro, is simply another example of how a growing market demands a new means of making payments that is acceptable to all persons.

The Corporation Emerges as a Challenge to the System

Many things have changed since Adam Smith first devised his system of capitalism. We have realized a standard of living that Smith and his early supporters never dreamed possible. The role of government in the economy has expanded, especially since the Great Depression of the 1930s.

The change with the most impact on capitalism is the emergence of the corporation. In a corporation two or more individuals combine to form a separate legal entity that can exist and conduct business as if it were a person. It takes on a life of its own and continues to exist even after the original owners have died. Beyond offering possible tax advantages, the corporation protects owners from being personally sued for the unpaid debts of the corporation if it fails. The courts accepted the legality of corporations as a way of organizing business in the nineteenth century. Corporations have multiplied rapidly since then, especially in industries where much capital is needed because of economic advantages to being large.

corporation, n. An ingenious device for obtaining individual profit without individual responsibility.

—Ambrose Bierce, *The Devil's Dictionary*

The corporation has changed the operation of the capitalist economic system significantly. First, because it allows owners of capital to combine and act as if they are one, the competition essential to control the possible bad effects of individual selfishness, such as exploitation of employees and customers, has been much reduced. The effect of the early corporation on employees was so harsh that it was only a matter of time—some eighty years in North America—until a majority of people accepted the right of employees to fight back by combining into a union so they could act as one when dealing with employers. In lower-income countries, however, where branches of the largest corporations operate, people have not been able to or have not been allowed to organize into unions or larger groups to gain greater equality in bargaining power.

A number of corporations have grown to gigantic size and have become powerful forces in our economies. Some of them outrank many countries in terms of the value of their production. One example would be Nestlé. It has such brands as Nescafé coffee, Perrier water, KitKat chocolate and Friskies pet food. Since 1985 it has spent $44 billion purchasing other companies. It now operates in eighty-four countries and has annual sales in excess of $50 billion.[5]

The second change brought on by the emergence of the corporation is that the important link between the ownership and management of resources has been broken. In larger corporations the managers are hired professionals who actually own very little of the corporation. As an unnamed middle manager within General Motors indicated, there is little difference between a manager's corporate role and that of a government bureaucrat.

> The salary of the chief executive of the large corporation is not a market award for achievement. It is frequently in the nature of a warm personal gesture by the individual to himself.
>
> –John Kenneth Galbraith, *Annals of an Abiding Liberal*

Third, the existence of corporations requires growth. Success is almost always defined in terms of growth. As a result, the problems created by corporations have increased while our personal control over what we would like to see produced has decreased considerably. Advertising has become a vital tool used by corporations to make sure consumer desire grows according to what the firms would like to produce. Though the unpopularity of Edsel car in the 1950s and the New Coke debacle in the 1980s demonstrate that advertising campaigns can flop, the successes greatly outnumber the failures. Further, because advertising subsidizes what we pay for our newspapers and magazines, what

we hear on the radio, and what we see on television, corporations have considerable control over what appears in each
of these media.   NPR now has to pay attention to Corp.

In conclusion, capitalism is a means to achieve both
greater individual freedom and increased production of
material things. It has done both. Its continued success has
been thrown into question, however, by the emergence of
corporations and, subsequently, of labor unions. Both of
these undermine the competition and freedom that Adam
Smith so treasured. In North America we have a strong
desire to maintain capitalism, so we respond to the threat of
corporations by asking government to do more, but this
causes government to grow ever larger and thus robs us of
some other freedoms. The economic price of these lost freedoms is the high standard of living we enjoy.

The discipline of economics is less a science than the theology of that religion, and its god, the Market, has become a vicious circle of ever-increasing production and consumption by pretending to offer a secular salvation. The collapse of communism ... makes it more apparent that the market is becoming the first truly world religion, binding all corners of the globe more and more tightly into a worldview and set of values whose religious role we overlook only because we insist on seeing them as "secular."

—*David R. Loy* p299

3

Sacred Values and the Worship of Abundance

The ideas of Adam Smith contributed to a major economic and industrial revolution in Europe. Smith lived at a time when the rights of the state and its supreme ruler, the king, were greater than the rights and freedoms of individuals. It was a time when merchants were glorified—both local traders and the international explorers who went off to "discover" new worlds for Europe. These merchants created new markets and opened up fresh sources of raw materials that made possible the increased specialization of labor that Smith observed in his visit to the pin factory.

Mercantilism

New Ideas Can Shape the Future

For ideas to shape the course of history numerous ingredients are required. In the case of Adam Smith, one ingredient was his penetrating critique of what was wrong with the existing system. The people who wanted the freedom to engage in their own businesses and to spend their own income cheered his critique of the state's visible and powerful fist. His concept of an invisible hand as the organizing principle for business was a most attractive alternative.

Second, Smith presented a clear alternative: the free enterprise system as a utopia that people could aspire to. We know today that heaven on earth is hard to achieve. But at the time, the promise of greater wealth coupled with the individual freedom to choose and to do business was an attractive ideal.

Third, the conditions were right to capture the imagination of a large number of people who sought a better life for themselves. By 1776, when Smith's *Wealth of Nations* was published, markets had grown enough to facilitate widespread expansion of labor specialization. Different forms of money had been created throughout the enlarged nation-states of Europe, and the resource base had expanded so much that many people other than upper-class nobles could taste the prospect of a standard of living well above mere subsistence.

Finally, the prevailing belief system, deism, conditioned people to believe that God had put in place a natural order that would benefit everyone if they let it operate freely. Deists saw God as a clockmaker who builds a fine clock and then lets it run without further tinkering. As Bob Goudzwaard argues, deism opened the door to the belief that human destiny is determined not by God, but by human beings.[1]

> The barrier of the divine shaping of history's destiny, which is part and parcel of the spiritual legacy of medieval society, had to be removed before the structure of modern capitalist social order could be crowned with success.
> This enormous task was accomplished by the spiritual movement known as deism.
> It fundamentally changed medieval faith in providence in two ways: first, by forcing the role of governing and intervening God back to the time before the beginning of human history; secondly, by couching this "indirect" divine control in a cloak of "providence" which guarantees only good results, at least for those who are willing to take the natural order into continuous consideration.[2]

The widespread acceptance of Smith's ideas, first in Europe and then in North America, contributed to an industrial revolution. This revolution made possible a higher standard of living for an emerging middle class as well as for the nobility. But by doing so it also ensured ongoing scarcity. Why? Because the new free enterprise system had no concept of enough; it promoted the worship of abundance.

Abundance as an Object of Worship

The industrial revolution wasn't the only thing happening to change life in Europe. Because the supply of natural resources was relatively fixed and the pool of available laborers was expanding only at the same pace as the population, something else had to become the chief resource to enable expansion of output to meet the rapid growth in demand. This task fell to capital. Hence the capitalist, who mobilized and employed capital, replaced the merchant as the key person in society, the one who would make "good things" happen. That is why Smith's free enterprise system is more popularly known as capitalism.

Historians are divided on one issue. A first school of thought argues that Smith cut economics off from its ethical foundation. This school gives Smith credit for doing what was needed to enable economics to evolve as a science: economists no longer had to be concerned with questions of what ought to be and could instead concentrate on studying what is.[3] The second school of thought denies that this occurred. Its proponents argue that Smith simply substituted one religion for another. They point to his concept of an invisible hand: rather than ensuring that all individual activity will work toward a larger social good, the invisible hand was a new kind of god. The quote from David Loy that opens this chapter illustrates this second school of thought.

Regardless of which school is correct, the reality is that we have come to worship abundance. One image, especially evident at Thanksgiving, is Mother Nature pouring her bounty from the Horn of Plenty. Another is the advertising industry's continual depiction of a normal lifestyle as something just beyond what the middle class can afford. The feminine character of abundance is asserted by advertising's prominent use of women as the means for selling this desired standard of living.

Values That Shape Our System

The intent of this study is to expand our understanding of the economic system, not to expand economics as a science. We need to ask some serious questions about this worship of abundance. Are we supposed to be served by our economic system, or dominated and ruled by it? We should do more than critique our system; we should ask instead, "Could it even be better?"

The Economist argues the prevailing values of Western Europe in Adam Smith's day favored an economic system dedicated to promoting growth.[4] This economic growth formed the basis for the progress we enjoy today. Other societies, less open to change or less interested in worldly goods, generated their own economic systems and have become low- and middle-income countries.

The Bases of Progress

Economic growth is a process of economic change. So an appetite for change, or at least a willingness to live with it, is essential if a society is to get richer. . . .

A readiness for change is only one of the values required. Acquisitiveness is another—an interest in worldly goods, a regard for the material as well as the spiritual, a will to exploit nature for man's benefit. Yet naked greed is no use. Growth requires investment—an investment is gratification deferred. The enlightened self-interest praised by Adam Smith combines the desire for wealth with prudence and patience.

Growth also requires another kind of self-lessness. A modernising society has to move away from self-sufficiency, in individual households, villages, towns, regions and states, towards interaction at all those levels, through specialisation and trade. This in turn demands that enlightened self-interest include an ethical component. Without trust and regard for one's reputation, the wheels of commerce do not spin.

Altogether, it is an improbable blend. Partly through religion, however, Western Europe developed a system of values that favoured all of the above. Other cultures, it seems, were less conducive to growth.

From "The Road to Riches," *The Economist* (December 31, 1999), 12. The Economist Newspaper Ltd. All rights reserved. Reprinted with permission. Further reproduction prohibited. www.economist.com.

Did we choose the better path to progress? How can we evaluate what constitutes better and what constitutes progress? To help us form a basis for such an evaluation, I propose a set of sacred values that are shared widely by people across numerous societies.

I have defined this set of values in conversation with a reference group that met regularly to advise on the content and approach of this book. Together we drew on our various knowledge specialties to formulate a basic core of principles by which to critically assess the performance of our capitalist economic system. They are sacred values in that they represent the transcendent promise of what can be as well as warning against the destructive potential of what might occur if we maintain our present course.[5]

The purpose of this chapter within the larger discussion of how our economic system operates is to identify those sacred values that overlap with or should impinge on our economic system. The set of seven sacred values is not exhaustive, but it is a good starting point. These values relate most closely to Christianity. Some of them are also shared by the other major religions.[6]

Sacred Values for Evaluating Capitalism

Human Dignity

The first sacred value is the dignity inherent in every person. The Creator, who granted a special status to human beings, bestowed this dignity.

The biblical account of creation describes this special status as being created in the image of God. While all created things express something of the creator,

> Then God said, "Let us make persons in our image, after our likeness; and let them have dominion over the fish of the sea, and over the birds of the air, and over the cattle, and over all the earth, and over every creeping thing that creeps upon the earth." So God created people in his own image, in the image of God he created them; male and female he created them.
>
> —Genesis 1:26-27

people explicitly reflect attributes of God. Think of an artist who is deeply inspired by a particular object and creates an abstract painting to express what she sees within that object. The painting does not depict the exact nature and dimensions of the object, but it does show us some of the features that first inspired the artist.

The psalmist's portrayal of the same idea in Psalm 8, communicates our dignity and our authority to represent God within the larger created order. We have been given a position of honor and an exalted responsibility to help sustain the order that the Creator has initiated.

Given this awesome task, any institution or system that we create should likewise maintain human dignity and help us carry out these duties our Creator has placed on us. An economic system that serves some people but denies the human dignity of others is not consistent with what the Creator intended. All of us, rich and poor, carry some aspect of the image of God.

> When I look at your heavens, the work of your fingers,
> the moon and the stars that you have established;
> what are human beings that you are mindful of them,
> mortals that you care for them?
>
> Yet you have made them a little lower than God,
> and crowned them with glory and honor.
> You have given them dominion over the works of your hands;
> you have put all things under their feet,
> all sheep and oxen, and also beasts of the field,
> the birds of the air, and the fish of the sea,
> whatever passes along the paths of the seas.
>
> O Lord, our Sovereign,
> how majestic is your name in all the earth!
>
> —Psalm 8:3-9

Living Together with Others

Not only have we been stamped with the likeness of God, we also have been created as social beings. We were not created to be hermits. Every woman and man has been created in such a way that our ability to live and be depends on being in relationship with each other within communities of people. As Robert Simons has written, individuals do not exist for the purpose of creating communities; rather, the community is the necessary context from which an individual identity can emerge.[7] Individual freedom is not an end in itself; one can become free to be only when one is in community with others.

To build community we need to respect each other just as God has respect for each human being. There are limits to how far we can go in making decisions for others. Dignity means allowing persons to err, to make decisions that may not be right for themselves or the community. Respecting people's dignity then requires holding them responsible for their decisions.

The dictionary defines community at several levels, as:

- a unified body of individuals such as a state or a commonwealth;
- a body of persons or nations having a common history or common social, economic, and political interests;
- people with common interests living in a particular area; and
- a group of people with a common characteristic or interest living together within a larger society.[8]

What do we mean by community? While the term has several shades of meaning, most people understand a community to be a group of people in a particular area who have some degree of interest in living together in relative harmony and well-being.

I propose that one goal of an economic system should be to help create an environment in which communities of people can emerge and flourish. Such a system has several elements.

- It incorporates all people; it is inclusive.
- It promotes the discipline of being attentive to the needs of others as well as one's own needs.[9]

- It creates the institutions required to enable all persons to participate within the community.
- It includes a shared political discourse that enables the participants to shape the aims of the community and to access the means to attain those aims.

In summary, an economic system should build and enhance communities in which mutual interdependence, human dignity, and the material well-being of all persons are promoted and, hopefully, realized. Economic policy should protect and strengthen such communities. The division of labor should demonstrate our mutual interdependence and underscore the importance of all human beings in a community.

Work as a Form of Creative Participation

Where human dignity is valued, everyone in the community has to participate. Having purposeful work is part of being created; we are called to till and keep the garden, the royal park of our Creator. We carry the responsibility to work the garden and to preserve it from damage.

Our physical, mental, and spiritual well-being depends on the fulfillment of our right to participate in a community. This right carries with it the responsibility to be an active, productive participant. And carrying out our duty calls for an appropriate level of reward for our labor.

Work gives us a way to express our creative spirit as well as a way to help develop society. When work fails to be this— for example, in the assembly line job described by Juli Loesch—it detracts from the dignity of the person performing it.

> Here's my machine, a plastic injection molder. It's not a tool, since it is in no way an extension of me or my skills. It isn't a co-worker, since there is no communication between me and it. No, when the mold snaps open and shut

and the plastic parts drop into the tray below, I spring into action. I scoop up the parts, throw away the plastic connecting "gate," put four parts on the cooling bars, and take four other parts off. Then I smooth their edges with a metal file. . . .

Anyway, the snapping open and shut of the mold is what springs me into action, like a reflex. The machine is, in a sense, my brain. I am its arms. I am its tool.

When my function is completed, it takes a few seconds before the mold snaps open again. During these few seconds, my mind is free. It's about long enough for three-fourths of a "Hail Mary."

But trying to pray while watching for the mold to open is like trying to make love while waiting for a bus. It lacks a certain presence.

I can't pray, since prayer is the activity of a thinking creature, and I can't think. But the problem remains: how to occupy that three-fourths-of-a-Hail-Mary's worth of time between the completion of my little function and the beginning of the next cycle.

The curse of this work is not its monotony. I've spent a day making furrows with a hoe and planting corn, but at least I could joke with Tommy Jean and his father, Mr. Woodard. "Gal, you work like a mule!" said Woodard— but I was not reduced to an animal: I was elevated to a friend and an object of affection.

And God knows that folding five thousand leaflets, chopping infinite and everlasting vegetables for the soup kitchen, or even walking a picket line are not stimulating craftsmanship or skilled labor. Yet in such activity one finds the possibility for either true sociability (singing and talking) or quiet and true solitude. Assembly-line work has neither sociability nor solitude, neither body-gratifying activity nor imagination.

"From the factory dead matter goes out improved, whereas (human beings) there are impaired and debased" (Pope Leo XIII).[10]

It's not that the type of work defines the dignity of the worker. Rather, the worker grants dignity to the work. Work does not have dignity in and of itself; it has dignity because a human person performs it.

This idea of workers granting dignity to work may sound strange today. We no longer value work in its own right; society values it on the basis of what the market will pay for it. As a result, we give much higher honor to multimillionaire athletes, movie stars, and corporate executives than to the parents, child-care workers, and teachers who shape the very future of our society.

Work needs to be redefined in much larger terms than merely how we earn a living; it is not good enough to judge the value of work by what it can earn in the labor market. Indeed, it's possible that today's version of tilling and keeping the garden may not always be found in a paid job. Our activities as volunteers in the community or during retirement may reflect this vocation better than the jobs we pursue throughout our "working life." The nature of what we name work needs to change so the term can more accurately reflect our vocation as human beings. We especially need to find ways to value the work carried on within the home and the service that is called "voluntary work." We need to recognize that these too are vital for human community.

We are all unique people who are called to develop our gifts in relationship with others. A just economy should encourage creativity, skill, and diligence. Human productivity and a sense of vocation will benefit all of society and give everyone a sense of accomplishment and participation. An economic system should call forth the creative and creating nature of human beings.

Sharing Responsibility for Ongoing Creation

As a form of creative participation within a community of people, work is not limited to the building of such communities. Included in our job description is the vocation, bestowed by the Creator, to share in the ongoing process of creation. The Genesis creation story gives us the dignity and authority to be God's junior partners in thus sustaining creation.

Genesis outlines several specific responsibilities within this general vocation of co-creator:

- We are instructed to be fruitful, to multiply, to fill the earth.
- We are given the honor of naming the other living beings that were created.
- We are called upon to till and to keep the garden.
- We are instructed to subdue, to exercise dominion over, the created order.

This is a shared responsibility: God calls on us to co-manage the ongoing process of creation. The mandate to multiply and replenish the earth establishes our responsibility to provide for ongoing life. Initially it required population growth, but that is hardly our need today.

Life and death are closely interwoven, each forming an important part of the natural process. Even though we have spent vast resources trying to extend human life, we are not able to avoid the reality of death. Still, we are called to consistently choose life over death, and not merely human life but all life. If we fail to do so we deny the co-management duties God has entrusted to us.

> So God created human beings in the image of God; male and female he created them. And God said: "Let them have dominion over the fish of the sea, and over the birds of the air, and over the cattle, and over all the earth, and over every creeping thing that creeps upon the earth." And God brought to them every beast of the field and every bird of the air, to see what they would call them; and whatever they called every living creature, that was its name.
>
> And God blessed them, and God said to them, "Be fruitful and multiply, and fill the earth and subdue it; and have dominion over the fish of the sea and over the birds of the air and over every living thing that moves upon the earth." And it was so.
>
> And God saw everything that he had made, and behold, it was very good. And there was evening and there was morning, a sixth day.
>
> —Excerpts drawn from Genesis 1 and 2

Our shared responsibility also authorizes us to name and identify all that is created. The naming process is a powerful means to create the various structures that serve and govern our lives. Where structures are created that destroy rather than create, it is our duty to expose what is named falsely.

Another aspect of our special vocation, to exercise dominion over the rest of the created order, requires interpretation. This does not give us license to destroy the created order. Rather, the term *dominion* implies the need to make decisions that affect life and death. God has given us both the ability and the responsibility to manage in a way that affirms life.

We may have carried out this role badly during the past two hundred years, but that's no excuse to shrug it off. Neither can we shrug off responsibility for the structures that have been created during this time, including the capitalist economic system. Our shared duty calls us not only to transform existing structures, but also to create spiritual as well as economic, political, and social order.

The exercise of dominion incorporates the responsibility to use natural resources for the benefit of all human beings. Our task is to care for the earth in the same way as the Creator does. We are called to ensure that future communities can also enjoy the bounty of nature.

An economic system is a major means to carry out this shared responsibility for sustaining life on the planet. A well-functioning economic system would recognize the integrity, fullness, and sacredness of creation.

In summary, economic decision making should incorporate environmental wholeness and an ethic that will ensure a sustainable future. Humanity is an integral part of an interrelated creation. People who abuse, exploit, and deplete resources or cause the extinction of species for economic gain violate the integrity of creation. They destroy what we are called to build and preserve. Unless their destructive behavior is contained, there likely will be few survivors of major, sustained ecological abuse. Along with the honor to name and the power to exercise dominion, our Creator also gives us the sobering freedom to fail, to disobey, to choose self-destruction.

Honoring the Sabbath

> And on the seventh day God finished the work that he had done, and he rested on the seventh day from all the work that he had done (Genesis 2:2).

From an economic standpoint our interest in the Sabbath has nothing to do with a specific religious observance of one day of every seven. Rather, it has to do with the need for periodic renewal of the created order. It means recognizing that there is more to life than greater efficiency in the production of material goods and services. If God finds time to rest, so should we.

The term *Sabbath* refers to the seventh day in the seven-day week of the Jewish calendar. It also refers to a sabbatical year every seventh year and to the jubilee, which was to occur after seven sets of seven years—every fiftieth year. The biblical term Sabbath derives from a verb that means to cease, to come to an end, or to finish. The concept of rest was added later when this day took on religious significance.

Some elements of the sacred value of honoring the Sabbath are:

In 1957, the average income of a person in the United States was $8,000 (expressed in today's dollars). The average income today is more than $16,000.

The average income doubled during this period. Yet the number of people who said they were "pretty well satisfied with your financial situation" dropped from 42 to 30 percent during these years!

If we compare ourselves with those who are richer than us, or think about how much we could possibly earn, we will never be happy or satisfied. "Enough" is an attitude we adopt, not a numerical goal.

David Schrock-Shenk, *Basic Trek: Venture into a World of Enough* (Scottdale, Pa.: Herald Press, 2002).

- promoting a concept of "enough" to challenge the assumption in economics that all human beings have an unlimited capacity to want;
- encouraging periodic means of contributing to the well-being of the larger community in ways other than merely striving for a greater material acquisition;
- renewing the human spirit by enabling everyone to rest from their labors periodically and reminding them that their Creator, rather than human endeavor, ensures the sustenance required for life; and
- accepting the principle that such forms of periodic renewal for humans will provide a form of rest as a benefit for all of creation.

Wide acceptance of the Sabbath concept would benefit the whole created order. Slowing down the acceleration of unconstrained wants of human beings would lessen the fear of scarcity as a driving force in our society. At the same time, it would free up human energy for activities that contribute to a communal sense of mental, physical, social, and spiritual well-being. Experiencing community in this way would open up new levels of satisfaction.

Obtaining some balance between our relentless pursuit of more and a radical trust in God to ensure that there will always be enough will require changes in the reasons for which we shop as well as in the institutions that make it so

A Busy Day for the Credit Card

In a few frenzied hours of consumer panic late this afternoon, Canadians will use their credit cards a staggering 500 times a second piling more than $1 billion in debt on their plastic. . . .

Consumers are already holding $20.4 billion in unpaid balances on credit cards, according to the Canadian Bankers' Association. That's an average of $1,337 for each of the 16 million Canadians who carry outstanding balances.

And the hangover will last well into the new year. Experts predict it takes the average shopper six months to recover from their Christmas spending. Many will still be carrying their Yuletide debt this time next year as they gear up for another shopping binge.

Doug Nairne, "Credit Card Busiest Day," *Winnipeg Free Press* (December 24, 1997).

easy to consume beyond our means. For example, pressure to buy and consume at Christmastime not only results in the satisfaction of our current wants, but also shapes and creates new wants. The explosive proliferation of credit cards makes it too easy for many families to commit a portion of future income to living it up now.

> Money may buy the husk of many things, but not the kernel. It brings you food, but not the appetite, medicine but not the health, acquaintances but not friends, servants but not faithfulness, days of joy but not peace or happiness.
>
> —Henrik Ibsen

Building Community with Fairness

How income and wealth are distributed is a key to maintaining a community's vitality, health, and human dignity. When wealth is distributed fairly, people are motivated to contribute to the community's well-being.

A desire to be fair is guided by the righteousness of God. Our covenant relationship with God means we want to be righteous too. Our place in this covenant covers our human relationships as well as our relationship with God. It means we deal justly with each other.

Building a fair society that facilitates community living will include:

- ensuring that all adult persons within a community have access to its means of production, or resources;
- employing resources in a way that favors the needs of the poor over the wants of the rich; and
- eliminating discrimination by pursuing equal opportunity, both in the use of resources and in the distribution of the goods and services produced.

The right of access to resources requires structures and institutions that enable all members to contribute to the overall well-being of the community. Conversely, community is betrayed if an elite minority of people can dominate access to resources so they will be available for their own use. Individuals have worth just because they are persons, not because they may be rich or powerful.

An economic system based on fairness will aim to invest the wealth, talent, and human energy of the community to increase opportunities for the poor, the weak, and those at the margins of society. Everyone's best interest is served when those otherwise marginalized are enabled to participate creatively and productively in community life. A fair economy involves all able people in responsible, participatory, and economically rewarding activity. If some members are excluded from productive and meaningful work and from access to the means of sustenance, neither individuals nor the community can survive.[11]

The concentration of capital in the hands of a few is widening the gap between the rich and the poor around the world. We now live in a world where the national income of all Tanzanians is less than what Americans spend on wallpaper.[12] This concentration of productive wealth increases the domination of the weak by the strong. A fair economy seeks continually to correct imbalances in wealth and power so that the poor and weak can have a hand in shaping their own future.

A fair economy ensures equal opportunity. Discrimination of any sort, whether based on race, class, age, ethnic origin, sexual orientation, physical disability, religion, or gender, contradicts the God-given dignity and worth of all human beings. When inequality and prejudice become woven into our social and institutional fabric, this constitutes a form of social sin.

Making Peace Possible

A just economy extended to the global realm would require and promote international peace and well-being.

There is no genuine peace without justice; nor can there be justice without peace. In a fair economy the intent of production would be to improve the lives of all citizens and not to produce more weapons.

Peace is promoted when all societies are given a chance to develop their potential. The structures and institutions that govern economic interactions among nations should strive for this end. This poses a special challenge to officials of multinational corporations, who sometimes seem to think they are immune to the laws and traditions of the countries in which they operate.

The realization of fairness at a global level will depend on being able to achieve fair agreements and fair exchanges among societies. Currently we lack the means to define and enforce such agreements. The void has been filled partially with the creation of some international agencies to govern global exchange, but they typically represent the interests of the wealthy countries. The achievement of a fairer way to regulate international exchange will require more democratic international institutions.

Summary

Our purpose in this study is to gain a "warts and all" understanding of the capitalist economic system. In examining the system's strengths and limits we have identified seven sacred values. These values call into question some parts of our system, such as the worship of abundance, and help us name those structures that enslave and destroy. With the help of these sacred values we can seek to transform our system in ways that will serve our society better.

Let us restate these sacred values in summary form:

- On each human being the Creator has bestowed dignity as a special status.
- Our ability to live and to be as human beings depends on

being in relationship with other persons living within communities.

- A person's physical, mental, and spiritual well-being depends on being able to participate in a creative manner within such communities.
- The Creator has bestowed on each person a vocation, a shared responsibility for ensuring the use of natural resources for the benefit of all human beings, for this and future generations.
- The exercise of our responsibility to ensure the ongoing process of creation requires honoring the Sabbath. This includes promoting a concept of enough and periodically renewing the human spirit by resting from our labors.
- The pursuit of fairness includes ensuring that all have access to the means of production and employing resources so that the needs of the poor have priority over the wants of the rich.
- Fairness extended to the global realm works for international peace by granting all societies the right and the opportunity to develop their potential and by defining a means to enforce fair agreements and exchanges.

Our enormously productive economy ... demands that we make consumption our way of life, that we convert the buying and use of goods into rituals, that we seek our spiritual satisfaction, our ego satisfaction, in consumption.... We need things consumed, burned up, worn out, replaced, and discarded at an increasing rate.
—*Victor Lebow*

4

Born to Shop

Capitalism advanced as a system when it succeeded in renaming people as consumers. Our place within society is now defined by our ability to consume. Someone who loses that ability becomes a nobody, a non-person. Collectively such people become "the homeless," "welfare recipients," or simply "the poor."

Persons who consciously choose a simple lifestyle by opting out of high levels of consumption typically also withdraw from society more generally. They are a useful fringe group, possibly a conscience for the larger society, but merely a fringe group nonetheless. This may change; more and more people appear to be considering this option.

What Happens When We Buy?

In this chapter I explain the role of the consumer in an ideal free enterprise system and in contemporary capitalism. In both cases the market, based on money as a medium of exchange, serves as the primary means through which consumers obtain the goods and services they desire. To make things easier for consumers, the prices in the market signal both the intensity of demand for each particular commodity and the different costs involved as firms mobilize resources to produce that commodity. In general the more

The law of supply and demand: if you don't want it it's cheaper.

—Jerry Kitich (1998)

intense the consumers' demand for an item the more they are prepared to pay. Conversely, if consumers lose interest in a good or service, the price they are willing to pay will decline.

In most cases when consumers express a more intense demand by offering to pay a higher price, firms enjoy higher profits. This then stimulates more production to meet the growing consumer demand. Resources for this increased production are drawn from the declining industries, where the decrease in consumer demand has caused prices, and hence profits, to drop. The market thus coordinates consumer demands through a process of price movements that induce firms to produce the quantity of each good or service that consumers are willing and able to buy.

An important question to be resolved here is why we as consumers choose to buy goods and services in the first place. What is the driving force that causes us to collectively run up a billion dollars worth of credit card debt the day before Christmas? I suggest three possible explanations for consideration:

- Each person has an uncontrollable desire to own and consume material things.
- We are influenced by peer-group pressure; the desire to keep up with our neighbors shapes our understanding of what we "need" to live comfortably.
- As consumers we have lost the freedom to choose what we want to buy because we have become helpless victims of producers and of their allies in the advertising industry.

Failing to Isolate a Consumption Gene

We Always Want More

The scholarly discipline of economics has not undertaken detailed biological or psychological study to understand human needs and wants. The underlying assumption of the discipline is that each human being has an unlimited capacity to want material things and services. Our desire to consume is part of our genetic makeup; we are all born to shop.

Does this assumption really hold true? There are, after all, exceptions. We decide to marry and have children. We share with others and we practice charity. And we derive pleasure and satisfaction from sharing an intimate dinner with a friend.

You have been invited to your friend's home for dinner. And he has prepared a wonderful meal. Before you leave, you take out your purse and give your friend an appropriate sum of money.

Who in the world would behave this way? Probably nobody in his right mind because virtually everyone knows that this would mean the end of the friendship. By paying, the relationship based on benevolence is basically transformed; if it survives at all, it is then a commercial one which all the people involved interpret quite differently.

Bruno S. Frey, *Not Just for the Money* (1997), 7-8.

Why Economists Don't Rock the Boat

Economists recognize the complexity of human motivation, but they tend not to question the underlying assumption that all persons have an unlimited capacity to want. After all, it serves economists well. There is no incentive for them to determine whether the assumption is an accurate portrayal of human nature.

If Adam Smith were alive today he might be surprised at where human wants have taken us. He and others in his day assumed that even rich people had limits as to what they would buy. After all, they could only eat a limited amount of food and wear a limited amount of clothing. Smith expected that a healthy, growing economy would eventually level off at a steady state once the economy provided each person with enough, because then everyone would be satisfied. In contemporary North America we have discovered that Smith's view of human beings was both too limiting and too optimistic. We have seen the proliferation of wants as advertising has fanned the flames of desire. Nowadays we know no limits; there is never enough.

In their study of demand for goods and services, economists are primarily interested in what they call relative
wants. The more we want something, the more we are prepared to pay. As the price rises, some can no longer afford to
pay that price, so they shift their demand to some less expensive way to satisfy a want. This human response enables the
market to channel demand away from those goods and services where resource inputs are becoming scarce (and thus
more expensive) to others where resources are abundant
(and thus cheaper).

Economists use this theory of relative wants to explain
why we spend our income as we do. Each of us gains maximum satisfaction from our income by buying more of those
goods and services that generate the largest increase in our
overall satisfaction. We are prepared to pay a lot for a diamond and very little for a glass of water because having a
diamond would be very satisfying while having one more
glass of water would add little to our satisfaction. Of course,
if we were wandering, lost, in a desert, our evaluation of the
relative value of a diamond and a glass of water would
change quickly.

Economists base their conclusions on studies of people
with adequate income. This often distorts the results of their
research. The fact that a rich person will pay more than a
poor person for water does not prove that the rich person
needs water and the poor person doesn't. Rather, in a free
market, when water becomes scarce, the poor person is eliminated from bidding for the water that is available. The poor
person ceases to be a consumer and is no longer of interest
to the economist. n businer person

Economists' consumer theory merely explains how consumers allocate their income if they are free to spend it as
they wish. It does not tell us what drives people to consume;
nor does it shed any light on whether consumers would,
given a free choice, ever choose something in life other than

purchasing more goods and services in the market. The drive to consume material things may be genetic, but so far that has not been proved.

Keeping Up with the Neighbors

Buying Because of Peer Pressure

Given our income, what we consume may be influenced by our peers, such as our neighbors, co-workers, or friends. We can see the effect of peer pressure on consumption behavior in the trendiness of certain products among the post-World War II baby boomers. Because this group represents such a large bulge in the population, markets have expanded rapidly for whatever has been in fashion for the baby boomers as they have passed from childhood to middle age. At one point in their childhood it was tricycles; later it was jogging shoes; then it was minivans. Without peer pressure directing baby boomers toward specific goods and services, their increased buying power would have been spread out over all goods and services available in the market.

> For over 40 years, your generation has been making or breaking products. Take a look at the Chrysler minivan. In 1979, Lee Iacocca was in front of the U.S. Congress, cap in hand, begging them to save his company. A decade later, Chrysler was smashing all its profits and sales numbers. Either Iacocca is a genius and figured out the market or he got lucky. In any event, Chrysler was first to the market with a minivan and the boomers bought them like hotcakes. Voilà–Chrysler was saved.
>
> David Cork and Susan Lightstone, *The Pig and the Python* (1996), 9 and 39.

Because our economic system tends to define people's value by their ability to consume, it is not surprising that acceptance into certain peer groups also depends on ability to consume. We buy certain goods and services not because we need them but because we want to gain acceptance among our peers. The desire to keep up with our neighbors is a powerful incentive.

Choosing Between Things and Leisure

At issue here is our motivation: What are the basic driving forces within our lives? Economists assume that each person seeks to minimize pain and maximize pleasure and that the primary way to maximize pleasure is to own and consume material things. But is this really the case?

The story is told of a proud taxi driver who worked sixteen hours a day. Because of his hard work he was able to give his daughter a new Buick for her sixteenth birthday. One wonders: Given the choice, would she have preferred more of his time while she was growing up, instead of the Buick?[1]

Juliet Schor has estimated that if we had limited our consumption to the levels North Americans enjoyed in 1948, the advances in technology over these years could have been put to use in such a manner that each working person could now work only half days or take every other year off.[2] The Europeans chose a more balanced approach during the same period, using part of the boost in productivity to achieve a higher material standard of living and part to increase the leisure time each worker can enjoy.

Robert Gordon estimates that productivity growth in a number of European countries has almost kept pace with that in the United States,[3] but the material standard of living, as measured by per capita Gross Domestic Product, is some 20 percent lower in these European countries. Partly this reflects smaller geographic space and better planned, more compact urban centers, which require significantly less expenditure on transport. It also reflects the fact that Europeans have opted to spend some of the benefits of productivity growth on increased leisure.

Finding 'A Lifetime of Work to Do'

[Betty Friedan] notes there has been no movement in the United States for shorter work hours in 60 years. "If anything, we're going in the opposite direction. People are holding two jobs. There's a lot of workaholism and overtime. We need a 'Get-a-Life' movement."

Marilyn Gardner, "Finding 'A Lifetime of Work to Do,'" *Edmonton Journal* (May 28, 2000).

Given that surveys show that North Americans are less happy now than they were thirty years ago, did we make the right choice to channel technology into increasing the output of material things? Or, is it time to reevaluate the way we spend our time?

Finding Happiness by Building Community

Does high consumption make it easier or harder to build relationships within a community? Many North Americans who travel to low-income countries are often surprised to see people who are as happy as we are despite a much lower material standard of living. Possibly the secret is in the relationships they enjoy within their communities. The human satisfaction and happiness that flows from such relationships doesn't depend on a material standard of living.

We need to think seriously about whether our ability to consume is essential to the achievement of relationships within communities that we require as human beings. We also need to examine whether we are being transformed into mere consumers with an insatiable desire to want material things. Are we being enslaved by a struggle to gain acceptance? If we choose not to be thus enslaved, we may find a new sense of liberty as we gain acceptance in a community that values us as genuine human beings rather than as mere consumers.

There is no denying that consuming goods and services provides certain pleasures and hence is satisfying. The question is whether being seduced by the pleasures of consuming leaves us in a second-best position. Could life give even more pleasure if we changed our priorities so that our behavior builds relationships and hence builds the foundation for a safer, better future?

Bought to Consume

At the time of Adam Smith there was little cause to question the assumption that consumer behavior was independent

of business influence. Firms were small in size. Potential customers lived nearby and typically knew the producers of the
products involved. It was the quality of the product and service to the customer that assured such small firms of an
ongoing existence. Advertising did occur, but it was primarily to inform people of the existence of a product, and possibly of its price.

Advertising: Making Us Want

Advertising today continues to inform people, but it also
does much more. It still enables firms to introduce new products they want to produce for the public. Without such information it would be difficult for a new product to break into
the market. There is, though, only a fine line between
informing the public of a new product and seeking to create
a need or a want for that product.

The need for firms to create wants for what they would
like to sell is not new. European explorers who returned with
new, exotic goods from foreign lands invented human ail-
ments that could be cured with the use of those exotic goods.
An example is chocolate from the American colonies, introduced into Britain in the seventeenth century as a drink with
ill-defined medicinal qualities. Among other things, it was
claimed that the Aztec ruler Montezuma had used it as an
aphrodisiac.[4]

A classic way for advertising to create new wants is to
prey on some insecurity people may be experiencing. A single person who hasn't had a date for a while is told by advertisers to wonder about bad breath, body odor, or dandruff.
For married couples the fear advertising exploits is that of
losing the partner's interest and affection. Attempts to market aphrodisiacs are as strong today as they were in the seventeenth century.

Another tactic employed by some industries is to periodically change styles and then promote the idea that smart,

fashionable customers simply cannot do without the new styles. For women's clothing and computer software such changes can occur several times a year. For cars, recreational equipment, and electronic devices model changes occur at least annually. Product quality and durability matters little, for producers hope we will discard the old well before its time is up.

Bob Goudzwaard argues that growth in the size of firms has generated the need for advertising to create new human wants.[5] It takes huge sums of money to build a big company. The risk involved is equally huge if consumers don't remain loyal to the firm's product. Advertising campaigns are designed to build such loyalty.

But as incomes of consumers rise, so does their ability to choose. The more choices available, the less likely it is that consumers will remain loyal to any one brand. Advertisers respond by creating new wants for these ever-hungry consumers. They cultivate the image of their products as vital ingredients of the good life, which of course always exists at the upper end of what people can afford.

People don't like to admit that they can be manipulated by advertising. But why else would firms spend so much money on it? Advertisers must have some evidence that their messages are being heard.

Eroding Our Freedom of Choice

If advertisers do, in fact, influence our buying habits, then an important aspect of the ideal free enterprise system— the freedom of each person to choose what is best for her or him—is broken. If individual producers can shape both supply and demand, then the price is no longer determined solely by the free market. Instead, it is controlled in part by the producer. The implications of such market control are serious if our goal is an economic system that serves the best interests of everyone.

Marketing techniques that go beyond simply informing potential customers interfere with our freedom to choose. This is an issue with significant moral dimensions. Should not firms be held accountable if they infringe on consumers' control over their own best interest? Influencing human behavior without any form of accountability is a form of violence against people. Lawsuits against tobacco companies and handgun manufacturers are current attempts to make producers more accountable.

Larger society will suffer both now and in the future if people are subtly coerced to cater to immediate desires. A hangover from excessive consumption of alcohol is one illustration of a short-term effect. Adverse health consequences of overindulging in tobacco and rich foods are examples of medium-term effects. Destruction of the ozone layer and global warming are longer-term consequences of obtaining goods for our convenience and pleasure today.

The issue is not whether any particular advertisement affects your or my behavior. Rather, it is whether the prominent place of marketing has caused us to accept without protest our loss of dignity as human beings by being renamed as consumers. Eva Weidman's reflection on the subject in her "Slice of Life" column likely speaks for all of us.

> I tried to deny being a consumer once through a week-long wilderness canoeing and hiking trip. . . .
>
> I wanted to purify myself somehow. Prove that I could indeed survive without using any modern conveniences. I wanted to become as one with nature, have deep spiritual moments with my surroundings and write an award-winning short story-all in a week. . . .
>
> A week of accounting for every bit of garbage I produced made me aware of how much of a consumer I really am. Having to lug my garbage back to civilization on the return journey doubled my awareness.
>
> I didn't become as one with nature. . . . I discovered the

simple satisfaction of a cup of tea made from water I carried and I did admire the silence of the wilderness—but I was still a consumer, still a greedy human in a natural world.[6]

We have been reduced to being consumers, and we no longer even bother to think about it. Going with the flow, living just like all the other consumers around us, is the easiest way to gain social acceptance. One reason we are so accepting is that we have been misled to believe we are completely free to choose and to control our own destiny.

Reclaiming Human Dignity

Being responsible consumers in community means rejecting our identity as mere customers and reclaiming our full dignity as human beings. At the personal level this means recognizing who we are and gaining a greater understanding of the external relationships that enable us to become who God intended us to be. This includes our relationships to things as well as our place within the communities that enable us to fully experience what it means to be human.

Being in Community Shapes Our Values

We need to reexamine whether we are indeed free to decide which goods and services will help us meet our personal and social goals. This will include avoiding being caught up in the lifestyle that the marketing industry seeks to create.

Our ability to accomplish such a reexamination depends on whether we are in a community of people who share similar values. First, we need to be in community to experience what it means to be fully human. Second, because it is impossible for a person to continuously swim against the stream, in order to resist all that the market offers and to hold the providers of goods and services accountable, we must work together with others.

As Mark Vincent indicates, each action we take in the market communicates to others something about our priorities, values, and worldview.

> Each time we make a purchase, decide on an investment, or give a gift, we communicate what we care about. Checkbook ledgers and stacks of receipts reveal our most tightly held values. Therefore, our use of money communicates our worldview.
>
> Worldviews influence more than one's moral code or priorities. A worldview combines our experiences, our perceptions, and our convictions with our faith, ethics, physical capacity, and network of relationships to form our view of life. Worldviews are seldom clearly thought through or consistent, but they determine our actions.
>
> Paul talks pretty plainly in his letter to Timothy. Notice Paul's conviction: that looking at a person's use of money reveals the heart. Jesus highlighted that truth, too, when he said, "Where your treasure is, there your heart will be also" (Matthew 6:21). Whether or not we talk openly about what is most important to us, how we use money gives us away.[7]

Do our actions serve to include others and build others up in this joint struggle to claim our rightful place within God's created order? Do they contribute to the struggle to once more make the economic system our servant rather than our master?

Shaping Consumption Isn't Easy

A good place to start is to become more informed consumers. We can seek out and support firms that serve our genuine needs and do not spend vast sums of money trying to distort our human wants. The concept of ethical shopping can be extended to include choosing producers that have good working conditions for their employees, consciously try to preserve the environment, and seek to build community with peaceful means.

Becoming informed will involve investing personal or community resources in gathering information. It will involve informing members of our own community and of other communities. It will involve identifying and encouraging firms that are guided by principles such as the set of sacred values summarized in chapter three. This kind of shopping may sometimes cost more, especially in terms of the time required to shop at a variety of smaller stores rather than the big-box discounters. And it won't always be easy to recruit others to this kind of activity if it doesn't yield results immediately.

Still, selected ethical shopping can have a significant impact. Large corporations can be vulnerable to joint action by consumers. One example is the successful boycott of Nestlé's products to protest its promotion of baby formula among low-income families who could not ensure appropriate sanitary conditions for bottle-feeding.

Substituting Relationships for Consuming

An alternative, possibly more productive approach is to opt out of obvious forms of excessive consumption and to create communities that can visibly substitute strong, healthy relationships for it. It will be important to demonstrate that such communities can provide what humans need for secure, happy lives. In addition, we will need to strive for these objectives in a manner that promotes the human dignity of all people and in which we exercise our dominion over the created order in a responsible way, as intended by God.[8]

When we speak of using our resources responsibly we are usually discussing either consuming with or saving our income. Actually there is a third option: we can share it in a charitable manner. Mark Vincent uses the term first-fruit giving to describe one way of exercising such charity. In some societies the first-born child was dedicated to God in a special way. Agricultural societies would offer the first fruits of

First-Fruit Giving

God's people brought their first and best to their places of worship. The money or goods were used first for celebration feasts, then for care of ministering people, and then for the support of needy people in the community. We become generous, not just with our first-fruits gifts, but in our lifestyle, because we have been treated generously. First-fruits living means we move away from individual use of money and possessions—we no longer see the money as "ours" alone—and we move toward a growing generosity in all of life. No longer are we consumers, but blessing-givers. We become generous with the families we are part of, and we become generous with the widows, orphans, aliens, naked, hungry, thirsty, imprisoned, and ill in our lives. We don't do it because it is our duty. We do it because we cannot not do it!

Mark Vincent, *A Christian View of Money* (1997), 82.

the harvest to a gracious God for meeting their physical needs.

A modern-day application of this first-fruit giving would be to take a portion of our regular income off the top and put it into service through the church or a charitable service agency. Alternatively, one could channel a percentage of income, each time it is received, into a special account. That account would then serve as the source for charitable actions we would carry out during the year.

It is liberating to make conscious decisions on how our income is spent. Rather than consuming first and saving or giving the leftovers, we reverse the process. By investing in others first, through our charitable actions, then consuming what is left over, we reassert that we are human beings, not just consumers. We also show the high priority we place on others and on being in relationship with them in community.

Removing the Incentives That Fan Our Flame

In addition to taking action to regain our full dignity, we need to ask whether specific corrective action should be required of business firms. If everyone in the world obtained the material standard of living enjoyed by North Americans, we would require the resources of three earths to meet the demand. Is it then morally responsible for firms to create ever more wants through advertising? What if government removed the tax-deductible status of these kinds of ads? This might be hard to enforce because firms could blur the line between informing consumers and creating new wants. An alternative could be to treat advertising like patents or copyrights, which have a built-in expiration date. The tax deductibility of advertising for a new product might be limited to a specified time period, possibly six months or a year.

The media would strenuously resist such a move. For some reason that we rarely question, most of our media is paid for by advertising revenue. In the end, we pay the bulk of the cost of producing newspapers, magazines, and radio and television programs by paying higher prices for the products we buy to cover the firms' advertising costs. If we were required to pay directly for our media we would, no doubt, demand much better service. Examples of periodicals that serve readers through subscription charges rather than advertising revenues are the *New Internationalist* and *The Marketplace*.

No Commercial Advertising

You may also appreciate that *New Internationalist* is free of commercial advertising. That means each issue is full of information—designed for our readers, not for advertisers trying to sell you their products.

Our independence from corporate advertisers means our price is a little higher than magazines that subsidize their subscriptions with ad revenue.

But our 85,000 subscribers around the world think our independence and quality are well worth a few extra dollars.

Wayne Ellwood, Co-editor, *New Internationalist*.

The task before us is large. But it is not impossible. The human race has demonstrated again and again that where there is a will there is a way.

Capitalism is an amazingly forgiving system. There's a logical reason for that. When things fail, the downside is limited to losing all of the money you put in. But when something works, there's no limit to how much money it can make. A thousand software companies can go bankrupt and it won't have as much impact on the economy as one Microsoft success.

—*Scott Adams*

5

The Visible Hand and the Bottom Line

Entrepreneurs—businesspeople and farmers—make things happen in our society. They are the capitalists set free by our system to undertake new economic ventures.

The capitalist system portrays these entrepreneurs as puppets, as servants responsive to the wishes of the puppeteer: the consumers. In reality, though, it is self-interest that drives them to provide a quality product with good service. If they don't, consumers will choose other suppliers. Firms that fail to serve their customers will wither and die.

This is the ideal of the free enterprise system. In this chapter we will look at some of the benefits of this ideal: the provision of a growing supply of the goods and services we need and desire as citizens of a society. We will then explore how this ideal is being eroded by a relatively small number of large corporations that hold immense economic power. Several suggestions are put forward on possible approaches to restoring a capitalist system that remains friendly to small businesses and family farms.

Making the Most of Profit

Adam Smith's primary intent was to explain the nature and cause of a nation's wealth. The prevailing view at the time was that a nation's wealth equaled the amount of precious metals, such as gold and silver, it possessed. Smith disagreed; he claimed a country's people determined its wealth. More specifically, it is the skill of the people, how they are employed, and how many of them are engaged in "useful" labor that determines a society's material standard of living.

Smith defines useful labor in terms of the quantity of capital—machinery and equipment—each person has to work with. The way such labor and capital is employed is also important to a society's standard of living. The desire to maximize profits is what drives the process of employing resources and producing output.

Supplying the Customer's Desires

One of the nice features of the free enterprise system is the ability of business firms and farmers to supply the goods and services people want. The market provides these at the right time, packaged in a convenient form, and located reasonably close to customers.

These desirable outcomes are the product of the personal self-interest or selfishness of every provider of goods or services. They make a profit from their efforts, and if they want to keep the profits coming, it is in their interest to continue to serve the consumer as best they can.

In general, society is well served by businesspeople's desire to advance themselves. Farmers and owners of small businesses continually respond to changing consumer demands as they are expressed through price movements in the market. It is their selfish desire to obtain a better living for themselves and their families that gives us access to the goods that make community life possible and enjoyable.

A firm doesn't have to satisfy all consumers. Many firms appeal to niche markets. A good example is the success of YTV, a cable network catering to "tweens." According to Shawna Steinberg, it is estimated 10 million viewers watch YTV every week. This tweens audience represents

$1.4 billion worth of buying power that advertisers are trying to exploit by sponsoring programming on the specialty channel.

Another niche market is the market for gourmet coffee. According to Randy Powell, CEO of Second Cup Coffee Company, Canada is a nation "that gets up every morning and drinks lousy coffee. . . . For most people, coffee is mere jet fuel, an essential

Tweens and Their Money

They're old enough to watch Alanis Morisette on MuchMusic, but too young to get into an AA-rated movie. Old enough to shop at the mall for themselves, but too young for their parents to let them ride the subway alone. . . . [They] are among the 2.4 million Canadians between the ages of 9 and 14 that marketers and sociologists now call "tweens. . . ". Tweens are swiftly becoming the newest—and the most influential—consumer group to emerge in today's marketplace.

Shawna Steinberg, "Have Allowance, Will Transform Economy," *Canadian Business* (March 13, 1998).

shot of caffeine to get—or keep—the day going."[1] With a string of 370 cafés across Canada, Powell intends to turn coffee drinking into a "pleasure, a time-out from a busy day to savor a brew made from the world's finest beans."

Some activities, like the scalping of tickets at a Super Bowl game, cater to highly specialized markets. Scott Taylor writes of football fans who were able to see Super Bowl XXXII only because speculators had had the foresight to buy up tickets and were willing to risk either being arrested or ending up with unsold tickets.

Tickets were $275 at the source and were selling for as high as $7,000 apiece yesterday, making brokers' tickets for the Super Bowl XXXII the most expensive of all time.

"Its nuts out there on the street," said Marcus Elton, 32, a ticket speculator from Chicago who had been fortunate enough to have come to San Diego with 20 tickets to the game.

"Early in the week, the best I could get was $800 for a $275 ticket. And those were tickets I'd bought for $450 each. I sold four this morning for $24,000 cash. I've been doing this for 10 years and this is the best week I've ever had."

Whether buyers got a $6,000 football game is in the eye of the beholder.[2]

The speculators' actions harmed no one and brought pleasure to a few. Of course, the people served were the rich; people with limited incomes could not afford to benefit from the speculators' foresight.

A commodity does not have to be legal to be part of the market. Take, for example, the many Cuban cigars that are smuggled into the United States. Even though it is illegal to import cigars from Cuba, an estimated 5 million banned cigars are consumed annually in the United States. In addition, *The Economist* reports, unsuspecting Americans consume 45 million fake Cuban cigars annually.[3] Whenever the demand for an item exceeds its supply, there is room for enterprising persons to produce imitations.

Poised for Change

A more typical example of how the market responds to changing tastes and supply conditions is the reaction of Canadian prairie grain farmers to the growing international demand for pork. When populous Asian countries developed a taste for pork, the world market for it grew substantially. As it turned out, major pork producers in Europe and Southeast Asia were experiencing serious pig-supply problems at precisely the time Canadian farmers were suffering from increased costs of shipping their grain to coastal terminals, and thus to export markets. Many farmers reasoned that it made no sense to pay a fortune to ship their grain when they could keep it at home and feed it to pigs. As a result there was a major switch to pork production to serve the growing Asian market.

When the subsequent Asian crisis brought this new market to a screeching halt many farmers who had invested in pig farming found themselves in trouble. As pork prices plunged, the weakest farmers, in many cases those with the most debt, were forced into bankruptcy or at least out of that market. Eventually the survivors prospered again as new markets emerged.

Such responses to changing market conditions are characteristic of small- and medium-sized businesses. Smith's confidence in their ability to supply society's needs and wants was warranted. Their freedom to undertake economic activity where and how they please has provided all of us with a greater freedom to select from a vast array of goods and services those that best meet our needs and wants.

The Drive to Grow in a Finite World

The ideal of Adam Smith's free enterprise system has been broken with the evolution of the corporation. Smith anticipated this result. He was critical of joint-stock companies, especially those to which the government gave monopolies to trade in a particular commodity or territory. An example still in operation today is the Hudson's Bay Company, which was granted a charter in 1670 by King Charles II that included the right to trade for furs in the whole region draining into Hudson Bay.

> The directors of such companies, however, being the managers rather of other people's money than of their own, it cannot be well expected, that they should watch over it with the same anxious vigilance with which the partners in a private copartnery frequently watch over their own. Like the stewards of a rich man, they are apt to consider attention to small matters as not for their master's honour, and very easily give themselves a dispensation from having it. Negligence and profusion, therefore, must always prevail, more or less, in the management of the affairs of such a company.
>
> Adam Smith, *Wealth of Nations* (1937), 700.

Keeping the Shareholders Content

Place yourself in the position of a senior corporate executive. You have two stakeholders you must satisfy. One is yourself. You have a personal ambition to maintain a secure job, preferably with a growing income. In order to achieve that, you have to satisfy the other stakeholder, namely your employers, who happen to be the shareholders of the corporation. They may want regular and sizable dividends, and they certainly expect to see the value of their shares increase.

For example, in 1998 the shareholders of General Motors reacted to the company's difficulty in adapting to the productivity changes needed to produce cars and trucks. General Motors shares were performing 70 percent below the stock market in general. The low price could be seen as shareholders' way of saying to the market, "Take these stocks off our hands."[4]

Continued invention and technological change can serve to ensure continued growth in production that is competitive in the market, thus enhancing profits. But the cost of producing new technology is high and somewhat risky.

A second way to improve profits is to cut the labor force. If a particular level of output cannot be maintained, the labor cost of each new item produced goes up. In the case of General Motors, reducing the number of employees cut the average labor cost per car, providing the opportunity for more profits.

The latter solution tends to be temporary. If many firms cut jobs there will be many more unemployed workers. People without jobs can't buy new cars, so demand will shrink. Then each firm will be back to where it started when it began to cut costs.

A third approach to improving profits is better management. By reorganizing and using knowledge technology, General Motors has overcome its productivity gap with Ford Motor Company. It is responding to consumer preferences by offering for sale a range of cars manufactured by firms that it controls but doesn't own. It also intends to enable consumers to use the Internet to find the specific car that is right for them—whether one made by another car manufacture or by General Motors itself.[5]

The Endless Struggle to Grow

The most obvious way to meet the dual objectives of job security and increasing profits is to grow. One way to grow is to increase market share at the expense of competitors. If the competitors are also large and powerful, they will fight back, making any growth short-lived. An alternative way to grow is to increase overall demand through a combination of offering an especially appealing product and conducting a strong marketing campaign.

Note, for example, what has happened in the market for blue jeans. Tommy Hilfiger and Ralph Lauren managed to steer the tastes of younger shoppers away from Levi's classic jeans to wide-leg jeans. As a result, the U.S. market share of Levi's declined from 31 to 20 percent.

Shawna Steinberg reported how Levi's successfully fought back. They scrapped plans for a new style of jeans, the product of a year of research and design, and revitalized a line of existing wide-leg jeans. This was combined with a massive "It's Wide Open" advertising campaign. The end result was that Levi's gained back some market share and expanded the overall market for jeans, and Levi's executives were able to keep their jobs.[6]

The struggle for continuous growth is not without problems. For one thing, it can be rather tempting to make a lower-quality product that is not intended to last, and then keep bringing out new styles, models, or updated versions to spur further sales.

Another peril of continual growth is the impact on the young. Advertising now reaches down to our children and grandchildren to make sure that they develop the appropriate shopping habits. Elizabeth Renzetti reports on the new school year starting with fourth grade girls resembling miniature Jackies and Dianas.[7] They are style-conscious and label-driven, and they would not be caught wearing last year's fashions.

Are kids born with a gene that makes them fashion conscious? Or are they socialized at an early age to think that way? Do large corporations encourage this process with advertising that exploits young people's need for peer acceptance? Should we be alarmed that firms use persuasive marketing to lure children into a shopping game in which the rules are defined by the corporation? Do we care?

What Do We Mean by Progress?

If you are concerned about the sustainability of life, then you do care. If you desire to live at peace with the many peoples who make up our earth, then you do care. Yes, we want the good life. We even want progress, but not at any possible price.

What, after all, is the goal of progress? Early in the twentieth century the economist Wesley Mitchell observed: "We boast of progress but lack the insight to see that the term means nothing because we have not thought for what destination we are bound."[8] Our economic incentive system promotes continued technological change, but it does not encourage or welcome questions about its purpose. Society has no way to set an overall direction for emerging technology. This has serious distributional implications as only a minority of the world's population can afford the new technology.

A good illustration of this point is the research priorities of the firms that produce drugs and vaccines. During the 1980s the number of large drug companies producing vaccines declined from twelve to four.[9] In part this is because companies do not want to go to the trouble to develop and produce vaccines that the primary customers in low- and middle-income countries cannot afford. In contrast, feel-good drugs, such as Prozac and Viagra, attract considerable research resources because wealthy consumers want them and are willing to pay for them. These are consumers who do not have to worry about many diseases because their parents could afford to have them vaccinated as children.

So, is it reassuring to have to trust our corporate executives with the decisions that shape our future? After all, they are just as selfish as the rest of us, driven in a particular direction because of potential profits. Just because they have the responsibility of running large corporations does not mean they have been transformed into virtuous and wise persons dedicated solely to the public interest.

Deep down, many of us just don't believe that the primary driving force is our own selfishness. William Pfaff allows for an additional driving force.

> And one reason they have shown this is that their religion has insisted that constructive work in this world pleases God, and advances the development of a history that is understood to have begun in the void from which God summoned matter and to end in the Day of Judgment, when we will all be held accountable for how we have used our talents and dealt with our fellow-men. The latter-day secularizations, political or ostensibly scientific, of this religious conception of history have changed little that is essential to it. Progressive humanists or Marxists, rationalists or scientific optimists, we in the West still go on working as if our immortal salvation depended upon it.[10]

There is reason to believe that Adam Smith sought similar comfort in his belief in a deistic God.[11] His faith that God would somehow take the sum of all of our vices and use them to work everything out in the end for society's well-being is commendable, but hardly reassuring.

Regardless of whose description of our motivation is right, Smith's view of human nature or Pfaff's interpretation of our culture, God has placed on us the co-responsibility to sustain creation. Part of this responsibility means we must analyze carefully whether large corporations in their present form can help us maintain the created order and promote its ongoing existence. It means asking whether any institution that requires continued growth to exist is likely to become a social cancer. As long as this danger exists there is a need to either transform such corporations or seek alternative institutions that can serve the larger interests of society.

The Corporate Visible Hand

Being Big Can Lower Costs

An important aspect of the ideal form of capitalism is the link between the ownership of resources and their management. In small businesses these are closely linked. Smith admired small operators who managed their resources with care and intelligence, constantly striving to improve their business.

Corporate executives, in contrast, typically own little of the vast resources under their care, and Smith thought they would not pay enough attention to detail. He concluded such mismanaged firms could survive only because government intervention protected them from having to compete against smaller, better-managed business firms.

Smith underestimated the potential of large corporations to survive even as they grew still larger. Whether they were efficient or not, their ability to raise large amounts of capital enabled them to take advantage of economies of scale. In certain types of manufacturing, producing enormous quantities can slash the unit cost of making an item.

A good example is a light bulb. Once the necessary machinery has been set up, huge quantities of bulbs can be produced every hour with very little labor. Of course, that's possible only if the firm can raise enough money to purchase the expensive machinery in the first place and then has the marketing capacity to sell all those light bulbs. The structure of the corporation is ideally suited to meet both conditions. By issuing more shares and corporate bonds the firm can raise the necessary money to purchase the machines, organize a large sales staff, and cover the cost of raw materials and labor until the bulbs are sold and paid for. Smaller firms, even if managed more efficiently, can't match the low cost of their giant competitors.

A Guiding Light of the Capitalist System

As corporations grew in size, more and more began to break free of the important control mechanism of Smith's free enterprise system, competition. Once our options as consumers have dwindled to a few firms from which to purchase, we have lost much of our ability to control their behavior. Some of our "puppets," the corporate giants, have risen up and wrested control from us as consumers.

The same is true for employees; in many cases they have lost their freedom to choose whom they will work for. Employees in large firms have limited bargaining power. Also, they no longer have a single person as an employer; they take orders from a foreman, who takes orders from a middle manager, and so on. People can identify with the characters in Dilbert cartoons because many middle managers are more anxious to advance themselves within a corporate hierarchy than to manage well the employees entrusted to them.

Over time, the visible hand of large corporations is replacing the invisible hand of Adam Smith as the guiding light of our economic system.

As large corporations emerged their goals changed.

The primary purpose of good corporate management is to keep a company in business indefinitely. They must look ahead and plan for depression risks, competition, obsolescence, exhaustion of natural resources, population movements, fashion changes and political attacks. They must grow reserves against hard times, improve and lower the cost of their products, stabilize the security of their workers as much as possible, and make the public like and desire their company as a community and national asset.

Charles Wilson as quoted by John McCallum in "New Managers, Same Old Skills," *The Financial Post 2000*, (November 22, 1997), 6. Material reprinted with the express permission of the National Post Company, a CanWest Partnership.

While small operators seek to maximize profits, this is not enough for the hired professional managers of corporations. Rather, the true corporate goal is to keep the company going. Profits are essential to long life. A firm that constantly loses money will not stay in business without government subsidies. Once minimal profits are assured, the corporation can use its massive resources to gain control of natural resources, develop a market for its product, and buy out competitors as a means of ensuring its ongoing existence.

So the bottom line for large corporations has changed. Maximizing profits is no longer the goal but is rather a means to the larger goal of preserving ongoing existence. To ensure its survival the firm must capture and exercise control over the consumer rather than allowing the consumer to dictate to the firm.

Where Is the Moral Compass?

As consumers we have lost much of our ability to shape the future in a way we would like because this right to decide has been taken over by corporate managers. The renewed interest in business ethics seeks to address some of this concern. For example, Max Clarkson defines business ethics as managing risk to create wealth without placing either human beings or the environment at greater risk.[12] In Clarkson's view, not knowing the potential risks of a particular business activity is no excuse.

The need for improved ethical standards to govern the behavior of corporate managers is clearly evident in the wake of the Enron, Global Crossing, and WorldCom scandals. Rodney Wilson argues that the corporate sector lacks the moral context for developing an ethic that serves more than merely the corporate shareholders.

> There is much talk of values, but little discussion of these values in a moral context. It is unclear what the

underlying morality is, or indeed if there is any. The human values seem one dimensional, concerned with self-fulfillment, but not personal responsibility beyond that to the company and its stakeholders. There are no laws to constrain management behaviour, just codes of practice worked out by the company itself, which by definition lack any wider legitimacy.[13]

As a result, there must be many managers in vast bureaucratic corporations who have asked, along with Dilbert, "Is it a bad sign if you spend the day wondering why there are no laws against what you do for a living?"[14]

Ineffective Competition Leads to Inadequate Control

The Powerful Temptation to Collude

Corporate leaders like to argue that the need to remain competitive will curb business behavior that is contrary to the public interest. The meaning of competitive, however, is subject to wide interpretation. When Bill Gates of Microsoft claims that the market is very competitive, he means something quite different from what Adam Smith had in mind. Economic analysis shows that whenever a few firms dominate a market there will be a powerful temptation to collude.

For example, imagine operating one of only two ice cream carts on a crowded beach, one mile long, on a hot Sunday afternoon. Where will you and your "competitor" locate your carts? If your primary interest is to serve the persons on the beach, you will each locate one-quarter mile in from opposite ends. In that way, no potential buyer has to travel more than a quarter mile for a refreshing ice cream cone. But if the interest is market share, firm growth, and business survival, each cart owner will be tempted to cheat on the other by moving closer to the center of the beach. Soon they will be standing side-by-side, forcing some people to travel up to half a mile. For this inconvenience, the customers now gain the advantage of two ice-cream carts to choose from. Because they are next to each other, the two cart owners will soon realize that reducing the price will not be in either one's interest.

A successful antitrust lawsuit brought against MasterCard and Visa in 2001 illustrates how real-life firms behave like the operators of these two ice-cream carts. While these two firms sought to project an image of vigorous competition, they were dividing up pieces of the financial services market between themselves. Specifically, they were found guilty of colluding to prevent banks that offered either MasterCard or Visa from offering any other credit card, such as American Express.[15]

Similarly, the major gasoline companies, banks, grocery stores and automobile dealers often locate their branches next to each other rather than spreading them throughout the community. Competing airlines cluster their flights at similar times rather than giving consumers a greater choice of departure times. If one firm drops its price, others usually follow suit; this clearly shows a form of collusion rather than competition.

Colluding on price is illegal. That is why golf is such a popular sport for business executives. Many agreements can be ironed out on the back nine with no one listening in or taking minutes. In other cases, the largest firm may exercise price leadership: it announces a price and the other major firms adjust their prices accordingly.

How Corporations Compete Without Lowering Prices

One important manifestation of nonprice competition is advertising. De Beers's marketing creates a feeling that we simply can't do without a diamond. It has been described as a "worldwide dealer in enchanting symbols" that rivals Disney in selling "myth and magic."[16] Other firms make changes in their products, often only in appearance rather than substance, then use advertising to persuade us that in order to be happy we must change to the latest style, version, or model.

In any market where one firm's action can harm other major firms, there are powerful incentives to collude with each other rather than compete. Gaining market share without undercutting the price of one's competitors is possible if an advertising campaign can generate and sustain brand consciousness. Some examples of widely recognized brands are Absolut Vodka, Ben and Jerry's ice cream, and Harley-Davidson motorcycles. These firms' advertising touches the emotions, creating fans rather than mere customers.[17]

The advent of the Internet has, temporarily at least, reintroduced more effective competition for large firms. With easy access to information, consumers can counter some of the effects of advertising. The cost of establishing and maintaining brand identification and loyalty is rising dramatically.

In the short term the Internet will provide new opportunities for enterprising smaller firms that cater to niche markets. In the longer term it will likely reduce competition even further as large firms take action needed to protect their markets and their future. Control of the Internet by advertisers will likely be one part of corporate strategy.

The Need to Limit Corporate Power

So where does this collusion masquerading as competition lead us? As Louis Emmerij observes, being more competitive is now a buzzword solution to many social and economic ills.

> Nobody would deny that a degree of competition is positive. Healthy competition—at school, at work, in research as well as in the economy—helps a society or an individual to progress and to remain innovative. The Latin

root of the verb compete is *competere,* which means "to seek together."

But the intense competition in today's global era is a far cry from this old ideal. Competition has become a weapon to wipe out the adversary. It has become an ideology and an imperative, and some even speak of the "gospel" of competition. . . .

Such an extreme system is bound to flounder. Indeed, extreme competition diminishes the degree of diversity existing in a society and contributes to social exclusion: individuals, enterprises, cities and nations that are not competitive are being marginalized and eliminated from the contest. This approach is unacceptable morally and inefficient economically. The more a system loses its variety, the more it will lose its capacity to renew itself. But above all, the ideology of competition devalues cooperation and seeking together. It wipes out solidarity, and therefore it is not surprising that this era is also witnessing heavy attacks on the welfare state.[18]

The experience of the past few years has demonstrated that such competition benefits primarily the managers, and only secondarily the shareholders, of large corporations. In the past decade competition has not been helping the employees. In the short term it may be helping some suppliers, but that will be only temporary. In the future, when there are many sellers and few buyers, prices for the suppliers will be dictated by large corporations. *Walmart*

Will consumers benefit? If there are benefits to consumers, they will be due to economies of scale, and some of these benefits will be lost to the inefficiencies that inevitably result when corporations eliminate the behavioral control mechanism of effective competition.

There is a pressing necessity to expand the interests of corporate managers to encompass the needs of the rest of society. If the interests of the employees, farmers, and small businesses that provide inputs to the large corporations are sacrificed continually for a few managers and shareholders, it makes little sense to pretend that consumers are benefitting. The bulk of consumers in any society are the families of employees, farmers, and firm owners who are the suppliers to large corporations.

As Emmerij concludes, unless this issue is addressed creatively, the end result will be more inequality, less diversity, and eventually the self-destruction of the capitalist system itself.

Alternative Ways to Boost Accountability

After retirement the occasional economist and some successful industrialists admit to fearing that the success of large corporations will ultimately destroy the capitalist system. Fanning this fear is corporations' compulsive need to grow. Can this need for growth be accommodated in a world that doesn't have enough resources to give everyone the high standard of living we enjoy? Can we afford powerful institutions that can survive only by expanding our wants?

Is Competition Still Enough?

Critiques of the capitalist economic system range from complete rejection to grudging acceptance. The position of Douglas Sherwin, as presented by Rodney Wilson, is an

Douglas Sherwin addresses these issues, at least indirectly, when he considers the ethical roots of the business system. He sees the purpose of a business as being more than serving its individual stakeholders, which for owners is profits and capital gains, for employees is remuneration and for consumers furnishing goods and services. Businesses also serve society more widely by being the most efficient means of securing given ends with least means. Through competition they come up with the economically efficient solutions which society expects, and which cannot be brought about by governments through command economies. Businesses are economically motivated institutions, but serve a larger social purpose in a pragmatic way which is more effective than alternative institutional arrangements involving state direction of production and distribution.

Rodney Wilson, *Economics, Ethics, and Religion* (1997), 177.

example of the latter. Whatever the system's shortcomings, says Sherwin, it is superior to any alternative we have seen so far. His confidence lives or dies on the premise that there is sufficient competition so that corporate executives will generally work to serve the larger public interest.

The favorable outcomes that Sherwin attributes to capitalism have, no doubt, a broad appeal to North Americans. But the corporate management crisis of 2002 has thoroughly shaken investor confidence. One market indicator that a crisis exists is the sevenfold increase in premiums for directors' and officers' insurance—to cover legal fees and settlements when managers are accused of failing in their duties—in scandal-prone high technology industries.[19]

The U.S. government has sought to address the management crisis by requiring the chief executive officer of every large corporation to swear each year that each annual and quarterly report of the firm does not contain an "untrue statement" or omit any "material fact." On the cover of its August 17, 2002, issue *The Economist* expresses its skepticism about the effectiveness of this legislation with an illustration of a corporate executive writing out: "I swear ... that, to the best of my knowledge (which is pretty poor and may be revised in the future), my company's accounts are (more or less) accurate. I have checked this with my auditors and directors, who (I pay to) agree with me. . . ."

There is a pressing need to question whether competition still serves as an adequate control mechanism. Too many industries are dominated by a few firms, eliminating meaningful competition. Further, our society does not appear to appreciate how vital competition is to our economic health. For example, there is a common perception that government-owned businesses are inherently inefficient. They are inefficient, but the reasons for that inefficiency have less to do with the fact that the businesses are government-owned than with the fact that governments typically grant a monopoly to their own firms. It is this lack of competition that leads to inefficient performance in government firms and in some privately owned firms as well.

The roots of our system of private ownership of property go back at least two hundred years to the ideas of Adam Smith and John Locke. The institution that has destroyed their ideal world is the corporation. The biggest threat to the ongoing existence of family farms, for example, is the corporations that buy the output; provide the inputs, including financing; and gobble up available land. Similarly, the biggest threat to small businesses is the suffocating economic environment created by corporations. The institution that consistently deprives workers of the output of their own labor is the corporation, which owns the machines and controls the markets. Governments, labor unions, cooperatives, and marketing boards have emerged or grown larger as a defense against such corporate power.

Marjorie Kelly puts forth an intermediate position, that although capitalism delivers many desirable outcomes, it has one serious shortcoming: it consistently favors shareholders at the expense of employees. The strike at General Motors in July 1998 is an excellent illustration of the classic conflict between these two major stakeholders—the desire to cut costs versus the desire to preserve jobs. The corporations' systematic bias in favor of cutting costs makes it difficult to build community and sustain democracy.

Questioning the Purpose of Capitalism

The social contract of capitalism is about paying workers less, so shareholders can be paid more. It's about reducing the wages of one person, so as to increase the profits (or capital gains) of another. It's called maximizing shareholder returns. . . .

It's not wealth I'm taking issue with here; I hope to have a good deal of it myself one day. And it's not capitalism as a whole that I question; I think it's the wisest economic system ever devised. What I take issue with is the current design of capitalism, which systematically favors the propertied class over the working class. Because in a democracy, such a system is a disgrace.

Marjorie Kelly, "Questioning the Purpose of Capitalism," *Business Ethics* (January/February, 1996).

The concentration of power in the hands of a few corporate executives is too complex a problem to address fully in the limited space of this volume. However, in the following proposals I suggest ways to bring corporate behavior more in line with the sacred values set out in the third chapter.

Loosening the Limits on Liability

A starting point would be a major change in corporate law, particularly the part having to do with limited liability. The limited liability provision guarantees that people who hold shares in a corporation will never lose more than the value of those shares if the corporation gets into serious financial trouble or goes bankrupt. The employees and creditors of the corporation cannot sue individual shareholders to gain access to their private possessions. This provision has enabled corporations to accumulate much more capital from selling shares than is possible for businesses owned by individuals, partnerships, or cooperatives.

The limited liability provision makes sense when applied to individual investors, but should it also apply if the shareholder is another corporation? Some corporations set up subsidiary companies or purchase enough shares to control existing corporations. It is too easy for an unscrupulous corporate entity to gain control of another corporation, arrange for it to borrow as much money as possible to finance the deal, then transfer liquid assets to the parent

Derek Bok, the former president of Harvard University, ... suggests that top corporate executives must be paid such outrageous sums to assure that they place the short-term interests of shareholders above all other interests that they might otherwise be tempted to consider—such as those of employees, the community, and even the corporation's own long-term viability. In short, top executives have to be paid outrageous salaries to motivate them not to yield to their instincts toward social responsibility. Viewed from this perspective, these salaries are an indicator of how distasteful the job of top corporate managers has become in an era of downsizing.

David C. Korten, *When Corporations Rule the World*, (1995), 242.

corporation and allow the purchased corporation to go bankrupt. Society would be better served overall if the parent corporation were required to cover all debts, including employees' earned wages and pension entitlements, of such a bankrupt subsidiary. The acceptance of full responsibility for the employees and debts of such firms would help to block this kind of attempt to reduce competition or to corner the market on supplies of strategic inputs.

A second area ripe for reform is executive compensation. To build community there has to be some link between the reward of the managers and that of the workers. The Japanese model might be instructive in this regard.

North American corporate leaders like to point to the willingness of Japanese workers to take a cut in pay whenever a business is in difficulty. Actually, such a cut is not a wage cut. Much of the Japanese worker's compensation is in the form of production bonuses that are paid only if the business has done well. If executive salaries here were similarly tied to a company's health, and if bonuses were extended to all levels of the work force, morale within the firm would be boosted and new levels of teamwork could be achieved.

A third area to be reformed is that of the annual meetings of corporations, where executives give account of their actions and boards of directors are elected. Since ours is a democratic society, we would expect an annual meeting to attract at least 25 or 30 percent of the shareholders. But that often isn't the case. Many corporations have a proxy system whereby shareholders sign over their vote to existing board members. This is the way they obtain a quorum. The effect is that management basically reports to itself and votes itself back into office. Even if some shareholders are dissatisfied, there is little they can do because they do not have the mechanism or opportunity to persuade absent shareholders to sign their proxy votes over to them. This lack of accountability for corporate executives is a significant problem.

In addition to being required to make their annual meetings interesting enough to attract a quorum of 25 or 30 percent of the shareholders, corporations should be required to have representatives of employees and customers on the board. Selecting the latter would be a challenge but not an insurmountable one. The form that assigns the proxy ballot would then allow the shareholders to indicate whether they want their votes to be cast by regular board members or by an employee or customer representatives. Such a practice would encourage more people to buy shares in corporations in order to let consumer representatives vote on their behalf.

Roger Parkinson, the publisher of *The Globe and Mail*, recommends that corporations donate 5 percent of their pretax profits to charities. He believes this would be an ongoing reminder to corporate managers and shareholders that there is a larger community out there and that their firms' ability to sell their output and to draw from a well-trained, dedicated labor force depends on the well-being of that larger society.

> The theory of capitalism or the purpose of a business is to increase the value for shareholders, not to make direct contributions to society. That is the role of government and of individuals. Personally, I distrust ideological purity. I am for what works. The important questions are: works for whom and over what time frame? . . .
>
> Some who accept the "for whom" as society in general and the "time frame" as mid- and long-term still argue that the most effective way to reach these goals is to reinvest the profits in the business to create new products for society, increase the size of the business, create more jobs, pay more taxes which the government can spend on charities. This is a legitimate argument. I think a more compelling public-policy argument can be made for donating 5 per cent of pretax profits to charities.
>
> From Roger Parkinson, "Notes from the Publisher," *The Globe and Mail* (June 22, 1998). Reprinted with permission from *The Globe and Mail.*

Exercising Our Power to Choose Alternatives

What other actions can we take to rectify the imbalance of power between corporate giants and the small local businesses that make the free enterprise system work as Adam

Smith intended? Where possible, we should patronize smaller firms. Big-box retailers may seem convenient in the short run, but they usually don't see the need to build community within our respective neighborhoods. These stores require a heavy stream of customers to pay for their immense advertising budgets and inventories. If we ignore their advertising, they will find it difficult to compete with smaller neighborhood firms.

We also can exercise some choice in where we invest our savings. We can seek out mutual funds that meet certain ethical or environmental criteria. These criteria can vary among ethical funds so it always pays to read the fine print. Some funds concentrate on companies that have good employee relations, demonstrate concern for the environment, don't discriminate against minorities or women, and don't operate in countries that violate human rights. Others screen out companies that produce weapons, alcohol, tobacco, pornography, and nuclear components.[20]

Setting such criteria is relatively easy; applying them is another matter. Many large corporations own subsidiaries companies or shares in other corporations. So even if a company's main activity passes scrutiny, the corporation may have other problematic linkages. Checking out all these

The Dilemma of Business Ethics

So if we don't know where our money is in mutual funds, we don't know whether it is supporting child labor, repressive regimes or any other unethical business practices. Which raises the question of whether we would care if we did know. Most of us would be horrified to discover that we are accumulating wealth through the labor of underprivileged, hungry kids or even obviously accelerating rot in the environment. But what would your reaction be if one of your target investments depended for at least part of its business on the military (at home or abroad)? Or if one of them regularly did business with authoritarian regimes in Asia? Or if one of them used chemicals to clean microchips and circuit boards at the time of manufacture without necessarily doing any kind of audit to make sure that the chemicals were disposed of safely? Or if one of them used aggressive, maybe intrusive, direct-marketing tactics?

From "The Dilemma of Business Ethics," Wayne Gooding, *The Financial Post Magazine* (December, 1998). Reprinted with the express permission of the National Post Company, a CanWest Partnership.

connections can be time-consuming because not all information is public. Also firms sell to many, varied customers. Would you eliminate a tire company from your portfolio if a small proportion of its tires were known to end up on army trucks?

As savers we want to get a good return on our investments, especially during times of inflation, when corporate shares usually increase in value while the dollar shrinks. We also want our savings to be secure. If we now add ethical concerns, our investment options narrow.

A weakness of selective shopping and selective investing is that the thrust is primarily negative. We are trying to avoid investments that do not meet certain ethical criteria. An investment strategy that seeks to implement the sacred values defined in chapter three would emphasize the positive. It would seek out desirable causes and opportunities that are made possible in part because our savings are invested there. In that way our values would be implemented. However, a price we may pay is reduced security for our savings and some risk of lower future earnings.

In summary, the ability of the many small businesses and family farms to meet the needs and wants of consumers is under serious threat from the concentrated wealth and power of a relatively small number of large corporations. To realize the values outlined in chapter three, we the people need to transform these large firms from institutions that dominate society into ones that serve us by building community.

The challenge of this act of transformation is similar to that faced by the mice that agreed they needed to bell the cat. Building a better future may mean a less certain future for some of us. It will be important to count the cost of moving from our present economic system to a new one that reflects the sacred values we deem essential for a better life. In the long run the benefits of a more sustainable, community-oriented life will be worth the cost.

The place to start is to resist, nay reject, the drive by business firms to re-name us as mere consumers. We need to reclaim our full humanity. We need to resist the temptation of using the possession and consumption of material things as means to stating who we are. We need to challenge the intent and the message of the advertising and marking institutions. When we consume we need to become much more assertive in directing business firms to produce and provide what is important to build community and to sustain life.

When work is a
pleasure, life is a joy!
When work is a duty,
life is slavery.
—*Maksim Gorky*

6

The Right to Work

Your labor and mine, all of our labor together, is a primary source of value in our society. The wages and salaries paid to labor account for some 60 percent of all the income generated in our economy. Working people are the heart, the core, of our economic system.

The discipline of economics does not deny the important contribution of labor, but labor is faceless: the human beings involved are reduced to merely another resource. This reduction is contrary to God's intent for all people. As I noted in chapter 3, God has bestowed dignity on every human being. A person's physical, mental, and spiritual well-being depend on the ability to contribute to community through creative forms of expression.

If we believe this, we need to ask fundamental questions about how people are employed:

- Does each person have a right to work? Or is this right controlled by business firms, labor unions, and government policy?
- If persons have a right to work, are they also obligated to do so and to contribute to the overall productive effort of our society?
- Is it enough for an employer to provide a job, or does that job have to be enjoyable?

Economists say the work we do happens in a labor market. Firms demand labor. The supply of labor is the people in that area who are willing and able to work. As in any market, the wage paid and the number of persons employed are defined by the point where the supply and demand for labor intersect. Many people think the wage you earn is your contribution to society, that it shouts to the world how much you are worth.

- Is your income a true indicator of what you contribute to society? If you devote your time fully to housework or volunteer work and earn no income, does that mean you are worthless?
- Does full-time employment always provide people with enough income to cover their family's basic needs of food, clothing, and shelter?

I address these issues in the present chapter, and I will pick up the discussion again in chapter nine, where I cover matters of equity and poverty. As part of the discussion of equity, I also discuss access to resources and whether access is high enough to cover a family's basic needs and enable its members to participate actively in their community.

Reducing Us to Mere Labor

The Place of Work in Religious Thought

The Bible presents a God who has given each of us personal dignity, who wants all of us to be creative, and who intends us all to have a living wage. But the Bible also says that life won't be easy. The ground produces thorns and thistles as well as food and other natural resources. It will take effort and sweat to realize the abundant life God wills for us.

Other religions also recognize that labor is important and that it is embodied in people. Islam, for instance, teaches that all people are given the capacity to think and to do physical labor. The ideal balance between these two enables persons to develop their full capacities.

Cursed is the ground because of you;
in toil you shall eat of it all the days of your life;
thorns and thistles it shall bring forth for you;
and you shall eat the plants of the field.
By the sweat of your face you shall eat bread
until you return to the ground,
for out of it you were taken;
you are dust, and to dust you shall return.

—Genesis 3:17-19

We're Diverse, but Still Mainly Workers

The discipline of economics recognizes that human capabilities are diverse. We are not all meant to do the same kind of work. Bob Goudzwaard summarizes this issue with a discussion of improving productivity.[1] For example, a group of workers can be organized so that together they produce more than if each one worked alone. The process of organizing labor more efficiently recognizes the important human capacity to manage. Moreover, productivity can be increased by combining labor with capital. Capital can range from the simple tools of long ago to the complex computers and machines of today. The evolution of such capital is the product of a third human dimension: a capacity to invent and innovate.

It's a Shame to Waste Creativity

With the evolution of technology and capital, the three resources—labor, land, and capital—became distinct elements of production. As illustrated by Adam Smith's visit to the pin factory, by the mid-1770s there was a movement toward greater labor specialization. By the mid-1870s, many workers were producing only one part of the actual product, such as the head of the pin. They no longer had the creative joy and privilege of literally holding in their hands the finished product to which they had contributed a part.

Karl Marx used the term *alienation* to describe what

happens to workers who become detached from the finished product. Many alienated workers ceased to be full human beings in the eyes of their employers. They were merely cogs in the wheel to increase the income of the employer and owner of the capital.

This alienation deprives workers of some of the dignity God has bestowed on them. They no longer see their daily labor as a means to express their creativity and contribute to the overall well-being of the community. Rather, it is the income they earn from their toil that enables them to live, to express some creativity, and to build community during their limited nonworking hours.

In an article titled "Monkey Business" *The Economist* describes how monkeys in Thailand are trained to pick ripe coconuts.[2] For their work they receive a "living wage," and they are given sick leave and retirement benefits. Many workers do not fare much better. Some fare worse. Not all people working for a large company could say with the Thai monkeys that their employer knew all their names.

Most economists in Marx's day did not object to people being called labor and thus losing part of their identity. His profound ideas on labor alienation were largely ignored. Goudzwaard observes that "under the influence of John Stuart Mill, Adam Smith's spiritual heir . . . economists introduced a significant modification: they regarded the possession of consumption goods as the most important type of 'utility' and the performance of labor as a clear instance of 'disutility.' All classical economists speak of the 'pain of labor.'"[3]

Labor has now been reduced to a mere input in the economic system. It is bought and sold like any other resource. Whatever humanity workers still possess is reduced to expressing themselves as consumers with the money they earn from their labor. For many people, their position at work is no different from that of a well-trained monkey.

Breakdown of Relationships

Between 1900 and the 1930s, the size of firms increased dramatically.[4] As a result, workers became alienated not only from the finished product of their labor, but also from their ultimate employer, the executives who control the corporation. Workers still relate to a supervisor, but the supervisor is merely another employee, one small part in a vast corporate bureaucracy called management.

During the Great Depression of the 1930s something else occurred in the realm of economics: output grew faster than incomes and demand. There were too many goods and not enough customers. Unemployment soared, businesses went bankrupt, and the economy became severely depressed. The economist John Maynard Keynes put forth a convincing argument that the free market, on its own, would not solve this problem. Instead, he urged governments to get more actively involved to ensure enough employment to maintain social stability.

In addition, Keynes helped focus attention on the unemployed as people. He argued that an important goal of economic activity should be jobs for everyone who wanted to work. A limited application of his ideas in the United States became known as the New Deal.

Labor Takes a Leaf from a Corporate Book

The response of laborers to their growing alienation was to join forces and organize as labor unions. The movement had started in the latter half of the nineteenth century. The reasoning was simple: if the owners of capital can form corporations, then the employees of these corporations should have the right to form unions. The law governing corporations allows the owners of capital to join together and form one firm. If the law provides this right to owners of capital, why shouldn't employees have a comparable right?

The Place of Labor Unions

The passage of the National Labor Relations Act (the Wagner Act) during the Great Depression gave the labor movement the legal framework required to form unions. But the struggle to gain acceptance, both from individual employers and from society at large, was long and bitter. Over time, however, the union movement has gained such benefits as grievance procedures, the eight-hour working day, annual vacations, workplace health and safety regulations, and significant pension rights.

In addition, during the past few decades the wages of union members have risen to 13 to 19 percent higher than nonunion wages in the United States, and 10 to 20 percent higher in Canada.[5] These benefits, though, vary a great deal by industry, occupation, and amount of overtime.

Often, the most powerful stimulus to the organization of a union is an unfair, indifferent employer, in addition to workers' general alienation from the finished product they are producing. The presence of the union steward enables an employee to communicate with the firm's manager without having to go through the foreman.

Not Going Quietly

In any economy, any time that health and safety, fair treatment and good pay are of importance to most employees, but of less concern to employers, then there will be a demand for unions—the old saying is that "management gets the union it deserves."

The issue of employee representation is so emotionally charged precisely because our work is vital to both our economic and social well-being. Our industrial relations system was designed to provide some balance among competing economic and social interests. If the evolution of the New Economy continues to unfold as it has, then the challenges to our existing labor market institutions will only intensify. As Canadians grapple with the challenge of reshaping the institutional arrangements we have inherited from the old economy, we ought not to separate the issue of how best to protect employee rights to freedom of association and workplace equity from debates about our future economic priorities.

From Richard Chaykowski, "Not Going Quietly," *The Financial Post 2000* (November 1, 1997), 13. Material reprinted with the express permission of the National Post Company, a CanWest Partnership.

No Room for Dissent

For a union's collective action to work, it needs to present a united front; dissident minorities cannot be tolerated. In this way, unions and corporations are alike. In a corporation it is very difficult, if not impossible, for an unhappy minority to take control. The system of proxy voting, according to which directors vote on behalf of absent shareholders, virtually ensures that the directors will get their way.

The labor movement has sought similar protection against minority viewpoints. The strongest position for a union is a closed shop, a situation in which no one can be hired without joining the union. An intermediate position is a union shop; employers are allowed to hire nonunion members but must still deduct union dues from each employee's paycheck whether the employee is a member or not. A third position is similar to the union shop, but employees can ask that their dues be allocated to a charity rather than to the union. The reason for collecting dues from employees who are not members of the union is that even nonmembers benefit from the collective activity of the union; therefore, they too should be "taxed," even if in a different way from union members.

The Big Stick Called "Strike"

The power of a union is its ability to withhold labor—go on strike—if an acceptable agreement cannot be reached with the employer. A strike is effective only if the vast majority of employees withhold their labor. As a means to this end, unions attempt to build up a strike fund from the monthly dues collected. If a strike happens, members who march on a picket line can collect strike pay. Union members who choose to stay on the job will be disciplined and likely will be harassed when they cross the picket line. Members who simply stay home lose their wages and don't receive strike pay.

Strikes can be costly in terms of both lost wages and lost production. The General Motors strike of 1998 closed down two hundred thousand jobs for almost two months. During this time the company lost sales worth more than two billion dollars.

Why would either side allow such a costly strike to drag on for so long? Part of the answer is found in an article featuring Mr. BoBo, a United Auto Workers member who is portrayed as a typical employee in the Flint, Michigan, plant of General Motors. Mr. BoBo, a loyal employee, felt the need to strike because he thought GM's managers had lost contact with the needs and priorities of their employees on the shop floor. Specifically, he saw the executives as so preoccupied with getting their bonuses that they lost sight of such important values as maintaining jobs for the next generation and preserving the ongoing health of small cities such as Flint.

The article goes on to indicate Mr. BoBo realizes things have to change. General Motors will find it hard to be profitable if it has to continue paying some employees $40 per hour for

A Man of Flint

Mr. BoBo is a good example of what might be called Flintman.... Like many of his peers, Mr. BoBo has been working for GM ever since high school, the only break being a two-year stint in Vietnam.... His father once worked for GM; his brother still does.... His wife comes from a GM family. Mr. BoBo would not dream of driving any other car.

Most employers envy such testaments of loyalty. But at GM, Flintman is disillusioned....

It is tempting to assume that Mr. BoBo is an industrial brontosaurus, prepared—thrilled, even—to hold his employer to ransom. He says he has no problem with managers being paid well, or with workers, if necessary, being replaced by machines; but he believes that the difference in attitudes between the boardroom and the shop floor is every bit as wide as the gap between himself and the people who protested about Vietnam 30 years ago. The last time the men at Flint made concessions, he complains, GM's then boss picked up millions in bonuses. "I think about how things will be when I'm dead; the guys in the boardroom don't. I'm worried about our children's jobs—and the towns around here. They just care about bonuses."

From "A Man of Flint," *The Economist* (June 20, 1998), 79. The Economist Newspaper Ltd. All rights reserved. Reprinted with permission. Further reproduction prohibited. www.economist.com.

eight hours per day in exchange for 4.5 hours of work per day. But a strike became necessary because Mr. BoBo and his fellow workers never heard these high-paid executives set out a vision for GM's future.

A similar argument is advanced in a *Globe and Mail* editorial that portrays General Motors as a company that is so successful it can avoid establishing the necessary trust between management and employees that is essential for a smooth-functioning free-market economic system.[6]

Contrast the experience of General Motors with that of Caterpillar, a company that has recognized the need to build trust with its employees.[7] It endured a strike that was on again, off again over a four-year period in the first half of the 1990s. The eventual changes reduced the time and effort to construct one large back loader from six thousand workers in twenty-five days to three thousand workers in six days. At the same time, management made the workplace cleaner and healthier, introduced forty-seven robots to do certain boring jobs, cut inventory costs, and reduced design-time lags from ten years to twenty-seven months. Such changes have restored labor peace and increased profits by 155 percent over a five-year period.

Union Pros and Cons

Defenders say unions continue to deliver workplace justice and improve workers' economic well-being—indeed, that they advance social and economic equity in society. They also point out that workers' rights to free association are critical to a healthy democracy.

Detractors say unions create economic inefficiencies, at the workplace level by constraining management from pursuing productivity—enhancing work practices and at the macroeconomic level by creating losses through strikes and by reducing the competitive capability of firms. For good measure, they add that unions create social and economic privilege for their members and that, in many cases, they are not particularly democratic.

From Richard Chaykowski, "Not Going Quiety," *The Financial Post 2000* (November 1, 1997), 8. Material reprinted with the express permission of the National Post Company, CanWest Partnership.

Did the union here contribute to the problem or to the solution? It's hard to say. We might argue they contributed to the problem by refusing necessary change. Even if that is an initial, contributing factor to the strike, one can conclude Caterpillar wouldn't have voluntarily improved working conditions without pressure from the union.

The advantages labor unions have gained for their members are being threatened by the growing ease with which companies can shop around to other countries to get their work done. This effect of globalization, forcing workers to compete against each other across international borders, is merely the latest step in the reduction of human beings to a mere factor in a production formula.

Organizing Work as if People Mattered

The dignity of the human person should be central to an economic system that intends to serve all people. If it is not— if the system uses some people for the benefit of others—it destroys part of the dignity of both the employer and the employee. We recognize this to be so in a master-slave relationship.

Ours is an economic system where the owners of capital hold the basic rights to manage and the employees have little influence over their working conditions. That is certainly better than slavery. But are there still traces of a master-slave relationship? We need to remember: it is not the type of work that defines the dignity of the worker. Rather, work has dignity because a human person performs it.

Keeping Dignity in Mind

A company that wants to foster the dignity of all persons in the firm must address several key issues:

- the nature of the work performed, including how it is organized;
- broad participation in making decisions about issues

such as job security and technological change and in dealing with interpersonal grievances; and

- fair distribution of the income generated by employees.

Work is part of God's plan. In Genesis we read that God assigns all persons the responsibility to join in the ongoing creation of the world. We are the ones granted the privilege of naming all the other forms of life that come into existence.

This assignment includes our daily work, which is more than simply what we do to earn a living. Our work is meant to express the creative spirit that God has given to each of us.

Whenever the nature of work or the way it is organized hinders people from being able to contribute creatively, those people lose part of their humanity. In Robert Simons's view, the capitalist economic system alienates employees from their spiritual need to create. Stated another way, providing work that fosters dignity is not natural to capitalism. As a result, we need to ask if the system is flexible enough to allow employers and employees to creatively develop a form of work that fosters dignity.

> Humans have a spiritual need to create. Most basically, it is expressed when they satisfy their physical needs. The satisfaction of physical needs, however, is secondary to the expression of human freedom as the primary manifestation of the spiritual need to create. In addition, the spiritual need to create is reflected in humanity's capacity for culture and for the cultivation and appreciation of the aesthetic.
>
> —Robert Simons, Competing Gospels (1995).

All Together Now: Flexibility

Can we reorganize work so that everyone can participate in a dignified manner? Any attempt to experiment or create new alternatives will have to take into account the new workplace buzzword: flexibility. As others have argued, flexibility can be positive for workers if it means continuous training, innovation, and adaptability to changing economic

No End in Sight

If stability was the core goal of industrial-age management, flexibility has assumed that role in the post-industrial era.

There are different ways organizations are now trying to become flexible. Some, but unfortunately not too many, are emphasizing challenging work, employee discretion and continuous training in order to establish a flexibility based on a multi-skilled and committed workforce capable of sustaining high rates of innovation and adaptability.

In most cases, however, flexibility primarily means minimizing costs, including fixed payroll costs. Thus the growing incidence of part-time, contract and temporary workers and, at the same time, the increased reliance on overtime....

Obviously, the concept of security changes in the flexible workplace. Even the most people-friendly organizations no longer have job security pledges, such as what we saw a decade or two ago. In fact, the best any employer offers workers now is a guarantee, not to a job for life, but to the kind of work experience and training that will leave them in good stead for the inevitable job searches in the future.

From Gordon Betcherman, "No End in Sight," *The Financial Post 2000* (November 1, 1997), 6. Material reprinted with the express permission of the National Post Company, a CanWest Partnership.

conditions. For most managers, though, it means little more than seeking ways to reduce fixed payroll costs and employment security.

To help make workers more willing partners in the move toward greater flexibility, some firms have developed effective personnel departments that have improved relationships between management and labor.

This model of labor management has some potential in that it gives groups of employees a greater role in defining work and working conditions and improves communication with management. Done properly, it could enable the flexibility that Betcherman favors: challenging work with employee discretion and ongoing training so they can generate the innovation and adaptability a firm needs to maintain a strong position in the market.[8]

In most cases, though, neither employers nor employees grasp the potential of this model of cooperation. Firms are attracted to this model not because it will develop their employees but because it may discourage them from forming a union and thus having the potential power to strike.[9]

Flexibility is sought by minimizing employees' power, not by enhancing cooperation and dignity.

Can Employees Help to Manage?

A Share of the Profits

Some firms have tried to enhance workplace human dignity by offering some form of profit sharing. In North America, profit sharing tends to take one of two forms: annually receiving shared profits in cash or investing shared profits in an enriched retirement or severance package. The former serves to motivate workers during the year in the hope of making the firm profitable. The latter bolsters employee stability and motivates employees to take an interest in the longer-term economic health of the firm. It may also give a firm some flexibility if the package is used to reduce the fixed costs of an employee retirement plan.

The Japanese approach involves a relatively low base salary, a high degree of job security—at least in the past—and a sharing of profits if the firm does well. This model has generated significant employee loyalty, has motivated employees, and has given managers the flexibility to absorb market downturns. In the Japanese model the base salary is lower and the proportion of shared profits is higher than in North America.

A further step, distributing shares in the firm, combines the issues of sharing profit and broadening participation. By owning shares, employees can, over time, gain some say in the management.

On a day-to-day basis, employees will be interested primarily in job security and a grievance system that allows them to bring work-related concerns to top management without having them filtered by immediate supervisors.

To have real impact, though, employees also need representation on the board of directors. This gives employees some say in vital issues such as the firm's process of technological change. It also opens the company's books to employees. While that may strike fear into the heart of management, a benefit is that employees see for themselves how their actions affect the financial picture. It places more responsibility on them to contribute to a firm's good management and profitability.

Profit sharing and employee stock ownership plans (ESOPs) tend to be most common in small and mid-size firms. They involve significant administrative costs related to the meeting of government tax and nondiscrimination regulations. Both approaches to profit sharing have two major weaknesses: they do not really address the first issue of organizing dignified work, and they are usually run by management.

Working With *and Not* For

One firm that has sought to organize work to involve the employees is DW Friesen and Sons of Altona, Manitoba.[10] Janis Thiessen notes the conscious use of the phrase "working *with* Friesens" to indicate an implied cooperation between labor and management. Building on a labor force that is ethnically homogeneous, Friesens have made a conscious effort to create a sense of community within the firm. They employ a form of the employee stock ownership plan to reward individual employees as well as distribute profits more generally within the firm. If an employee dies or leaves the

---

"Working with Friesens"

Working with Friesens is the title of the 1993 employee handbook of the printing and stationery firm DW Friesen & Sons of Altona, Manitoba. The choice of preposition is interesting. One does not work for or even at Friesens, but with the company. To explore the meanings underlying this word selection, these three prepositions are placed on a continuum of the relationship of labour to the production of value. At one end of the continuum, working "for" a company implies that labour is merely one of several inputs or resources. The word "for" denies any creative role to labour. At the other end, working "with" a company implies that labour is essential to the production of value. The preposition "at" occupies the territory in between. Clearly, Friesens wish to convey the idea that labour is a partner in the business.

From a paper by Janis Thiessen (1995), 1.

firm, the accumulated shares are "bought" by the Friesen Employee Trust.[11]

The level of job satisfaction among Friesens' employees is above average for firms with four hundred to five hundred employees, and outside observers are impressed with the quality and dedication of the workforce.[12] This approach to employer-employee relations has served the firm well and can be a model for others.

How Much Do You Contribute?

In any firm, it is people who produce output. For the business to remain on a healthy path there has to be some way to divide the value of this output among owners, managers, and employees.

When you look at your income and the income of others around you, do you think the portion you earn fairly represents what you contribute to society? If your boss makes one hundred times as much, does that mean your boss is contributing one hundred times as much?

The Paycheck as Motivator

Does income motivate people to work? Would you work harder if you were paid more? As your income goes up your taxes go up even faster. Does that discourage you from wanting a promotion or a chance to work overtime?

In the United States, estimates of the income of chief executive officers (CEOs) relative to that of employees range from 28 to 1 to 326 to 1.[13] These estimates show that the average CEO makes 728 times more than someone earning minimum wage. If the U.S. minimum wage had risen as fast as executive incomes since 1960, it would now be $41 per hour rather than $5.15.

One explanation for relatively high executive incomes is that executives work long hours. With downsizing, managers have to work harder to make up for the thinning of the work force. In addition, globalization forces them to travel much more, and they have less time to spend with family and friends. Even so, these differences in pay cannot be explained or justified on the basis of productivity.

Peter Drucker, a management studies guru, calls the CEO wage gap a disaster and predicts a significant backlash. Drucker cites the successful industrialist J. P. Morgan, who claimed that whenever after-tax income of management is more than twenty times that of the employees, it becomes impossible to build a team. Morgan saw that as corporate mismanagement.

Executive Pay Backlash

"In the next economic downturn there will be an outbreak of bitterness and contempt for the super-corporate chieftans who pay themselves millions.... Few top executives can even imagine the hatred, contempt and fury that has been created."

Predictions of class warfare from Buzz Hargrove, president of the Canadian Auto Workers? A call to arms from the Communist Party?

Actually, it's a quote from management studies guru Peter Drucker, hero to many CEOs in big business around the world....

Prof. Drucker adamantly believes the CEO wage gap is a diasaster for employees, companies and shareholders.

From Bill Tieleman, "Executive Pay Backlash," *The Financial Post* (January 4, 1999), C4. Material reprinted with the express permission of the National Post Company, a CanWest Partnership.

Measuring Productivity

The discipline of economics seeks to explain these income differences with a theory of something called marginal productivity. According to this theory, it is possible to measure how much each person contributes to the output of the firm and then pay each person accordingly, even if it means a lopsided distribution of money.

Although this theory is embraced by some economists, it has numerous weaknesses. For one thing, what wages really reflect is the relative bargaining power of the employer and the employees. When we see a huge gap between executive and employee salaries, what we are really seeing is the limited bargaining power of employees.

Another fallacy of this theory is that it judges the value of a job solely on the income earned from that work. That is shortsighted. What really gives work value is the contribution it makes to our primary vocation of being responsible to God for the ongoing creative process. People should be set free to express their own creativity as they pursue this vocation. The real value of their creativity is much more than income; it is the contribution they make to building, maintaining, and sustaining all that has been and is being created.

Suzanne McBride illustrates what such freedom can mean. Her ability and education enabled her to obtain a high-paying, secure job. The money she was able to earn should have set her free to enjoy all that life had to offer. But what she really wanted was the freedom to express herself and contribute to society. After becoming a full-time artist, she discovered that life becomes a joy when one's work is a pleasure.

The fallacy of equating the value of work with income is most obvious when it comes to volunteer work and work in the home. Likely the best way we can contribute to building community and a better future is through the care we offer our children in their early formative years. In our society, though, persons who set aside several years for this important task are made to feel second-class, as if they are guilty of not contributing to the production of output. We don't even count this labor as worthy of a pension or other means of old-age income security.

> ### Climbing Corporate Ladder Loses Its Appeal for Some
>
> Suzanne McBride's paper sculpture rests on an easel at the Carving Arts Center in old downtown Plano, Texas. Intricately designed with upward-reaching swirls, it is titled Freedom's Dream.
>
> The piece could be a symbol for her new life. Ms. McBride, who has a master's degree in computer science, abandoned her lucrative career as a software engineer last year to become a full-time artist. "This has given me the freedom to do whatever I want on a given day," she said. "It makes me feel good to get up in the morning again."
>
> From Diane Kunde, "Climbing Corporate Ladder Loses Its Appeal for Some," *The Ottawa Citizen* (June 20, 1998).

The same holds true for volunteer work. Take the case of Carol Ann Cole. Did she contribute more to society as a vice president at Bell Canada than she does in her current role as a volunteer fundraiser for cancer research and treatment? If measured the value of her contribution as we normally do, on the basis of income earned, the answer would be yes. Her salary at Bell Canada enabled a lifestyle that made a statement: I am somebody; I am significant.

Another example is the countless hours of volunteer time offered at the community club level. Community club volunteers help make some of our neighborhoods great places to raise a family. Similarly, when young people spend two or three years as volunteers on an overseas relief or development assignment, they typically find the experience enormously worthwhile. Frequently it shapes their values for life. Society grants very little recognition to such forms of work.

Why is this so? Because to place a value on volunteer labor would seriously challenge a central tenet of capitalism: the use of income to motivate human effort. Capitalism does not expect everyone to have the same income. It rewards according to differences in talent, education, and willingness to take risk. It also contends that over time there will be more goods and services for everyone to share if income

Carol Ann

Carol Ann Cole believes in a well-ordered universe—one in which everything, no matter how awful, happens for a reason. She has to believe something good came from the lump she found in her breast in 1992, just five days before her 76-year-old mother, Mary, also learned she had cancer. Otherwise, the long treatment they both endured and her mother's death 11 months later would be without purpose. And Cole might still be a high-flying vice-president at Bell Canada, instead of finding deeper purpose as a tireless cancer crusader and fund-raiser. "I work just as hard, I get no salary and I'm forever on the road," she says, smiling from amid the clutter of her small apartment-office in a Halifax highrise. "But at the end of the day, I've never felt so fulfilled."

From John DeMont, "Carol Ann," *Maclean's*, (December 21, 1998).

differentials are used to attract and retain people with the appropriate mix of skills and to motivate individuals to contribute more productive effort.

Enjoying the Fruits of Our Labor

Wouldn't workers be motivated to contribute more if they were given more time off to enjoy their income? Juliet Schor cites two examples to illustrate this:

> When the Medtronic Corporation in Minneapolis decided to give its employees forty hours' pay for thirty-six hours of work, it hired no additional personnel but found that output increased. On balance, the company saved money. Ideal Industries, a small family-owned business, shifted to a four-day, thirty-eight hour week—almost at forty hours' pay. Again, productivity did not decline. But absenteeism did.[14]

Another example is the move in France to a thirty-five-hour workweek. Companies are required to pay the equivalent of thirty-nine hours of wages for a thirty-five-hour workweek or for a thirty-nine-hour workweek and two additional weeks of holidays during the year. During the first two years of the policy employment increased, more women were encouraged to enter the workforce, economic growth exceeded the average for the euro currency area, labor productivity increased, and payroll costs fell because of lower social charges and greater flexibility in labor use. The improved labor productivity, at least in the short term, has been attributed to the fact that firms were forced to use the time of the workers more wisely.[15]

It is too early to consider the French action a success. The program of implementation included tax concessions that may have been the stimulus for the economic growth that occurred. Labor unions initially advocated the move to a shorter workweek but are having second thoughts as opportunities for overtime work are being reduced. The initial success occurred in large firms, which welcomed greater flexibility in organizing work. Small firms are now being phased in to the plan, and they are finding it much harder to replace the labor lost with a shorter workweek, so the initially reported advantages may not be repeated in the smaller firms.

Both examples illustrate work as duty, and the source of pleasure from a job as the spending made possible by the income generated. Economists assume spending is the source of pleasure for the vast majority of people with jobs. If so, then a shorter workweek merely inserts some balance between income and time to enjoy it to ensure the continuation of the desired motivating effects of income derived from a job.

But if we believe that our work is a creative vocation, as God desires, we need to prove economists wrong by organizing work differently. This is not unrealistic. As Bruno Frey observes, we do many things without expecting or receiving payment. We do them simply because we enjoy doing so—"playing cards with friends the whole night, jogging for miles, climbing high mountains, spending hours solving crossword puzzles, contributing anonymously to a charitable organization, or working without compensation in a developing country's hospital."[16] He calls this inner reward intrinsic motivation. If we organize work in such a way that we see ourselves as God's partners in the ongoing work of creation, then Frey's intrinsic motivation may complement income as a motivator.

In her discussion of Frey's ideas, Monique Jerome-Forget argues that payment of money can actually crowd out intrinsic forms of motivation. Further, she says that employees may be better motivated if they can work with the employer rather than being governed by rules and time clocks. Recognizing employees as human beings, building on their desire to contribute creatively to the building of a better society, and encouraging them to develop their capabilities may well reduce the role of income as the chief means to motivate a fair day's work.

Work as an Expression of Our Reliance on God

Seeing high income as the gauge of our contribution to society can have severe consequences: we may find ourselves making work an idol in our life. The Old Testament tells many stories of people striving to be totally self-sufficient without any reliance on God. This desire for self-sufficiency is portrayed as idolatry. The word *idolatry* sounds harsh, yet that is the result when we make work our whole life, even drawing our entire identity from it.

Take the example of the taxi driver picking up passengers at the station: the price paid is the sole outcome of the transaction. Now inject an element of personal relationship, say, a host picking up her guests from the same station. The dynamic is quite different, although the action is superficially similar. The more important personal relationships are in a given situation, the greater the influence of intrinsic motivation.

Within the family or in a friendship, an untimely monetary payment—say, for a favor rendered or an act of love—can completely erase this motivation. Compensation can also crowd out intrinsic motivation in the workplace, for example, in cases where employees are highly motivated by the content of their jobs and where they perceive the monetary incentive as overly controlling.

The crowding-out effect applies not just to the specific target of an intervention, but spills over into related areas.... The child paid to mow the lawn has not only less intrinsic motivation to do that job, but is also less willing to do any other housework for free.

From Monique Jerome-Forget, "Taking a Closer Look at Personal Motivation," *The Financial Post* (August, 16, 1997), 23. Material reprinted with the express permission of the National Post Company, a CanWest Partnership.

While we may pay lip service to the importance of a well-rounded and balanced life, the fact is that our society heaps honors on those who are obsessed with advancing their firms. Take, for example, the selection of Canadian National Railway's Paul Tellier as the *Financial Post's* Chief Executive Officer of the Year. In an article celebrating this honor Kathryn Leger describes his role in completing the privatization of the

railway and turning it into an expanding, profitable corporation. He has accomplished this with a lot of hard work and by
reducing the work force by one-third and the number of vice
presidents from eleven to five. Leger quotes Tellier as saying:
"You've got to be resilient. You've got to keep pushing. I'm
more motivated than ever. . . . Instead of winning the lottery,
what I would love to have is a 26-hour day."[17]

An effective counter to this attitude is the biblical
Sabbath. Keeping one day a week (and for some, one year in
seven) free of work reminds us that the ongoing existence of
life, business, or job does not depend on ceaseless, furious
work. It allows us to say that a certain level of income is
enough. It opens the door to having our identity shaped by
our relationships with our Creator and with one another, in
the communities God has willed for us.

Alternatively, rather than striving for ever higher income
and incurring debt to buy the "good life," some are opting
for simpler living. At the end of a day they still have leftover
human energy and time to build and maintain communities.[18] Their security and well-being is based on being in
community.

Workaholics, as well as all business executives who have
tried to advance their firms by eliminating the competition,
need a sabbatical. Indeed, society likely would be served well
if winning the *Financial Post's* CEO of the Year award
required a one-year sabbatical from the job.

The opposite of idolizing work is being unable to work
because of discrimination or lack of jobs. The victims of job
destruction and discrimination are denied not only income,
but also the opportunity to contribute creatively to the building of community. Our society would be very different if
CEO of the Year awards were given on the basis of the
achievement of cost-effective ways to create employment
opportunities for all persons rather than merely the maximization of profit and physical production.

In summary, our society needs to rediscover the people who make up our workforce. This will involve addressing both how work is organized and the purpose for which people are employed. If we want to retain the human dignity that God intends for each person, we will need much greater flexibility within our economic system. All people should have more freedom to choose their preferred material standard of living as well as the means to earn the income to support it.

Neither present economic theory nor the incentive system that drives many entrepreneurs points the way to this greater flexibility and choice. If we want to achieve a dignity-enhancing new vision in which we all have a creative role in building community, we will have to work concertedly to make that dignity and creativity a priority of a renewed economic system.

In the pursuit of commercial wealth, we have cleared land of natural vegetation and planted monoculture crops, dammed and diverted most of our major water courses, moved mountains to extract mineral wealth, replaced native wildlife with imported domestic animals, unleashed a toxic brew of complex organic chemicals into our ground and surface water, air, and food supplies. We have been intrepid in our experiments with nature, making radical changes without knowing the full consequences, hoping that whatever they are, we will be able to cope and still reap some benefit. However we think of ourselves politically, we have been anything but conservative. We are among the most radical people in the history of civilization.

—Thomas Michael Power

14.6

7

The Entire Creation Sighs and Throbs with Pain

We now come to the third major input, after capital and labor, to the productive efforts of all contemporary societies: natural resources.

The analysis of natural resources is quite different from that of the other two inputs. Labor is unique in that all of it is owned by persons. Capital is also owned, although primarily by corporations rather than directly by persons. Many natural resources are not owned in this sense. Jurisdiction over oceans, for example, is shared by countries, who often get into vigorous disputes over who owns the rights of resources, such as fish stocks, within these bodies of water. The air that we breathe and that absorbs many pollutants is not subject to private ownership. The same holds for much of our landscape that we call wilderness.

How to exercise stewardship of these natural resources within our capitalist system has become a major challenge. Failure to meet the challenge could massively disrupt our livelihoods and standard of living.

The Landscape of Our Lives

Natural resources are much more than mineral ore, farmland, forests, and fish. They are our total environment, the natural landscape of our lives. They include a plant in full bloom, a soaring bird, a majestic mountain peak, a cascading waterfall, the vast sky filled with stars. They include the feverish activities of insects that pollinate our plants so the plants can bear fruit. They include the silent work plants do to separate carbon from oxygen to give us a continual supply of air to breathe. They include an atmosphere that brings the moisture back from the sea to provide us with the water we need for life and for the replenishment of our lakes and rivers. They include the complex biodiversity we need to sustain life on this planet.

Our Misuse and Abuse of Nature

This natural landscape can no longer be taken for granted. Our misuse of it threatens to extinguish numerous forms of life. As noted in this chapter's opening quote from Thomas Power, we have engaged in radical experiments with nature. Richard Welford claims that the "Damage to the environment of the planet over the last few decades has reached the point of causing untold suffering for human beings and other species."[1] Relating this directly to fishing prospects in the Atlantic Ocean, Richard Cashin states: "We face a disaster of monumental proportions."[2]

> **A Clarion Call for All Earth's Creatures**
>
> Did you know that within two millennia of his arrival in North America about 12,000 years ago, man had hunted 57 species of the continent's largest mammals to extinction? That earth's forests are being cut down at a rate of more than one acre a second? That homo sapiens—a tiny minority of the planet's fauna—annually consume half the energy needed to sustain all the planet's life forms?
>
> From a book review by A. C. Grayling of *The Sixth Extinction*, by Richard Leakey and Roger Lewin, in *The Financial Post* (March 10, 1996). Material reprinted with the express permission of the National Post Company, a CanWest Partnership.

Even though there is mounting scientific evidence of an impending disaster caused by global warming, we tend to take little notice. The automobile, oil, and coal industries have effective political lobbyists urging our legislators to resist specific actions such as implementing the Kyoto Accord. As it did in the case of exhaust emissions, California is taking the lead to counter such political forces with legislation intended to address major causes of global warming. In July 2002, Governor Gray Davis signed a law extending the requirement that car manufacturers reduce exhaust emissions; the new law calls for them to reduce the emission of greenhouse gases.[3]

We tend to downplay the negative effects our actions may have on the environment. After all, the actions of each one of us are so insignificant in a global setting. This is a convenient rationalization for our unwillingness to stop greedy, careless activities. We'll only live to be seventy or eighty; why worry about the long-term future?

A Sustaining Mission from God

In the Bible we read that the entire creation sighs and throbs with pain (Rom. 8). We, humanity, are the cause of this pain. We have failed to recognize the integrity, fullness, and sacredness of what God has created. We have not grasped our divine assignment to continue the creative process and to sustain life on this planet. It has been edged aside by our relentless pursuit of abundance.

In this chapter I look at how the market impacts the environment we all share. Specifically, I examine the tragedy of common-owned property, the problem of setting a price on our priceless landscape, and I consider how we can motivate one another to tend our garden for the benefit of our children. I conclude by discussing how to move from our current destructive path to the healing and restoration God intended.

The Tragedy of the Commons

Paying for the Air We Breathe

What if Mother Nature charged a fee for all the services we receive from her on a daily basis—like turning carbon dioxide into the oxygen we need to breathe? Some ecological

Putting a Price Tag on the Planet

A couple of economists have gotten together and added up all the free services and goods provided by Mother Nature. This "natural capital" included soil formation, regulation of atmospheric chemical composition, nutrient cycling, pollination, production of raw materials and other marvels.

After a mighty bit of figuring, the economists concluded that Creation provided things for free that would probably cost anywhere from US$16 trillion to US$54 trillion on the free market. In other words, according to Nature's economists, if Mother Nature ever sent capitalist society a bill, it would total an average of US$33 trillion a year, or almost twice the world's annual economic production.

From Andrew Nikiforuk "Putting a Price Tag on the Planet," *Canadian Business* (August 1997), 83.

economists have calculated that the price would be more than the value of all of the labor employed and all of the capital used to produce the goods and services that humanity counts in its Gross Domestic Product (GDP).

That's a staggering sum. And it's something we rarely consider because no one ever sends us a bill. Much of what nature has to offer is not paid for because no one person or firm owns it. This lack of individual ownership gives rise to what is called *the tragedy of the commons*.

When the Usual Rules Fail Us

Adam Smith had a pragmatic view of the ownership of private property: we take better care of something we own than we would if others owned it. In Smith's time, the commons referred to a common grazing area either owned by the community or not yet developed. All community members could use such an area to graze their livestock or hunt wild animals. If more animals grazed there than the land could support, the grazing area would begin to deteriorate. Or if too many animals were hunted, they would become scarce or even extinct.

Since no one owned the property, no one had a personal incentive to take charge of conserving its resources. No individual herder would reduce the number of animals grazing there, and no hunter would feel personally responsible to cut back on hunting. The general principle is that if no single person can benefit from careful, sustainable use of a resource, then that resource will eventually be abused through overuse and misuse.

Our Waste of Water

A pressing example of the suffering of a natural resource that is held in common is that of our oceans. Scientists tell us

these vast water reservoirs are dying, and human behavior appears to be the culprit. And since the oceans beyond the two-hundred-mile coastal limits are open-access, no one country can address the problem adequately on its own. Nations will have to act together to reverse this process of dying.

> **Our Dying Seas**
>
> From the polar seas to the tropics, fish populations have collapsed or teeter on the brink. In a third of the Pacific, plankton that form the foundation of the marine food chain are vanishing.... As science scrambles to make sense of uneven data, evidence points to an alarming conclusion: the sea, the cradle of life, is dying.
>
> From Chris Wood, "Our Dying Seas," *Maclean's* (October 5, 1998), 50.

In the Pacific Northwest the northern spotted owl is threatened with extinction. A conflict has arisen between the commercial interests of the lumber industry, both owners of firms and their employees, and those who are concerned about the maintenance of the owl's habitat. It is claimed that up to a hundred thousand jobs in Washington, Oregon, and northern California could be at stake in the dispute.[4]

The owl cannot hire a public relations firm to make its plight known. Nor do persons concerned with its survival have a direct way to express concern within the market. If this owl vanishes, no corrective action will ever bring it back.

Wanted: a New Economic Theory

The tragedy of the commons is not new. What is new is the number of people who are making claims on our common property as the world's population continues to grow.

To deal with this ravaging new reality, Herman Daly calls

for radical changes in the discipline of economics.[5] Economic theory generally is based on what happens normally, or on average. It does not typically address what happens in the market as the environment approaches its limit in more and more areas. Daly argues that as we add up the value of the fish we catch, we also need to subtract the loss associated with a dying sea. As we add up the profits and wages earned from the lumber industry we also need to subtract the loss of species that become extinct because of how this industry operates.

Canada's environment provides an illustration of what happens when a relatively small number of people encroach on the vast territories of nature.[6] The country is bounded on three sides by oceans, and within its borders is 9 percent of the world's supply of fresh water. One would think this is enough water for any country, but Canada has exploited its supply so thoroughly to aid in the exportation of raw materials and to raise its standard of living that "experts fear Canada's cavalier attitude towards water will prove calamitous."[7]

The effect has been that people on all three coasts who earn their living by fishing have lost their livelihood. Canada is now faced with the multibillion dollar cost of trying to maintain and restore sources of drinking water for its population. Meeting this challenge is pitting the powerful within the market against the weak. The First Nations people in Canada are being denied access to one of their staple foods, salmon, to ensure that there will be an adequate supply for wealthy Americans and Canadians who will pay $3,500 per fish to engage in sport fishing there.[8]

Paying for Priceless Resources

What Market Prices Don't Include

The market does a poor job of handling the cost of those aspects of our landscape for which there is no price tag. In economics we refer to this as a social cost, an externality, or a spillover effect. Social costs are additional, hidden costs of producing the goods and services we enjoy. They often are some aspect of nature that is essential to produce the output, but for which no one is charged.

For example, if a firm dumps its waste into a stream or river, it avoids the cost of clean up or disposal. Similarly, if it pumps smoke into the air through a tall smokestack, it saves the cost of removing the pollutants. You and I do this whenever we drive. Our vehicles belch exhaust into the air but we do not get charged for this pollution.

If your car is the only one on the road, somewhere out in the country, nobody will ever notice that you are polluting the air. But many cars around the world all emitting exhaust at the same time, combined with other forms of air pollution, created vast clouds of smog in 2002, one that covered much of Asia and another across northeastern North America. If such clouds form on an annual basis, they will gradually increase the average temperature of our earth, causing enormously costly global warming. If this happens, the additional social cost of driving a car will be large, but likely paid by other people at some time in the future.

The air we breathe is only one of many essential aspects of our landscape that cannot be owned or sold. Since these resources are priceless, our use and misuse of them does not really enter the pricing system that the market uses to guide our allocation of resources and the distribution of goods and services.

The sacredness of the economy implies, with only slight exaggeration, that only economic value has any reality. That is, only the value of economic goods is specifiable; comparisons of economic value are the only ones that can be made; the money metric is universal, readily understood and assessed. Non-economic entities—non-commodities such as peace, personal relationships, and a star-filled sky—have no value because they cannot be exchanged. . . . They are, indeed, priceless.

John Boli, "The Economic Absorption of the Sacred" (1995), 106.

The Losers Pay Tomorrow

The existence of social costs has two immediate effects. One is that we use up or abuse resources faster than we would if we had to pay for them. We will pursue this issue in the next section when we discuss the importance of leaving enough oil reserves in the ground for our children.

The second effect is that social costs redistribute income in favor of the consumers, owners, and possibly employees of the firms that can charge lower prices because they are not fully paying for the resources they use. The losers are the people who end up suffering the negative effects of the resulting pollution. Some of the effects, such as diseases, may appear only many years later.

An extreme example of this redistribution involves a house with toxic waste buried in the yard. An unknown firm buried the waste and saved itself the price of proper disposal. The losers are the owner, who has lost the value of the property; the bank, which has lost the value of the mortgage on the property; and the local government, which has lost all tax revenues from the property. In addition, the two adults and three young children who live in the house may become losers in the future if they suffer health problems as a result of living there.

An economist analyzing this situation would typically

No One Wants Toxic House, Except Family That Lives There

A family living on a property that has 50 barrels of toxic waste buried on it has refused to move out of the house, even though the soil is so contaminated zinc pollution readings are more than 200 times the provincial norm.

The estimated $500,000 that it would cost to clean the property is so great that the bank won't repossess it, the municipality will not seize it for nonpayment of taxes, and even the owner has said he doesn't want it.

Claiming his house is worthless, owner Richard LeBlanc hasn't paid municipal taxes or his mortgage for years and the town and the bank have vowed to steer clear of the mess....

Mr. LeBlanc bought the property in 1988. He said he discovered the barrels while landscaping. The government tried six years ago to track down the source of the pollution, but failed.

From Charlie Fidelman, "No One Wants Toxic House, Except Family That Lives There," *National Post* (December 3, 1998). Material reprinted with the express permission of the National Post Company, a CanWest Partnership.

conclude that the market had failed to operate properly. If all the firms were playing by market rules, the cost of burying chemical waste would have increased the value of all potential burial sites. With this land-price increase and the consequent increase in the cost of waste disposal, the firms burying waste would have been motivated to either switch to processes that produce less waste or find ways to recycle it.

Cornelis van Kooten's response to this analysis is that economists should really say that if firms are given enough time they will develop the technology required to reduce or eliminate a particular pollutant. He notes, for example, that urban land can eventually revert back to usable farmland.[9] But it takes a very long time. Current economic theory is weak in factoring in the length of time required for the market to motivate appropriate responses to sustain our landscape.

Economic theory also lacks the concept of irreversibility. Once a species is extinct we cannot bring it back by reversing our actions. Should global warming become a reality, it will require considerable time to make the changes needed to reduce its causes plus enable the temperature to drop back to normal. The globe can eventually heal itself, but by then we and our children may well be dead. *7 generations*

More Taxes or More Regulations?

Economists and politicians alike recognize the existence of social costs. Economists typically recommend raising the price of the output—for example, by imposing a tax on the product—to cover the added social costs. Europe is pursuing this route. In Sweden a sulfur tax was introduced a decade ago. One effect was a decline in the sulfur content of fuels to 50 percent of minimum legal requirements.[10] In North America, imposing new taxes tends to strike horror in the hearts of politicians; they have been more prone to regulate fuels by passing laws to limit emissions from trucks and cars.

One promising prospect is the development of a new fuel cell that will burn hydrogen and produce water vapor as exhaust. But clearly something will need to be done until the fuel cell is ready for widespread use. So far the options of either increasing taxes on gasoline and diesel fuel or imposing tougher fuel-economy standards on new vehicles have been resisted effectively by the oil and automobile industries. Voluntary standards plus some tax incentives to encourage conservation of energy, reduction of greenhouse gas emissions, and development of alternative energy sources appear to be the politically preferred strategy at present.

Will There Be Enough for Our Children?

Another issue the market does not address well is how to allocate resources so there's enough left for future generations. The market provides little guidance on whether our generation carries any responsibility to ensure ongoing life for our children and their children.

Resources That Can't Be Replaced

To analyze this issue it is helpful to divide our natural resources into two types: renewable and nonrenewable. Renewable resources include streams of water, forests of trees, schools of fish, and electricity generated from hydro sources. Nonrenewable resources include bodies of mineral ore and reservoirs of petroleum oil, things that cannot be replaced once we've exhausted their supply.

The concept of sustainability focuses especially on non-renewable resources. As the supply of a resource dwindles it is important to conserve it. This can be done in one of two ways: making a technological change that allows us to substitute other resources, or reducing consumption so the scarce resource lasts longer.

The market moves us toward one of these solutions or the other by increasing the price of the scarce resource. This causes the price of all goods and services dependent on that resource to increase. As these prices increase, customers may shift to other goods that have not increased in price, and producers will seek other ways to cut costs. When oil prices soared in the 1970s, customers began clamoring for more energy-efficient homes and smaller cars with better fuel economy.

Raising prices for relatively scarce goods and services slows down the use of nonrenewable resources but does not guarantee an adequate supply for the future. If oil prices rise faster than steel prices, this just tells us that supplies of oil are lower than supplies of iron ore relative to demand. It tells us nothing about whether our usage of these resources has slowed to a sustainable pace. To learn that we may have to use additional measures beyond price.[11]

Finding a New Business Hero

Daly calls us to recognize that our natural resource base—the name he uses is natural capital—has become the limiting factor for future economic growth.[12] During the time when markets had to be developed and enlarged, economic theory focused on the merchant as the central player within the economic system of that time, mercantilism. Once markets had been enlarged, physical capital became the limiting factor. In response, economic theory focused on the capitalist as central to the new free-enterprise system.

But now we face a new era with new challenges. According to Daly, economic theory must replace the current hero, the capitalist, with a hero for the future, the environmental conservationist. We need an economic system that recognizes our natural landscape as the factor that can limit continued and sustainable growth. To achieve this our society must elevate the role of those who devise sensible ways to conserve our natural resources. In other words, the prudent environmental conservationist must replace the buccaneering capitalist as the new key player in our economic system. We must change our focus from trying to become rich to trying to be safe from environmental disaster.

A New Kind of Economic Math

According to Andrew Nikiforuk, ecological economists are concluding that we need to replace Gross Domestic Product (GDP) as the measure of economic activity so we can substract the depletion of our natural resources from the market value of the goods and services produced. He points to Indonesia as an example. From 1971 to 1984 its economy grew by more than seven percent a year. But adjusting for the reduction in Indonesia's natural capital during this time, the real rate of growth was only four percent. Indonesia was purchasing current economic growth at the cost of reducing the potential for economic growth in the future.

Ecological Economists

The folks driving home this message in *Nature* and other science publications call themselves "ecological economists." Many own businesses, and some are architects. Most want to reform capitalism, not with regulation but with smarter thinking. And they all start with the simple premise that every economy is but a small room in the greater house of Nature. Foul a room and the house quickly becomes unlivable, if not unsellable.

From Andrew Nikiforuk, "Putting a Price Tag on the Planet," *Canadian Business* (August 1997), 83.

Nikiforuk goes on to portray ecological economists as entrepreneurs who recognize the role businesses will need to play in working toward a sustainable future. They propose, for example, that durable goods such as cars, refrigerators, televisions, and computers remain the ultimate responsibility of the original manufacturer. As long as the product is in use by the purchaser or is sold second-hand to someone else it remains the possession of an individual consumer. As soon as it becomes obsolete, ownership reverts back to the original producer, who will have to rebuild it or recycle its parts to make new products.

The intent is to bring the life of a product full circle, back to the design stage. Product designers would gradually learn not to create waste because who brought a new product into being would be responsible for its ultimate disposal after its useful life was over. This would be a revolutionary change in the way our economic system operates.

Economic Incentives Are Not Enough

Along with exploring such a shift in responsibility, we might also ask whether economic incentives alone are the best way to motivate personal behavior. Bruno Frey argues that such incentives have their place but can be counterproductive and do more harm than good. The incentive he criticizes is the tradable license. Because the environment can absorb a certain amount of pollutants, some firms are given licenses to do a certain amount of polluting. Firms that want to pollute more than their license allows can buy unused polluting capacity from other companies. For example, in the United States companies that generate electricity can trade their right to emit sulfur dioxide into the atmosphere.[13] Companies that exceed government-defined emission levels can buy the right to emit more from companies that emit less than government standards allow.

Frey asserts: "Economists should change the attitude with which they argue for incentive instruments. Most people concerned about the environment find it cynical to state that once one has paid the price, one is free to damage the environment."[14] Economic incentives, he continues, aren't enough. We also need moral appeals. A long-range environmental ethic must be based on the idea that something is the right thing to do rather than merely that it pays to do it. A place to start for all of us, including business leaders, is to recognize that we share a desire to have a pleasant natural landscape in our immediate neighborhood. We should not infringe on others who want the same thing.

The Human Factor

Who Is to Blame?

Humans appear to be the primary cause of the decline in our natural landscape. When one mentions the problem of teeming populations, the Western mind automatically thinks of countries in Asia and Africa where such growth is the fastest. But that sidesteps an important issue: the role of per capita income in defining our use and misuse of the environment.

The World Wildlife Fund has predicted that if China is transformed into a clone of the United States, it will generate an ecological disaster.[15] But that is not the case now. The countries with the highest population growth also tend to have lower standards of living, so nature can handle the relatively low demands their people make on the environment. Their needs put far less pressure per person on the environment than the overheated wants of the West.

Aggressive action to slow the population growth creates some painful side effects. For example, China's one-child policy has created the prospect that by 2030 all workers will have to support a set of parents plus their own children.[16] This will be a high dependency ratio. Who knows how far China will lag behind other countries in the 2030s because it took commendable action, from a global population-control perspective, during the last two decades of the twentieth century?

We All Want More

The immediate cause of the growth in demand that has led to our environmental crisis is not the population of low-income countries. Rather, it is the attempt by the corporations in the high-income countries to create a demand for a Western lifestyle among the emerging middle class in other parts of the world. Demand has grown not because there are so many people in Asia and Africa, but because more and more of them want to live the way we do. Their appetites for the Western "good life," with all its excesses and hidden perils, have been whetted by the advertising messages of the multinational corporations.

While large corporations are part of the problem, some believe they could be a source of solutions for an improved natural landscape. *The Economist* remains optimistic that businesses will respond favorably to calls to protect the environment if the price is right.[17]

Not everyone is so optimistic. According to Richard Welford, studies at the United Nations Research Institute for Social Development do not spark hope that large corporations will seriously address the root causes of the environmental crisis.

> We are in the hands of large corporations which must be persuaded, cajoled or even forced to change. Few of them have recognized the crisis and are committed to change. The reality is that corporations duck and dive, invest in smoke screens, hide behind science and technology, espouse gradualist solutions, and attempt to derive maximum publicity from piecemeal changes in environmental management systems.[18]

With their huge advertising budgets, corporations can trumpet the smallest environmental modifications through massive publicity campaigns. By doing so they divert attention away from more significant questions such as their role in promoting consumerism.

From Exploitation to Creation

Putting Limits on Our Growth

Our free-enterprise economic system is geared for growth. Where swelling populations have combined with the corporate drive to increase per capita consumption, we have quickly bumped into the environment's limited capacity to absorb the additional waste generated. Heavy pollution and galloping deforestation now threaten to produce dramatic climate changes. Far-reaching changes in human attitudes are needed if we are to begin to heal past injuries and make possible the sustaining of life on this planet.

Moving from Being Exploiters to Being Co-creators

In this last section I focus on the changes in values and attitudes that are needed for us to move from being exploiters of the earth to being co-creators as God intended. An economic system should:

- recognize the integrity, fullness, and sacredness of the created order; and
- help us balance our relentless pursuit of abundance with our responsibility to ensure the sustenance of life on this planet.

Our religious traditions have typically understood these values in the context of the concept of stewardship. This concept affirms that the natural environment does not belong to us: it is a gift of God (or a gift of nature). Its wise use is a responsibility entrusted to us by the Creator.

When Stewardship Isn't Enough

Wesley Granberg-Michaelson argues that a concept of stewardship is not enough. It does not adequately define our responsibility to nurture and sustain life on this planet. The practical application of stewardship has focused too heavily on technology alone as the way to address environmental deterioration.

As a replacement for the concept of stewardship, Granberg-Michaelson proposes a theology of interrelationship in which creation has value because of its relationship to God rather than its utility for humanity, and in which creation offers a trustworthiness and reliability that expresses the presence of God's grace upholding the world. Such a theology can open for us a possibility of recognizing that we are part of a continuing process of creation rather than managers of something God completed a long time ago.

A starting point for building such a theology of rela-

Renewing the Whole Creation

From this view, technologies are evaluated in light of their environmental side effects. Further, the answers to problems of bad stewardship usually are given in terms of better technology and regulation. Scrubbers on coal-burning smokestacks, catalytic converters on cars, and superfunds for toxic waste cleanup are the kind of responses prompted by responsible stewardship.

From Wesley Granberg-Michaelson, "Renewing the Whole Creation," in *Sojourners* (February-March, 1990), 12. Reprinted with permission from *Sojourners*. (800) 714-7474, www.sojo.net.

tionships is to keep the Sabbath in a manner as proposed by Mary Evelyn Jegen. Many regard the Sabbath in legalistic terms, applying a set of do's and don'ts. She focuses on the healing dimension of the Sabbath rather than on the religious observance of a particular day.

Just as there is a place for work, there is also a place for rest and healing. In the Bible's creation account, God's rest was an opportunity for him to contemplate what he had created during the time of work. Similarly, we are called to set aside a time of rest during which we contemplate our natural landscape, rediscovering our place within the process of ongoing creation and rejoicing in our bond of mutual care with our environment.

Maintaining Diversity for Life

Let's contemplate for a moment our bond of mutual care with that part of nature called oceans. Joseph MacInnes describes the three oceans that border North America as a defining symbol for the continent. They supply food, shape weather and climate, serve as a highway for transport, and provide a vast, irresistible playground. The beauty of the oceans consoles and inspires us.[19] But our actions have caused the oceans to sigh and throb with pain. Drastic action is needed.

Contributing to the gradual destruction of the oceans is our rapidly growing population and our ever-increasing demands. This raging, hungry humanity is like a tumor and the planet like a cancer patient.[20] The actions of humans and cancer are both seen as uncontrolled growths that invade neighboring territory and lead finally to death. The analogy is frighteningly apt, at least as it applies to the uncontrolled wants in high-income countries.

Concern about population growth and increasing wants usually focuses on our natural landscape's capacity to provide resources and to absorb waste. But there's more to worry about than whether we will run out of nonrenewable resources; a related concern is diversity within nature, or biodiversity. The various species of plant and animal life were created for a purpose. The well-being of the total depends on the health and existence of the various parts.

Cornelis van Kooten reminds us of the importance of preserving biodiversity:

- Unknown species could contain genetic material that may someday be valued, perhaps as a cure for disease. If such species become extinct, these benefits are lost forever.
- The fate of some so-called minor species serve as an ecological warning of environmental changes that could be costly to correct, much like the fate of canaries in coal mines warned miners of the presence of dangerous gases.
- The web of species is needed for the generation of soil, regulation of fresh water supplies, disposal of wastes, and maintenance of atmospheric quality.[21]

Building a Sustainable Future

A Call for Community Action

There is an environmental crisis because we are saddled with:

- a dysfunctional economic system;
- a corporate business structure dependent on the expansion of human wants beyond the environment's capacity to deliver; and
- an economic theory that still promotes capitalists as the key to a happier future for all.
- the theology of the market

To correct all three of these basic problems, we need to change our system and our theory so that responsibility for sustaining the environment rests with those persons who are the primary decision makers on the use (and misuse) of natural resources. In addition, we need a new incentive system that motivates all of us to recognize and contemplate the integrity, fullness, and sacredness of the created order.

A good starting point would be a shift in attitude for all of us caught up in the work ethic of Western society, striving for more as if our eternal salvation depended on it.

We work so hard in large part so we can expand our capacity to consume. In previous chapters I have outlined ways to overcome this addiction. In the chapter on labor I suggested seeing work as an end in itself rather than viewing it merely as a way to earn income. In the chapter on the consumer I called for an approach to consumption that builds community rather than excludes some people from it. I also proposed changes in the incentive system such as elimination of the tax deductibility of advertising that aims to create wants. In the chapter on business firms and capital I made a case for ethical investing. These principles can be extended to environmental issues.

Investing for Sustainability

With the availability of a variety of ethical investment funds we can achieve our long-term savings objectives while supporting more sustainable approaches to meeting human needs. What do we seek to accomplish through such changes in our behavior as consumers, savers, and investors? We hope to encourage a fundamental shift in the attitudes of our business leaders.

One aspect of this shift is captured in a "Punch" cartoon.[22] Two business executives in pin-striped suits have parked their limousine below a waterfall in a beautiful valley. As they stand there admiring the beauty of this part of the natural landscape, one says to the other: "Out here a guy could be lulled into thinking that there is more to life than just power or money." Executives like that need to be motivated to conserve and improve our natural landscape rather than viewing it as merely one more input in the productive process.

A Motivator Called Taxes

Earlier I suggested that manufacturers should remain responsible to reuse items they produce. I also called for replacing capitalists with environmental entrepreneurs as the key persons in our system. In addition, different accounting and tax practices could promote more environmentally friendly business decisions.

Welford urges a variety of actions to reshape our economic system and influence business behavior toward achieving a more sustainable future.[23] He advocates using taxation to promote the conservation of natural resources and the productive use of labor. He also favors more realistic measures than current profit-and-loss statements and GDP data as tools to guide our decision making. This might mean adding accounting costs for the depletion of nonrenewable resources or emission of pollutants into the environment and then allowing such costs as tax-deductible expenses.

Finally, we need experiments in community living that demonstrate the feasibility and attractiveness of sustainable approaches to use of the environment. We need new models that show there is more to life than consumerism and individualism.

A Vision for the Future

UNESCO offers a vision for the future in which every generation leaves resources—water, air, and soil—as pure and unpolluted as when it arrived on the earth.[24] Richard Leakey and Roger Lewin express their fear that human beings will cause the sixth major extinction of other species and ask, "Does it matter?" "While there is hope and perhaps time, we have no right— we the species that can reflect, understand, make choices—to take so many other species into the abyss with us."[25]

Fortunately, nature has a tremendous capacity to renew itself if given the chance to do so. But it also has limits. We can demand too much of our environment. Once a part of it dies, it cannot be revived, restored, or fully replaced. In addition to applying our vast analytical, technical, and entrepreneurial skills to pressing environmental issues, let us consider the admonition to keep the Sabbath. Let us contemplate the Creator and all that has been created, and let us realize there is indeed more to life than power or money.

Is your local public library a public service for tax-paying citizens, or a service for library customers? The answer to that question will affect every aspect of its operations—from library hours to the books it has on its shelves. How many copies of Madonna's book *Sex* should a library stock? Based on consumer demand, lots. But based on public service, perhaps not so many.
—*David Zussman*

8

The Role of Government

What's so bad about government? To hear politicians during election time you'd think government—the state—was a villain that needed to be vanquished, or at least brought down to size.

While the state has become a convenient target of ridicule, just about everyone—from Adam Smith in the eighteenth century to the World Bank today—agrees that government is necessary for a well-functioning free-enterprise system.

In this chapter I discuss why a public institution like government is needed in order for a private economic system like capitalism to work, and how the state operates in that system. Since the market is primarily concerned with private goods and services, we should define what we mean by a public good or a public service. We need to ask whether public goods and services are merely extras that some societies choose to provide, or whether they are required for the ongoing well-being of a society that chooses to operate with a capitalist economic system.

We'll start with the World Bank's position on the essential role of the state within a market-based economy. Since the countries of North America are democracies, it is assumed that voters like you and me have a hand in deciding what role the state should have. But that raises the puzzling question of why voters seem to have little interest in whether they have a well-functioning state. After all, the clamor we hear is to reduce the size of our governments and distribute the savings in the form of tax breaks. We hear very little public discussion of a positive role for the state in building a better future for our children and us.

The Minimal Functions of Government

The Role of the State in Eastern Europe's Transition

The struggle to develop market-based economies in the former Soviet Union and other eastern European countries has demonstrated how important a well-functioning state is in society. The World Bank has helped guide many of these attempts at transition. Initially it was thought if the role of the state were reduced, a free market would take over automatically.

We now realize that was much too simplistic an approach to a serious problem, and in the meantime we have seen some countries, especially in eastern Europe, deteriorate into criminal activity. Hard experience has shown us there is no such thing as a completely free market. A basic set of governing institutions is essential to the smooth operation of a market that is central to capitalism.

In order to function well the market requires a particular social and cultural context as well as a particular legal framework. It is not enough for each person to behave as an isolated economic agent. There have to be specific social understandings and commitments that are tacitly agreed upon as well. For example, a tradition of telling

---

No Isolated Economic Agents

The market cannot function in the smooth and efficient way that economists say that it should if people behave as thoroughly economic agents. For in order for the market to work, people must make moral commitments to agree on what can be bought and sold, to tell the truth, and to honor their contracts. In the absence of these commitments, the market will grind to a halt. And as the market grinds to a halt, so will our system of political democracy.

Robert Simons, *Competing Gospels* (1995), 70.

the truth and honoring contracts, at least generally, are essential elements of capitalism.

Given its experience with countries that are moving from one economic system to another, the World Bank has concluded that the problem often isn't the state's involvement in the development process; rather, it is the state trying to do more than its capabilities allow. Therefore, the World Bank now has a two-part strategy: match the state's role to its capabilities and raise the state's overall capabilities by reinvigorating public institutions.

The World Bank goes on to list five fundamental tasks every state must accomplish:

- establish a foundation of law;
- maintain a policy environment with minimal market distortions and with macroeconomic stability;
- invest in basic social services and infrastructure;
- protect the vulnerable; and
- protect the environment.[1]

The Evolution of the Role of the State Within Capitalism

These five tasks are more than Adam Smith envisioned as the minimal role of the state: he listed only the first and third tasks. This amounted to defining the rules of the game and providing a referee plus providing those services that the private sector could not or would not provide. The latter included national defense and expensive projects such as the digging of canals and the building of bridges. Over time societies added other functions that the private sector would not readily furnish, ranging from the construction of streets and highways to the exploration of space.

In many societies public benefits funded by general tax revenues. Examples of these benefits are fire departments in major urban areas and public schools, libraries, and parks. At the university level, the public good element is declining as we reduce subsidies to the universities and expect students to pay a larger share. *N p ≥ 46,,∙∙*

The post office uses revenues from selling stamps to provide a public service. We in North America take it for granted that mail service is available to every citizen. We pay the same price to send a regular letter no matter how far it has to travel within the country. So those of us who buy stamps to mail letters to people in the same city subsidize the mail service of people who live in remote communities where it costs much more to provide the same service. We won't mind doing that if we believe preserving rural communities is desirable. If we don't share that value, we may be tempted to use private firms that promise to deliver letters at a cheaper rate than the post office within the same city or between major cities.

The World Bank has added additional roles for the state: to provide stability to the market, to protect persons who are vulnerable, and to protect the environment. These additions reflect two hundred years of experience with capitalist economic systems that Adam Smith did not have. We have learned over time that markets can fail and that markets can produce results that are both socially and environmentally harmful.

When the Market Fails to Deliver

Besides the minimal roles listed above, the World Bank identifies additional, intermediate functions a state should carry out (see table 8.1). Especially prominent is the need to step in when the market fails to operate adequately or efficiently.

The Existence of Spillover Effects

The market falls short whenever there are spillover effects: benefits or costs beyond those paid for by the buyer of the good or service. For example, every time a person is vaccinated against a communicable disease the spillover effect is that others' chance of catching that disease goes down because the pool of carriers has gotten smaller. That may cause me to think that if everybody else in society gets vaccinated, I don't have to bother. This type of thinking causes too many people to avoid vaccinating their children and themselves, so such diseases remain a real threat to society.

Similarly, if my neighbor's house is on fire, I benefit if the fire department comes immediately and prevents the blaze from spreading. The option of allowing private sector firms to compete for the right to put out a fire, each bargaining with the owner of the burning house for an acceptable price

Table 8.1: Functions of the State

	Addressing Market Failure			Improving Equity
Minimal Functions	*Providing pure public goods:* · Defense · Law and order · Property rights · Macroeconomic management · Public health			*Protecting the poor:* · Antipoverty programs · Disaster relief
Intermediate Functions	*Addressing externalities:* · Basic education · Environmental protection	*Regulating monopoly:* · Utility regulation · Antitrust policy	*Overcoming imperfect information:* · Insurance (health, life, pensions) · Financial regulation · Consumer protection	*Providing social insurance:* · Redistributive pensions · Family allowances · Unemployment insurance
Activist Functions	*Coordinating private activity:* · Fostering markets · Cluster initiatives			*Redistribution:* · Asset redistribution

Source: *World Bank, World Development Report 1997: The State in a Changing World* (New York: Oxford University Press, 1997), Table 1.1. Copyright 1997, The International Bank for Reconstruction and Development/The World Bank. Used by permission of Oxford University Press, Inc.

before the firefighters start fighting the fire, has not proven particularly attractive.

On the cost side, a good example of a spillover effect is that of cigarette smoke. Whenever anyone enjoys a cigarette within a space shared with others, the other persons in the room suffer the effect of the smoke generated.

Free-market extremists who oppose all forms of government involvement would like us to believe there are no significant spillover effects. They would argue that wherever minor spillover effects exist, the people involved can resolve the issue through negotiations with each other. For example, if you feel like smoking in a public place, you can negotiate a bribe to be paid to the others in the room for the privilege of being allowed to smoke there. Such a process of bargaining for a solution works when the compromise requires only one decision for a number of years. It is difficult to apply if decisions are required every day. The time and effort involved is just not worth it.

Governments typically respond to negative spillover effects by making rules against undesirable activity rather than by providing incentives designed to change human behavior. Some examples of such regulations are the creation of no-smoking areas in public places; the requirement that people in vehicles use seat belts and that motorcycle riders wear helmets; and the requirement that cars and trucks reduce exhaust pollutants.

Such prohibitions may have their place, but it would be better to use market incentives to motivate behavior. An excellent example is the move by Groupe Commerce Inc. to add an extra fifty dollars to the insurance premium of drivers who have cellular telephones in their vehicles.[2] The drivers either pay fifty dollars to have a cell phone in their vehicle or remove the phone and save the money. The extra premium is based on research indicating that drivers using phones are more likely to have accidents.

The story also illustrates why governments frequently have to become involved. Other insurers may refuse to follow the lead of Groupe Commerce Inc., choosing instead to spread the extra costs generated by cell-phone drivers' accidents among all their policyholders. If the insurance industry can't solve the problem of dangerous cell-phone drivers, the state may have to resort to its customary role of prohibiting this kind of behavior.

A policy based on a price-incentive system allows greater freedom of choice but may result in society ultimately bearing the burden of costs incurred by those persons who persist in their behavior despite the incentives. For example, a manufacturing plant could be offered a tax incentive to reduce the source of a pollutant. If the plant's managers elected not to seek the tax incentive but to continue polluting, the plant's neighbors would bear the health risks associated with the pollution. Similarly, we could offer motorcyclists a discount on their insurance if they chose to wear a helmet, but if a motorcyclist decided to forego the discount and sustained a catastrophic head injury, society would bear some of the burden of his medical care.

The Need to Promote Adequate Competition

In addition to situations where spillover effects exist, markets fail when there isn't enough competition to protect society from firms dominating certain industries. The public was sufficiently concerned with this problem by the end of the 1800s that the Canadian and U.S. governments took action to prevent the formation of monopolies. Canada passed its first anti-combines legislation in 1889. The comparable legislation in the United States was the Sherman Antitrust Act, passed by Congress in 1890.

These laws, which seek to ensure the continuation of workable and effective competition, have evolved over time. The more recently passed Competition Act in Canada (1986) broke new ground by establishing a tribunal that can assess the effects of a proposed merger or takeover before the deal can be completed.

In addition, "lemon" laws have been passed to enable consumers to take legal action against producers of cars, cookers, medical devices, computer software, and many other products to hold them accountable for product quality and safety.

In those industries where effective competition cannot be maintained, states have opted either for a government-owned institution—called a Crown corporation in Canada, a parastatal in many other countries—or for government regulation of the private firms providing these goods or services. For example, electricity and telephone service, public transport, and broadcasting are tightly regulated in most regions.

In some industries—airlines, telecommunications, and banking—the degree of regulation has been much reduced in recent years. Some are advocating deregulation of electricity generation and distribution as a means of addressing the energy vulnerability of major economies, especially that of the United States. One of these advocates is *The Economist*, which highlights tax incentives, changes in existing regulations, and exemptions from

A Lemon Law for Software?

If Microsoft made cars instead of computer programs, product-liability suits might by now have driven it out of business. Should software makers be made more accountable for damage caused by faulty programs? . . .

Techniques such as "extreme programming" or the "five-step capability maturity model," which require programmers either to work in pairs or to follow rigid sets of rules, can produce remarkably clean code first time around.

But the disciplined approach is alien to the software industry's quick-and-dirty culture. Software firms prefer to bash out code and then try to catch as many bugs as possible while racing to ship the product. Unfortunately, that means the customers end up doing much of the quality-assurance work—as they track down and report errors, install security patches and buy upgrades. According to the Standish Group, a market research firm, faulty software cost American firms $100 billion last year.

environmental regulations that need to be put in place to allow micropower to enter the market as a new provider of energy services.[3] As was the case in telecommunications, new technology separates the functions of local creation and delivery of service—in this case the generation of electricity—from the transmission of the service over vast distances. Achievement of the beneficial effects of allowing micropower producers to compete in the market requires undoing what governments have done in the past to regulate large electricity utilities operating within local or regional monopolies.

The Need to Provide Adequate Information

A third area where the market tends to fail us involves those goods and services for which there is not enough information for each consumer to make a sound market decision. For example, it would be unwieldy—and unsanitary—for all customers to examine the kitchen of a restaurant before deciding whether to eat there. So we have instituted health inspections as a public service to protect the eating public. Similarly, safety inspections are required for many facilities used by the public. This is justified because most of us do not have sufficient information or access to evaluate the safety of elevators, airplanes, or ships.

There is also the issue of whether governments need to intervene to augment or correct inadequate or inappropriate information provided to consumers by business firms. For example, 60 percent of the adults and 25 percent of the children in the United States are overweight; 27 percent of the population is obese.[4] In reporting these statistics for 1999, *The Economist* raises questions about the role of businesses and farmers in this problem. Their marketing strategies promote a lifestyle that leads to being overweight, and they take action to limit the ability of government to educate the public about the dangers and the causes of being overweight.

The provision of financial services is another area in

which the government seeks to assist the public. Without government involvement, we would not have access to the relevant documents of banks, insurance companies, and trust companies to assess whether each is a secure institution to which we can entrust our hard-earned savings. The history of bank failures has caused us to move to a form of deposit insurance to maintain consumer confidence in the system.

Public Enterprises and Alternative Forms of Service Delivery

The privatization of government-owned firms has generated some gains but the overall effect has not been impressive. A more recent approach is to transform the service delivery mechanisms of publicly owned enterprises into alternative forms that seek to maintain the essential element of a public service but deliver goods or services with a businesslike efficiency driven by profit maximization. If all government services were handled this way, the government's role would be reduced to the mere steering of the overall course of economic activity. Private-sector firms would carry out the provision and delivery of the actual goods and services.

Government's New Style

Every imaginable kind of government service, from scientific research to parks management, is now being actively explored for alternative service delivery opportunities by federal, provincial, and municipal governments. Although they may differ widely in form and function, all alternative service delivery organizations have one thing in common: they try to combine public service with a bottom-line orientation—including independent revenue generation.

The trend toward providing government services through independent agencies is global. "The role of government should be to 'steer, not row,'" argues Ted Osborne, in *Reinventing Government*, now viewed as the bible of government reorganization. . . .

What's different about the new breed of organizations is:

- They go far beyond the traditional range of services provided by Crown corporations.

- Their governance structure does not depend solely on government, but on a mix of government, commercial and local community interests.

- There are a lot more of them.

Excerpts from an article by David Zussman in *The Financial Post 2000* (October 18, 1997): 5. Material reprinted with the express permission of the National Post Company, a CanWest Partnership.

In his critique of alternative service delivery programs, David Zussman expresses the fear that citizens are in danger of being reduced to mere consumers of the state. He sees governments' move to reduce taxes while imposing user fees for public services as a clear step in this direction. Two dangers stand out: the overall morale of government employees would suffer, to the detriment of public service; and the employees would be forced to cater to the interests of the immediate consumers of the product or service rather than serving the public in general.

The central issue here is whether we accept that there is such a thing as a distinctively public good or service. Zussman presents public libraries as an example.[5] Some people can afford to buy any book they desire; many cannot. A library can stock at least one copy of many books so that every citizen has access. The library enables even those who can afford to buy books to read much more widely than if they had to buy every book they wanted. Given that reading is valued socially, paying for a library as taxpayers, rather than only as users, serves a useful public purpose.

Providing a Safety Net

Another function of governments—a role that horrifies some fervent capitalists—is that of providing a social safety net. If you've watched trapeze artists perform in a circus, you may have seen a safety net in action. It's there to catch someone who fails while trying to perform a daring feat. The very existence of the safety net may actually improve the performance, as it gives the high-wire artists the confidence to take more chances.

The Role of a Safety Net

According to the World Bank, the government function of providing a social safety net falls into the category of improving equity. It recognizes that the market system's way of rewarding producers will not necessarily result in an equal or fair distribution of goods and services.

Others, such as Paul Martin, see safety nets as a contribution to capitalism, not a detriment.[6] People will have a greater incentive to reach for the very top of the corporate and social ladder if they know a safety net will catch them if they fail.

Providing safety nets to offset the extreme effects of capitalism goes back to the beginning of the nineteenth century. The first area in which the system abused people beyond society's level of tolerance was in the use of children in the workplace. England passed a law in 1804 to limit the number of hours that orphans were required to work in underground mines. At twelve hours per day, the limit was not particularly humane, but it was a start. In many countries the misuse of children as laborers is still a problem today. With increases in trade interaction and tourism we are becoming more aware of the conditions under which children are employed in some countries.

Hubert Humphrey extended this concern to persons who normally are not expected to work for their living. A test of a society's concern for others is its willingness to ensure at least a minimum standard of living for all the elderly and for persons who are unable to work because of illness or serious handicap. Old-age security and veterans benefits programs fall into this category. Both Canada and the United States also have some form of family or child assistance.

> It was once said that the moral test of government is how that government treats those who are in the dawn of life, the children; those who are in the twilight of life, the elderly; and those who are in the shadows of life—the sick, the needy and the handicapped.
>
> —Hubert H. Humphrey (1977)

The Role of an Unemployment Insurance Fund

Another area of shared concern in our society is for persons who are temporarily unemployed. For a free-enterprise system to function properly there has to be the flexibility for growth industries to expand production. It's hard for a company to hire new staff if no one is looking for a job. Therefore, it is generally agreed that some level of unemployment is necessary for our system to operate properly. We call this frictional unemployment. The frictionally unemployed are people who are temporarily between jobs. Because they serve a useful purpose for all of us, it's hardly fair that they carry the full cost of being unemployed. Therefore, we have devised unemployment insurance programs as society's way of easing the burden of temporary joblessness.

No one knows precisely the level of frictional unemployment needed for the system to work. Generally, economists accept that it has to be about 3 or 4 percent of the labor force. It certainly should be much lower than the 8 to 10 percent many employers prefer so their employees will be more docile and less likely to look around for greener pastures.

The Place of a Safety Net for the Employed

Yet another area in which society's tolerance is sometimes exceeded and government intervention is welcomed is the case of open discrimination in the workplace. Examples of interventions in this area are equal opportunity laws to curb discriminatory hiring and promotion practices based on race, gender, or disability.

A situation that governments have not addressed well is that of the working poor—people who are employed but don't earn enough to climb above the poverty line. Minimum wage laws helped, but increases in the minimum wage over time have not kept pace with inflation. People who are working at the minimum wage tend to remain in poverty even if they are employed full-time.

Forms of Social Welfare as a Last-Resort Safety Net

Where all else fails, there is still welfare. People receiving welfare are essentially segregated from all other active participants in the economy. As a condition for receiving welfare they typically have to give up ownership of assets they own and strict limits are set on how much income they may earn. In exchange, they receive a bare minimum amount of money to live on. And since we tend not to trust people on welfare with actual cash, we give them food stamps, subsidized housing, and selected health services.

There are two serious flaws in our approach to welfare. First, it has fostered the attitude that the government must take care of whatever the free-market system messes up or cannot handle. This is a no-win situation for governments.

Second, governments are expected to address the problem without interfering in any way with a basic thrust of capitalism: that distribution of the output is used to motivate initiative and production. As a result, we have come to expect that some people will be cast aside and given only enough to merely keep them alive. The best we can hope for is that this will involve only a small percentage of the population.

During some periods of our recent history, the percentage of people receiving welfare has been too high, generating a tax burden politicians find easy to attack when voters cry out for a tax cut. In the United States and Europe, various forms of retraining and workfare were introduced to lower future welfare costs.

The only option left for many of the unemployed who are not covered by insurance tends to be welfare. The serious social stigma of being on welfare and receiving a bare minimum to live on is deemed necessary by government and business firms. They want to ensure that the option of welfare does not become attractive enough to stop people from looking for jobs—even in companies where working conditions are bad. If we devised a socially acceptable way of providing for the persons cast aside by our economic system, employers would have to work much harder to make their jobs more pleasant, providing each person with some satisfaction of contributing to the well-being of the community.

Just Give Me a Tax Break

Prosperity Is Lulling the Voter to Sleep

Even though the World Bank's experience in many countries makes the case for an essential role of government within a capitalist economic system, this does not mean we voters have to agree. Indeed, public trust in politicians appears to be at an all-time low. Richard Finlay suggests that the prosperity capitalism has brought to many of us has made us less alert about and demanding of our government leaders. He recognizes that the freedom to choose within capitalism is intimately tied to the exercise of our civic duty as voters within a democracy.

Civic Decline an Unnecessary Cost of Capitalism's Success

Joseph Schumpeter, meet Monica Lewinsky. Not even the renowned economist who predicted capitalism would eventually become a victim of its own success could have foreseen the latest example of his theory: the moral amnesia of prosperous citizens in the face of ethically wayward politicians. . . .

One of the remarkable virtues of capitalism is it enables people to acquire the wherewithal to appreciate choice and hold institutions responsible for their actions. It is no coincidence the rise of the middle class in western society paralleled the groundswell of public demands to open civic institutions and make them more accountable.
Capitalism was never intended as an opiate that dulls people's sense of their democratic duty. While capitalism itself cannot be blamed for the apathy that

besets public governance today, it has a vested interest in ensuring that people are soon awakened from their civic slumber. . . .

It is time for the voices of responsible capitalism to speak out about principles of moral leadership and civic duty. They can take their share of credit for the current boom.

But they also need to make the point that just as capitalism works best when stakeholders, shareholders and customers exercise the choice and decisions to which they are entitled, democracies work best when citizens are vigilant and involved.

From J. Richard Finlay, "Civic Decline an Unnecessary Cost of Capitalism's Success," *The Financial Post* (June 27-29, 1998), 23. Material reprinted with the express permission of the National Post Company, a CanWest Partnership.

He observes further that we have lost sight of the intimate link between our democratic responsibilities and rights and the way capitalism functions. It seems that most people would rather urge more tax breaks than engage in spirited public debate over how well the government is carrying out its essential functions in order to ensure the smooth operation of our economic system.

The Case for Lowering Taxes to Offset a Decline in Savings

Many business leaders prefer tax cuts for companies as a way to stimulate the economy and generate more employment. This proposed solution to the unemployment problem is based on one of two major competing theories. It assumes that the reason for unemployment is that society is not saving enough to allow the necessary investment in capital goods to take place. The case is then made for a tax cut for the wealthy because they do not consume all of their income—because they have so much more than they need that they are the ones who save and invest.

This approach to unemployment is evident in the tax cuts offered during the Reagan administration and the George W. Bush administration in the United States. The Harris government in Ontario and the Campbell government in British Columbia have tried to imitate it. Critics of the approach compare the unemployed to chickens in a barnyard. Cutting taxes for the wealthy is like feeding more oats to the horses so the chickens can get more "recycled" oats from the horse manure.

The Case for Lowering Taxes to Stimulate Consumer Demand

A competing theory argues that the needed investment is not occurring because businesses are not experiencing a persistent growth in demand for their output. For example, the Asian financial crisis reduced overall demand in a number of countries, causing those economies to slow to a crawl. Similarly, the September 11 tragedy has contributed to a major economic slowdown, especially in North America. The solution is to either have the governments spend more or to grant tax cuts to consumers so they can spend more. The economic booms associated with wartime expenditures can be cited in support of increased spending.[7] Advocates of a tax cut to stimulate demand favor reduced taxes for lower-income groups because they are sure to spend the money rather than save it as the rich are prone to do.

Cutting Taxes Involves Difficult Political Decisions

Forming a government budget is a daunting challenge when the public is more interested in tax breaks than in good government. A tax cut must please the majority of the voters. Even if a tax cut to business would somehow solve the unemployment problem, the cut itself would go to only a small minority of the voters. The people who constitute the voting majority want some of the tax cut money to flow into their own pockets. Spreading tax cuts that widely, however, means no one gets very much in the way of tax savings.

George Bernard Shaw once observed: "A government which robs Peter to pay Paul can always depend on the support of Paul."[8] But there have to be enough Pauls to make it worthwhile for the government. People on welfare, the unemployed, children, the sick, and people with disabilities do not constitute a majority able to organize effectively and to vote as a group. Their interests are likely to be submerged within the larger agenda of the majority of the voters. The public debate has been largely diverted from the essential role of government within a capitalist economic system to addressing the short-term greed of voters.

Kenneth Bagnell, in his review of Hugh Segal's book *Beyond Greed*, notes Segal's concern that many contemporary conservatives truly reflect Adam Smith's view that

Segal Laments Lost Conservatism

Hugh Segal, the thoughtful Progressive Conservative, has a major concern these days. The mainstream conservative movement so central to his life has been almost taken over by a narrow band of selfish forces. Some people call them the far right, others the new right, others the neoconservatives or simply neocons. He doesn't like them. He regards them as greedy, divisive and, worst of all, destroyers of the real nature of conservatism that values the broad welfare of people over the bottom line.

"I am not thinking," he writes by way of explanation, "of Thatcher, Reagan, or Mulroney. . . . I am thinking of today's purveyors of barbed wire politics, one that seeks to destroy the conservative ideal that places order at the centre of the universe where individual freedom and social responsibility coexist in real balance."

Segal almost feels that if the neocons are left to their destructive devices, they "dismantle anything that isn't produced by free-market forces, including medical care and public education. If that happens, we'll be left with a society in which a few have it all, the rest nothing but yesterday's hopes and today's poverty."

From Kenneth Bagnell, "Segal Laments Lost Conservatism," a review of Hugh Segal's *Beyond Greed*, in *The Financial Post* (November 15, 1997), 32. Material reprinted with the express permission of the National Post Company, a CanWest Partnership.

people are driven by greed. According to Segal, conservatism is therefore in danger of losing its very essence: "conservatism that values the broad welfare of people over the bottom line."

The Place of Minorities in a Democracy

Social Capital

The World Bank also allows for an activist role of government. Existing forces within a society can hamper a market-based economic system. If the ownership of resources is skewed—for example, if a few families control almost all the farmland—there may be a need for land reform. If criminal elements extort protection money from successful businesspeople, there clearly is a need for some kind of official intervention. If corruption is evident at all levels of society, there will be a need to bolster pride in the public service and to implement ways to ensure accountability for decisions made. Problems such as these are endemic in a number of societies, and the World Bank is recognizing that the political process can help bring about the changes necessary for a free-market to flourish.

Similarly, the process of economic advance depends on the existence of such institutions as "firms, families, contracts, markets, rules and regulations, and social norms. . . . Institutions can consist of both formal entities like laws, constitutions, written contracts, market exchanges and organizational by-laws and informal ones like shared values, norms, customs, ethics and ideology."[9] A good government can play an active role in creating and promoting such needed institutions.

These institutions constitute what is called social capital, which is produced when people work together for a long time and develop shared norms, values and benefits. According to the United Nations Development Programme (UNDP), countries with adequate social capital have governments that are open and transparent and therefore less likely to be corrupt and more likely to be efficient. Sweden and Japan are cited

People Acting Together

But beyond its contribution to community life, social capital has a much wider influence—affecting the whole process of governance. When local and national institutions are firmly grounded in shared norms and values, they are more likely to be run in an open and transparent fashion, reducing the chances of inefficiency and corruption.

Social capital has played an important part in the human development success of many countries. In Sweden, for example, decades of successfully combining economic progress and advances in human welfare were based on a broad consensus among many parts of society—including churches, trade unions, employers, political parties and government. In Japan the extraordinary advances of the past 30 years were deeply rooted in social customs of cooperation. Other countries

have had a less happy experience: part of the reason for the Soviet Union's collapse was the lack of any kind of effective "civic space" outside the government system.

So, how can social capital be developed? In many respects this is not a matter for government—most forms of cooperation are spontaneous and thrive without outside government influence. But governments can contribute, both through expenditure on education that gives people the capabilities to act together, and by ensuring that the many disparate parts of civic society have the space and freedom to develop their full potential.

as countries with ample social capital; Russia as a country where the social capital is depleted and needs to be replenished.

Minority Rights in the Building of Community

The realization of the sacred values I set out earlier requires appropriate social capital and the use of the political process to shape our economic systems accordingly. On its own, our economic system will not necessarily build community, provide for productive participation by all, guarantee access for all to the goods and services produced, ensure the ongoing existence of our environment, and build relationships to other societies on the basis of peace and justice. The challenge is to devise ways to make sure the economic system serves these ends while still providing for a higher material standard of living.

An important element in this agenda will be protection of the rights of minorities within our midst. Building a community calls for being inclusive. Being inclusive can be stifling if conformity is required. Rather, we need to recognize the richness inherent in diversity. Where diversity is accepted and valued there will be minorities, and minorities always run the risk of being challenged, possibly even persecuted, by the majority. The political process needs to protect the interests of minorities.

> Governments exist to protect the rights of minorities. The loved and the rich need no protection: they have many friends and few enemies.
>
> —Wendell Phillips (1860)

Related to safeguarding minorities is the need to protect against what Simons calls economic imperialism.[10] The concern here is with the use of money to buy nonmarket "services" such as influence and opportunity. This use of income and wealth raises the distinct danger that the political process will be corrupted for the advantage of a few. An important role of the democratic process within capitalism is to hold government accountable for its actions and ensure that it devises and enforces laws against such corrupting influences.

Homelessness in the end is intimately intertwined with hopelessness. We cannot generate much confidence for the future without the security and sense of social cohesion of roots. And we cannot fully capture the opportunities of the new economy without addressing the most rudimentary needs of our current society. Companies who do business within a community, and derive their profits from its people, are linked economically and morally to its well-being. Rebuilding a sense of home is therefore an obligation of the market as well as of society.

—*John Dalla Costa*

9

Penalizing the Achiever, Rewarding the Parasite?

The capitalist economic system rewards people who succeed. In the 1990s multibillionaire Bill Gates was the shining example of what is possible if we try hard enough. But not everyone is a winner. For every Bill Gates there are many who cannot afford daily shelter. The persistence of homelessness in North America shows that the capitalist system has some who lose as well as some who win.

Why do some lose? In my discussion of labor and the right to work in chapter 6, I concluded that there is no objective way to measure the contribution of either Bill Gates or a homeless person to the overall productive efforts of our society. The wide income gap between a Bill Gates and a homeless person is primarily the product of the resources they own and their relative bargaining power in the market. I also argued that money was only one way to motivate human effort.

Can this vast difference in income be justified in any way? The answer cannot be based simply on a concept of justice, since there are various understandings of what we mean by justice. Some, like Scott Powell, argue that the enormous income of Bill Gates is just, that he deserves it. The Committee of Catholic Bishops, meanwhile, can also appeal to justice to condemn our economic system because it generates so much poverty and need.

Powell's position typifies that of many contemporary defenders of our economic system. It has become a powerful rationale for eliminating public goods and reducing the role of government in society. Because this argument is used so widely, I devote the first two sections here to examining it. First I look at the need to reward the achiever, and I consider why the nonachiever is seen as a parasite. Then I argue that a minimal standard of living should be a basic human right—an expression of responsibility and fairness in our society. Finally, I move to the important human need to be in community and consider fairness as a means for building community.

<u>Justice advises men to reward good and punish evil</u>. It is the guiding principle behind the multi-billion dollar fortune of Bill Gates. The payment made to Mr. Gates by every software purchaser is a reward for having his life made easier by Microsoft's products.

Earning money is a form of justice. By contrast, giving unearned money to the destitute is unjust, not because poverty is immoral but because paying for it is: it contravenes the basic principle of justice by rewarding a man for his lack of value.

From Scott Powell, "Did Foster Miss the Point on Justice," a letter to the editor of *The Financial Post* (November 3, 1998), C7. Material reprinted with the express permission of the National Post Company, a CanWest Partnership.

Having made a case for fairness, I conclude by asking whether the capitalist system can generate the required fairness. Can it adapt sufficiently to address such basic values as human dignity for all and opportunity for everyone to build and participate in community? Or will we destroy the system if we try to modify it to achieve fairer, community-building outcomes?

Redistribution as a Penalty

A central element of the capitalist economic system is that output is distributed as a reward for contributing to the productive effort. The more one contributes to the growth of the pie—the total material goods and services in our society—the larger the slice of pie one deserves. If society gives slices of pie to persons who have not contributed to the pie's production, those who contributed are hurt in two ways. First, the active producers receive a smaller slice than they earned because some free pie is being shared with those who did not contribute. Second, the size of the total pie is not growing as fast as it would if none had been given away. This double loss—a smaller piece of a smaller pie—is the penalty placed on the achiever.

Distributing Output to Promote Human Dignity and Build Community

Some authors allege that there is a biblical basis for a system that rewards the achiever. One example is H. Gossen, who believes egoism, or self-interest, is the true force that moves the human family.[1] His ideas have been used to argue against minimum wage laws, social security, and all forms of relief to poor people. Peter Bauer, meanwhile, declares that humanitarian efforts are a cause of envy, one of the seven deadly sins.[2] According to this argument, when Christians help poor people, they arouse envy among them, which, in turn, does harm to their beneficiaries' soul. Margaret Thatcher has argued that there is no such thing as society. This would suggest that we have no social responsibilities to anyone beyond our family.

British Prime Minister Margaret Thatcher thought she could kill the idea of community when she declared, infamously, in 1987: "There's no such thing as society. There are individual men and women, and there are families."

But social interconnectedness is a hard thing to kill, it's something that seems to be hardwired into the human brain and heart. Just 10 years after that statement, Thatcher's successor Tony Blair won a landslide victory in Britain by articulating exactly the opposite vision: "We are not simply people set in isolation from each other, but members of the same community, the same human race."

From Cameron Charlebois, "A New View of Volunteerism," *Winnipeg Free Press* (December 5, 2000).

In the earlier discussion of sacred values I said that human dignity is a gift granted to us by God. I also said that living in community is the way to realize our God-given dignity. In other words, I directly contradicted the fundamental tenet of egoism and therefore cannot accept it as the source of good. Nor do I seriously believe, with Bauer, that humanitarian assistance generates envy. Rather, I favor the position taken by Tony Blair, who recognizes that we are members of a community.

Distribution, Motivation of Production, and the Level of Poverty

If the primary goal is to motivate productive effort, to enlarge the size of the pie, then giving away free pie to non-contributors will be discouraged. Those who hold this view concede that poor persons are getting a shrinking proportion of the pie, but argue that over time the achievers will create a bigger pie. Then the poor people will be better off because their slice of a bigger pie will be larger than before.

Another version of this position observes that the incomes of poor people are rising simultaneously with those of the rich and at approximately the same rate. This is the conclusion David Dollar and Aart Kraay offer in their World Bank study of eighty countries.[3] Of course, when the same percentage increase is applied to a low income as to a high income, the disparity between the income of the rich person and that of the poor person grows over time.

Those who put forth arguments such as these see poverty in absolute terms, with no regard for how people compare with each other in society. Instead, these arguments say that we should compare our situation today with our situation yesterday. If our slice of pie includes more material goods and services today than it did yesterday—even if it represents a smaller proportion of the pie—then we are less poor. If we want to make comparisons, this argument says, we should compare poor people in high-income countries to poor people in low-income countries. Then we would really understand how fortunate poor people in a high-income country are.

Ensuring Open Opportunities to Contribute to the Productive Effort

Michael Novak casts the advantage of being poor in a rich country in terms of open opportunities rather than material standards of living.[4] The possibility of upward mobility is an attractive feature of our society, though it implies the risk of downward mobility as well. Of interest is Novak's presumption that the reward given for effort constitutes a just wage, where superior work should be rewarded with superior pay. He does not use either a more equal or a more fair distribution of income as the basis for defining what justice means.

The need to continuously reward the achiever arises from a coordinated struggle to ensure progress without questioning the present or future content of progress. This view holds that wealth is a constructive force that funds a particular type of society that values excellence, achievement, and compassion. Tinkering with or redistributing wealth in any way would dilute or destroy wealth's constructive capacity to build a better future. Hugh Segal argues that some of the wealthy families of our time have done much good by using their riches to create jobs and opportunities and to support the arts and charitable organizations.[5] Our economic system should not dampen the creativity of the wealthy or their efforts on behalf of society. Rather, the system should concentrate on deterring nonproductive uses of wealth such as hoarding and tax evasion.

Human Beings as Parasites

When we exalt and reward the achiever, we tend to consider the nonachiever a parasite. Even normally productive persons can eventually end up being branded as parasites. As people age and retire they may begin moving downward in terms of economic activity but they typically still expect a slice of the pie, regardless of how little they now can contribute to the productive effort. When that occurs, they meet the definition of a parasite: someone who "lives at the expense of another or others without making any useful contribution in return."[6]

The Place of Innocent Suffering

Such parasites exist in every capitalist society. Affluent people typically embrace the view that people are poor because of laziness or inherent defect. The alternative view, which sees poverty as a by-product of our economic system, has been articulated by what is called liberation theology. Many of us find this latter view disturbing because it clearly implicates all of us as part of the cause of poverty.

Some try to reduce their guilt by discrediting liberation theology. But they seldom face up to a central liberationist theme: the issue of innocent suffering. Gustavo Gutiérrez, one of the "founders" of liberation theology, notes that we in the West cannot comprehend that someone could suffer for external reasons and not for any fault of their own. We have so effectively combined views of human individualism with our belief in a loving, all-knowing, and all-powerful God that we tend to see suffering as God's way of

Human suffering, involvement with it, and the questions it raises about God are in fact one point of departure and one central theme in the theology of liberation. But the first concern in this context is not with the "evil of guilt" but rather with the "evil of misfortune," the evil suffered by the innocent. I am here using a distinction made by Adolphe Gesché, who remarks:

The West has not had a theology of the evil of misfortune, the evil suffered by the innocent. In my view, the basic importance of the theology of liberation, that which gives it a major importance that I hope it will not lose, is that it takes into account the widespread, objective evil that entails no fault in the sufferer.

I myself believe that we must not forget the responsibility of those who may be the cause of the evil suffered by the innocent. But Gesché's point is well taken: the suffering of the innocent and the questions it leads them to ask are indeed key problems for theology—that is, for discourse about God. The theology of liberation tries to meet the challenge.

—Gustavo Gutiérrez, *On Job* (1988)

disciplining people for some personal reason. We have lost sight of a suffering God who allows people to make choices and who enters into the pain of those who are innocent victims of the selfish activities of others.

We also downplay what the Bible calls "principalities and powers." These are the social, political, and economic systems that were created to govern us but have gone astray and now operate on behalf of the selfish and powerful.

Creating Open Opportunities for Those Who Fail

There is an element of truth in both approaches to poverty. Many suffering people contribute in some way, willingly or unwillingly, to their own plight. But such suffering occurs within a larger environment that also is a contributing cause. Those who find themselves downwardly mobile are unduly punished and prevented from rising again. We must not dismiss these "losers" as mere parasites, living off of the diligent efforts of the achievers. The environment that contributes to their failure needs to be changed as well. For the "losers" to accept responsibility for their own part in bringing about their condition and move toward healthy relationships, the norms and mores of our society that also contributed to bringing about their condition must be challenged and transformed as well.[7]

A Moral Alternative: Responsibility and Fairness

Poverty Grows When Employment Declines

Downward mobility always gets more public attention during periods of economic recession. The Committee of Catholic Bishops created quite a stir with their New Year's message in 1983. The immediate context was the general recession of the early 1980s, but their critique is just as applicable to the economic downturn of a decade later, when one of every ten adults willing and able to work was being denied access to employment opportunities: there were no jobs available, they lacked the skills needed to fill available jobs, or they lacked the resources needed for self-employment. People with years of company service were being thrown out on the streets. Businesses were declaring bankruptcy. Not only was this a personal tragedy for the owners, employees close to retirement were seeing their jobs and their accumulated company pensions vanish.

The effects of these recessions fell disproportionately on the weak and the poor. In the midst of all this turmoil, many in need exhausted their unemployment benefits and had to sell or mortgage their homes as a condition for receiving welfare. The rich, in contrast, did not appear to be seriously inconvenienced. Jaguar dealers and upscale tailors claimed that their businesses were unaffected by the recession.

The Needs of the Poor Versus the Wants of the Rich

The Committee of Catholic Bishops drew from the Bible two moral principles that related to the depressed economy of the time: each person has the right to some form of creative activity, and the needs of the poor should take precedence over the wants of the rich.

The bishops hit a raw nerve. Political and economic leaders lambasted them for meddling in non-spiritual matters. They were also criticized for proposing methods to achieve these moral objectives. But nowhere did economic and political leaders actually debate these two fundamental values. The concerns of the bishops were swept under the rug.

Problems arise not when economics extends knowledge, but when it restricts it. Those involved in welfare economics are often socially motivated and well-intentioned, but factoring normative questions into mere equity and efficiency trade-offs may result in other moral questions being overlooked. Some of those with few possessions, such as monks, may have arrived at their position by choice, and may not want to "benefit" from an income redistribution from those who are materially better off, but perhaps spiritually worse off.

Rodney Wilson, *Economics, Ethics and Religion* (1997), 18.

The Link Between Spiritual Values and Economic Activity

There are two fundamental questions here. In the debate about unemployment and poverty, who decides the agenda? And what are the basic values and principles that define the agenda? The Catholic bishops were accused of meddling in politics and economics. This implies that spiritual values can and should be separated from the rest of life. Do we believe that?

The major religions of our time do not support separating life into the secular and the sacred. In his brief survey of Judaism, Islam, and Christianity, Rodney Wilson describes these faiths' position on justice and equity:

• Judaism: "Jewish sources deal distinctively with two important issues, the prevention of poverty, and the plight of those who once had an adequate income, but who have become poor. The implication of the first is that short-term measures to prevent people falling into poverty are preferable to long-term unemployment or social security benefits to those who are already, and perhaps have always been, poor. It is best to maintain the dignity of those who have suffered a temporary setback, rather than assist those who had little dignity in the first place. The poor should not be treated as a social group in need of permanent assistance, but rather as individuals who may need to be treated differently."[8]

• Islam: "The two overriding principles of Islamic economic justice are equality and fairness. Moderate inequality is acceptable, but not extreme disparities in income and wealth. Fairness means that economic gains are to be earned and losses deserved. Injunctions such as the inheritance laws and the prohibition of riba [charging interest] ensure equity and fairness."[9]

• Christianity: "The poor did not have rights or claims upon the rich, but the rich had a religious duty to make charitable donations. These were to be freewill offerings, there being no question of compulsion either by the state, or indeed by the church laying down a fixed formula. Augustine recognized, however, that riches could result in licentious living and excessive pride in possessions. If Christians were to differentiate themselves from pagans, they should resist the temptations that wealth brings. There was, however, no sin in wealth itself, it was its potential for misuse that was the problem. A restriction and reorientation of wants might be necessary for the rich, as their excessive consumption demands could not, and arguably should not, be met out of material growth. Wealth brings responsibilities for wise stewardship, and for charitable deeds."[10]

Several major themes emerge here. First, preventing poverty before it occurs is better than dealing with it afterward. In either case, it is important to preserve the dignity of the persons involved. A second theme is equality and fairness. This sets limits on the extent of inequality and calls for periodic correctives. Estate and inheritance taxes are examples of ways to redistribute wealth. Fairness also relates to how wealth is gained or lost, and large disparities of wealth are contrary to the will of God. Finally, there is an emphasis on responsibility. The poor are not automatically entitled to a claim on the wealth of the rich, and the rich are to act as stewards of their wealth and must exercise charity liberally, but without being compelled to do so.

The Christian tradition is not in full agreement on the rights and responsibilities of the rich. In the sixteenth century, the early Anabaptists exercised communal sharing of goods in the spirit of Acts 2:43-47 and 1 Corinthians 9. In contrast to other religious groups of the time, they made a point of ensuring that there were no beggars in their midst. Destitute members had the right to expect the more affluent to meet their basic needs. Laziness, however, was not tolerated; all members were expected to work diligently for the material and spiritual advancement of the church community.

The Catholic church also has a tradition of encouraging justice by redistributing wealth more equally to ensure at least a minimal standard of living for everyone.[11] Such redistribution is warranted as a step toward open participation for all within a community.

Still, the prevailing attitude of contemporary Christians is that the rich are to *voluntarily* act responsibly and exercise charity liberally. Major charitable acts of wealthy Americans are often seen as an illustration of the "religious" virtue of the rich who exercise wise stewardship over the distribution of their wealth. The debate within church circles does not consider an alternative use of such wealth; it doesn't consider the society that could have been if wealthy entrepreneurs had employed more workers, paid those workers more, paid regular taxes on income, and donated one-seventh of their time in voluntary service to build better communities.

In summary, mainstream religious teaching sees no problem with individual wealth. Rather, what matters is how individuals handle that wealth.

Does Money Have a Soul?

This emphasis on the wealthy being left alone to exercise good stewardship over their possessions causes Margaret Randall to ask whether money has a soul.[12]

In Praise of the Unspeakable

The landscape of America is littered with monuments to business philanthropy. Look at great universities like Stanford or Chicago. Or great art galleries like the Getty or the Frick. Or great medical institutions like Rockefeller University. Every one of them is the product of a large private fortune translated into a large public good. Andrew Carnegie and John D. Rockefeller were hard-faced men who destroyed their competitors and crushed trade unions. But they were also great philanthropists. Carnegie's dictum that "the man who dies rich dies disgraced" created a fashion among his fellow robber-barons for pouring money into universities, art galleries, and medical schools.

For better or worse, this philanthropy has allowed America to tackle its social problems without building a European-style welfare state, and to embrace modernity without abandoning its tradition of voluntarism, decentralization, and experiment.

She observes that our society has evolved myths that link poverty with purity and godliness as a means to rationalize the acts of the rich. Especially as they are applied to females, Randall concludes, such rationalizations have served to socialize the gender roles evident in our society. What is seen as wise stewardship by the wealthy is, in many cases, seen as exploitation by those who receive the charity.

A Minimum Standard of Living as a Human Right

If we redistributed everything so that everyone had an equal amount, it wouldn't take long, in a free market setting, before that equality would again be broken. This raises the question whether the rich could be relied upon to make sure this inevitable inequality wouldn't get too far out of hand.

The Definition of Poverty Involves More Than Income

A discussion of poverty must go beyond the issue of a more equal distribution of income. It also needs to include values such as the dignity of every person and the importance of being in community as defining elements in human well-being. Economic concepts such as efficiency and equity take on meaning only in the context of a community of people. This means we need to go beyond the discipline of economics because economists are not in the habit of considering whether activity contributes to building such communities.

The values of dignity and being in community require us to speak for all human casualties of our economic system. This is especially so during times of recession and downward mobility. Amartya Sen sees the basic issue as one of relationships between *primary goods*—such as income, resources, and goods and services—and *well-being*—such as liberties, utilities, other achievements, and freedoms.[13] He argues that if the two sides of this relationship can be defined in more than one space, then inequality cannot be defined by only a single variable or measure, such as income.

Given that individuals have different equality preferences, freedom of choice becomes important. Sen emphasizes
the equality preferences of an adequate diet, good health,
and a reasonable life expectancy.[14] He observes these are
much more likely to exist in societies where basic freedoms
are evident.

Constructive Changes in Welfare Rules

Since our economic system frequently fails to provide
enough paid jobs for all who are willing and able to work,
we need to find ways for everyone to earn enough to afford
the basic freedoms of an adequate diet, good health, and a
reasonable life expectancy.

A traditional approach to ensuring that a minimum standard of living is met is the use of transfer payments such as
welfare. A serious limitation of such programs is their high
marginal tax rate. Usually a welfare recipient is permitted to

Out of Sight, Out of Mind

Changes in the [U.S.] law since 1984 have increased funds available to low-income working families almost tenfold, from less than $6 billion in 1984 to over $50 billion in 1999. About half this rise comes from the Earned Income Tax Credit (EITC). Introduced in 1975 and expanded three times since then, this refundable tax credit tops up the earnings of the poor Americans: it can be worth as much as $3,800 a year, or $2 an hour, to low-income workers with children. At least ten states have their own EITC programmes that add between 4% and 46% to the federal credit.

Public health insurance for the poorest (Medicaid) has also expanded greatly. Medicaid used to be limited mainly to those on welfare. Now states have to provide coverage for all poor children. Add in other new federal programmes, such as tax credits for child care and a general child tax credit—as well as vastly increased spending by the states on the working poor—and it is clear that incentives for the poor to work have multiplied. . . . In 1986, a single mother with two children who received $8,459 in welfare would have gained only $2,000 from taking a full-time job at the minimum wage, and would have lost her family's health insurance. In 1997, by contrast, the woman would have gained over $7,000 from working full-time, would have kept her children's health insurance and would be above the poverty line.

earn a small amount each week without losing any welfare benefits, but earnings beyond that minimum trigger a reduction in welfare payments. Reducing welfare payments dollar-for-dollar according to income earned has the same effect as taxing that income. This amounts to a marginal tax rate of some 90 percent on the income earned. If other benefits are lost, the cost of earning extra income can go even higher. Note, for example, the report in *The Economist* that prior to 1986 a person on welfare in the United States who took a full-time job at the minimum wage would earn an additional $2,000 annually but would lose Medicaid benefits.

The rich complain about negative incentive effects of marginal tax rates in the 50-to-60 percent range; why then are poor persons subjected to a tax rate much higher than that?

The Economist's survey article illustrates some creative initiatives to encourage people on welfare to seek employment. Some states, by allowing the working poor to retain more of their earnings, keep Medicaid coverage, and earn tax credits, have made it possible for a minimum-wage worker to earn income that exceeds family welfare benefits by $7,000 annually. The article reports that these changes, coupled with strong employment growth, have reduced the poverty level in the United States from 15 percent in 1993 to less than 13 percent in 1998.

Fairness as a Means to Community

In the name of fairness we have emphasized the minimal responsibilities of society to each member. But fairness needs to be balanced with each individual's responsibility to society. How can society ensure that its members behave responsibly?

We Can Afford a More Fair Society

At the outset, we can agree that we have more than enough to meet all of our basic needs plus many of our wants. That is largely a product of our capitalist economic system. But, the success of capitalism can lead also to spiritual poverty and a spiritual hunger.[15] Being successful at the individual level can lead to feelings of disappointment. Material abundance is not necessarily satisfying to the human spirit.

Is there more to life than bettering one's condition in a material sense? One wants to shout: "There has to be more!" Our search for more, for meaning, cannot be limited only to us. Our having more will be sustainable only if the others in our society feel that their conditions are improving as well.

The Need to Build Social Capital

Ensuring that the poor people in our midst are included as we work together to build communities requires that we all create social capital together. With time, enabling values, norms, and beliefs can be shared by all members of the community. Building social capital involves creating a climate of trust and cooperation. The United Nations Development

---

People Acting Together

When people have been together for a long time—developing shared norms, values and beliefs that enrich the way they live and work—they possess social capital. This complements physical and human capital—enabling them to be used and managed more efficiently. Creating a climate of trust and cooperation, for example, reduces the transaction costs of doing business and creates an environment in which investment, saving, and employment can grow. Thus, it makes a significant contribution to economic growth.

Even more important, social capital is crucial to human development. People acting as a strong, cohesive community—whether through community groups or other non-governmental organizations—can achieve more than individuals. And

this also tends to offer more space for those who otherwise would be weak and powerless.

When people work together in this way, they help develop a virtuous circle as one form of social capital builds on another. The alternative—when social capital decays into individualistic, self-seeking behaviour—is more of a vicious circle, leading to greed, violence and crime.

A secure communal identity also encourages sustainability. When people identify with their community today, they want to see it survive.

From United Nations Development Programme. *Human Development Report 1996* (New York: Oxford University Press, 1996), 75. Copyright 1996 by the United Nations Development Programme. Used by permission of Oxford University Press, Inc.

Program characterizes such a climate as the exact opposite of one dominated by individualistic and self-seeking behavior.

In short, the productive use of the human and physical capital generated by the free market requires the operation of complementary institutions based on values quite different from those the market itself promotes and nurtures.

Fairness as an Opportunity to Enjoy One's Capabilities

The pursuit of fairness should be based on variables much broader than mere primary goods, such as income. Again, following Sen's lead, we could pursue a capability-based approach to justice.[16] Here fairness includes capability as one of the freedoms an individual chooses to exercise and enjoy. Fairness can then be understood as the freedom or opportunity to enjoy one's capabilities.

This means we need programs and policies that set people free to enjoy their own capabilities. Where do we start? Julia Bass has suggested some ways to assist people who depend on food banks.

- Reinstate national standards on welfare to provide an effective safety net for poor persons.
- Create jobs to address the primary cause of poverty, a lack of jobs.
- Develop work-sharing solutions to address the needs of the unemployed and underemployed persons in our communities.
- Renew federal involvement in housing to assist poor people directly and to create jobs.[17]

Employment Opportunities as a Priority

With the possible exception of redistributing holdings of wealth, the most effective way to achieve greater equity is by providing new employment opportunities. In addition, as John Dalla Costa argues, secure employment removes the corrosive effects of the uncertainty associated with unemployment and homelessness. Moreover, labor income leads to increased consumption, so investing in job creation pays off through higher sales revenue.

John Dalla Costa tells a story that relates employment to improved housing and hence better communities.[18] When the Chief Executive Officer at General Motors, John Smith, took up a challenge to visit the homes of low-paid workers employed in his plant in Mexico and saw that they were living in metal shacks without electricity or running water, he was moved to action. General Motors subsequently came up with an initiative designed to make affordable housing available to them.

One wonders what would happen if every corporate CEO paid visits to the homes of employees. Ensuring proper housing for their employees would be a significant contribution to the development of community: more jobs and better homes.

At Home and Homeless

Of course, it is not just those who lose their jobs who experience this emotional dislocation. The mere threat of joblessness, like the reality, creates a corrosive uncertainty. Beyond that, the dehumanizing practices of recent re-engineering have largely destroyed what was left of employee loyalty and commitment. For most people who spend years building careers with the same company, work had the regularity and the sense of home. Now, Dilbert-like, we inhabit temporary cubicles and improvise temporary roles, fulfilling ever-changing job descriptions while fully expecting to be the next victims of outsourcing.

The re-engineering of companies has profoundly re-engineered the very customers that support the corporate economy. Wages for the average worker have been essentially stagnant since the mid-1970s. Already financially stretched, the experience and threat of being uprooted from their jobs have only intensified uncertainty and a sense of caution. In trying to come to terms with this hostile economy, people have displayed two tendencies. First, they are significantly less loyal to companies as consumers. In effect, by making people disposable to companies, companies have made their products and services disposable to people. Many managers bemoan the loss of customer loyalty without understanding the negative reciprocity at its root.

From John Dalla Costa, "At Home and Homeless," *The Financial Post Magazine* (March 1998), 34. Material reprinted with the express permission of the National Post Company, a CanWest Partnership.

Investment in Education

Another profitable investment to reduce poverty is education. *The Economist* documents impressive returns on university education in the United States: average income is 74 percent higher for college graduates than for high school graduates and the unemployment rate is 50 percent lower.[19] Education can benefit the community as a whole by making citizens more informed, generating higher tax revenues, lowering the amount needed for transfer payments and social programs, and developing skills that can lead to technological advancement, better administration, and entrepreneurship. Additional benefits that economists cannot readily measure flow from advanced study in the arts and the humanities.

Investment in building community tends to have cumulative effects. In an article reporting on a study edited by Miles Corak, *Labour Markets, Social Institutions, and the Future of Canada's Children*, Luiza Chwialkowska notes that every additional thousand dollars in parental annual income adds only some fifty dollars per year to the later income of the children. In contrast, parents' actions to strengthen family life, create lasting roots in a community,

Earnings Not Limited by Income of Father

Parents of all income levels can improve their children's financial future. . . . A stable marriage, roots in the community, and setting an example of saving and investing helped children grow up to be wealthier.

Children whose fathers received some interest or dividend income in 1982, for example, earned $3,000 more in 1994 than children whose fathers had the same overall level of income but did not report any asset income. . . .

On the other hand, income from certain government transfers had negative or no correlation with the adult earnings of children. Those children with fathers receiving income from employment insurance, regardless of the amount, ended up making less.

Community ties were also important. Teenagers who had moved from one neighbourhood to another earned anywhere from $500 to $2,000 a year less as adults than their counterparts who did not experience a move.

From Luiza Chwialkowska, "Earnings Not Limited by Income of Father," *National Post* (November 6, 1998). Material reprinted with the express permission of the National Post Company, a CanWest Partnership.

and invest in the future made a much larger contribution to the subsequent earnings of their children.

In conclusion, a high material standard of living is not an end in itself. More significant values are to ensure human dignity for everyone and to build inclusive communities. The larger the differences in income and wealth and the greater the destruction of dignity, the more difficult it becomes to build and maintain communities of people. Greater equity does not produce community automatically, but it facilitates a move in that direction. It enables communities to be more inclusive, and it tends to make them more stable and enduring.

Can Our Economic System Generate the Required Fairness?

Thus far I have sought to challenge the underlying premise of our economic system: that distribution of income is the only way to motivate people to advance their material standard of living to ever-higher levels. I have argued that responsibility and fairness are important ingredients in the fostering of human dignity, the building of community, and the provision of opportunities for all to contribute to the overall well-being of the community.

Can these means of fostering dignity and community be achieved by a capitalist system that continues to generate unequal income, wealth, and power? The system has no built-in way to generate or ensure fairness. Purposeful action will be required to make sure our economic system serves us rather than enslaves us. In this concluding section I outline ways we might work together to direct our economic system toward greater responsibility and fairness.

The Need to Ensure Access to the Means of Production

The first issue of concern is our current distribution of wealth. If we want to build communities in which all people are free to enjoy their respective capabilities, we must deal

Wealth and Possessions

There is provision in the Torah for addressing the inequalities which inevitably exist in any economy. This is not so much a matter of redistribution, but rather one of creating a level playing field for each generation so that material advantages acquired through one generation's acquisition of wealth are not handed down. In the Torah there is much discussion of land rights, land and labor being the crucial factors of production in ancient Israel rather than capital. As the ultimate owner of land is God, humans do not have the right to sell it permanently, or indeed to acquire a freehold through purchase. In Leviticus the implications of the year of Jubilee for land are spelt out: "Consecrate the fiftieth year and proclaim liberty throughout the land to all its inhabitants. It shall be a jubilee for you; each one of you is to return to his family property and each to his own clan." This would seem to imply that all slaves are to be freed, and that those who have leased or purchased land should hand it back to the original owner.

Rodney Wilson, *Economics, Ethics and Religion* (1997), 29.

with the concentration of wealth in the hands of a few families.

The Israelites in Old Testament times were known as people who placed a very high value on being in community. To ensure that all families would have some access to the primary means of production, periodic provision was made for slaves to be freed, debt to be forgiven, and land to be returned to the original owners. These redistribution practices, known as the Jubilee, was to occur on a seven-year cycle or on a seven-times-seven-year cycle.

Land was the primary resource. To prevent the population from being divided permanently into the landed and the landless, people were given a chance every fifty years to gain back their family's land. Over time this gave them a more or less equal opportunity to make a living comparable to that of others in the community.

Is this basic principle of guaranteed access to the primary resource essential for the equity required to build community? In rural communities, land is still the primary resource. If the family farm is essential to maintaining community, new approaches need to be devised to ensure its preservation. The communal approach of the Hutterites, the intergenerational approach of the Amish and Old Order Mennonites, and community-based land trusts are possible models.

Not all of us own land. Our comparable resources may be knowledge and ownership of the various forms of capital. A broad-based, quality education made available to everyone would be a good start on the knowledge resource. The role of patents and copyrights, which allow individuals to claim monopolies over parts of our knowledge base, would need to be evaluated continuously.

Ensured access for all to capital as a means of production is a major challenge. Those who own capital traditionally also have the right to determine who has access to it. Maybe that right is necessary to make sure the capital is used in the most productive way during the lifetime of its owner. But should that right necessarily be transferable to future generations? Does passing this capital to heirs necessarily mean it will continue to be used in the most productive way? Capital gains taxes and inheritance taxes, unpopular as they may be to the wealthy, may need a second look because they are effective ways to reduce the concentration of power that comes with owning capital.

At a more basic level, though, we must ask whether taxing wealth is the most creative way to address this issue. Here is a real challenge: to redefine ownership rules for accumulated capital in a manner that periodically gives all members of the community a chance to work with capital and to help earn their livelihood. Whoever comes up with alternative, practical ways to accomplish this will have made a major stride toward achieving the fairness we need in order to build communities.

Implementing the Values of a Sabbath

The Jewish Sabbath and the Christian Sunday are the other side of biblical Jubilee. The Jubilee enables some to reduce control over the means of production so others have a fresh opportunity to participate. Similarly, the Sabbath and the Sunday are pauses in our feverish drive to gain an ever-higher material standard of living for ourselves. Such a pause in consumption and production can be a significant step toward freeing up opportunities for others.

We tend to think of the Sabbath (or Sunday) in religious terms. That is important, but the concept has much wider implications than the timing or format of our worship. It is a time to say "I have enough." There are limits to your and my wants. Our contribution to the well-being of our community goes beyond simply what we produce or consume.

This periodic pause is also a time to acknowledge that the productive aspect of God's creation can get along without us for a day. It's a time to realize that it is not merely human endeavor that has brought our created order into existence. Nor is it human endeavor alone that maintains and sustains the created order. Honoring the Sabbath provides a form of rest as a benefit for all of creation.

We can extend the spirit of the Sabbath by confronting honestly the questions about ethical business posed by Jesus M. Cruz, a Mennonite with long experience as a banker in New York City and Lancaster, Pennsylvania.

> Many of the conflicts between business practices and Anabaptist faith ethics arise out of the following questions:
> - Fairness. Do I pay a fair wage? Do I pay a fair price for goods or services I purchase? Am I asking a fair price for goods or services I sell?
> - Integrity. Am I providing the value I am advertising? Am I dealing in good faith?
> - Stewardship. Am I saving or hoarding? How much profit is enough? Am I sharing my blessings?[20]

Source of security. Do I look for my security in my business, my profits, my power or my faith? The wages paid to employees help shape both the living standard of the employees and the community in which we live. Similarly, the level of profits, the use of those profits, and the manner in which savings are invested can play a significant role in the shaping type of community we live in.

Limiting the Range in Wages and Salaries

We noted earlier the problem of excessive executive compensation. We need greater clarity on the role that pay incentives play in motivating us to make productive contributions to the well-being of our community. Is it unreasonable to suggest that entrepreneurs pay themselves no more than ten times the income of their lowest-paid employees? Herman Daly points to army, civil service, and university salary structures as examples.[21] Extending this principle to business firms would go a long way toward the building and maintenance of community.

Unfortunately, any intervention in society's normal method of compensating people is derided promptly by some as penalizing the achiever and rewarding the parasite. This attitude seems to hold true for all kinds of assistance to the poor. Whenever income or resources are transferred from the achievers to those who have limited access to the means of livelihood, poverty is seen as a social burden.

Addressing the Vulnerability of Persons Living in Poverty

The poor are often blamed for their poverty, which is thought to result from alcoholism, limited education and job skills, a lack of drive or initiative, an unwillingness to save, or a failure to spend wisely.

But there is more to being poor. A basic characteristic of all poor persons is their vulnerability. They do not control the economic and social forces that shape their lives. They are constantly at the mercy of social forces that keep pushing them around.

Many poor people compensate for their vulnerability by learning to rely on each other. They often have stronger relationships than others and a higher degree of mutual concern and sharing. Success is shared—whether that success is a good income from a new job, success in self-employment, an inheritance, lottery winnings. Each act of sharing can be seen as willingness to bear burdens together.

The intrusion of welfare, though desirable in certain cases, reduces the level of sharing. So our welfare programs, while providing a security net and a minimal standard of living, end up destroying individual initiative.

Poverty is also a burden to the larger society. Transfer payments, though beneficial, represent income that is not earned in the conventional sense. In Canada such transfer payments account for a major portion of federal, provincial, and local government budgets. They include supplemental incomes for the elderly in poverty; all forms of welfare; family allowances and other forms of tax credits for children; unemployment insurance; and veterans benefits. In addition there are transfers at the personal level and numerous charitable programs such as United Way agencies and food banks. Poverty also adds significantly to the cost of health care. Another cost is increased crime as the distribution of income and wealth becomes less equal.

Making the Human Dignity of All Persons a Priority

To break down the barriers between the "achievers" and the "parasites" we will need to move boldly to modify our behavior and change certain aspects of our economic system. This discussion is one attempt to outline some steps that might point us toward building community and being at home in community. We cannot guarantee that any of these steps will work. Dare we concede that our economic system is beyond repair? If we can muster a personal and a social will to do so, we will find a way to build community. Our will, though, needs to emerge from a conviction that every person is worthy of human dignity, that human dignity is nourished in community, and that every person deserves the opportunity to contribute creatively to the building of that community.

For if the eagerness is there, the gift is acceptable according to what one has—not according to what one does not have. I do not mean that there should be relief for others and pressure on you, but it is a question of a fair balance between your present abundance and their need, so that their abundance may be for your need, in order that there may be a fair balance. As it is written, "The one who had much did not have too much, and the one who had little did not have too little" (2 Cor. 8:12-15).

Corporate leaders
are truly men
without a country
as they strive to
overcome irrational
nationalist
constraints and
integrate the world.
—*John Ralston Saul*

10

Our Place in the Global Market

Our discussion so far has focused on two countries, the United States and Canada. But the buzzword of our time is globalization. The market that serves as the nervous system of capitalism has become global. In this chapter I explore what this global market means for the economic system that drives North America.

Globalization: The Next Stage in Specialization

Defining Globalization

Globalization is like an elephant: an elephant is not easy to explain to someone who has never seen one, but once you have encountered one you know exactly what it is. Vijay Govindarajan and Anil Gupta recognize this complexity by providing a definition that applies at the worldwide, country, and industry levels.

- Worldwide level: "the growing economic interdependence among countries as reflected in increasing cross-border flows of goods, services, capital and know-how"
- Country level: "the extent of the inter-linkages between a country's economy and the rest of the world"
- Industry level: "the degree to which a company's

competitive position within that industry in one country is interdependent with that in another country."[1]

Why Is the Price of Natural Gas Going Up?

Recently, a number of factors have continued to increase demand for Western Canadian natural gas. One factor is the opening of new natural gas markets in the United States. New markets mean increased demand and Western Canadian producers can meet that demand because of new pipelines built to supply U.S. markets.

From "Notice of Rate Change," a Centra Gas statement enclosed with its natural gas bills to Manitoba customers (December 1, 1999).

When it comes to business, no country can be an island unto itself. The prices we pay in our local community are shaped by demand and supply forces in other countries as well as our own. Similarly, business managers making production decisions locally have to be aware of production costs and market conditions in other countries far away.

Globalization Is the Next Stage in the Evolution of Specialization

The word *globalization* is a recent addition to our vocabulary, but the market and the activities it describes are not new. Rather, globalization is the latest stage in the evolution of specialization that has been occurring for centuries. In the example of Adam Smith's pin factory we observed the revolutionary change in production that occurred when the job of making a pin was broken down into ten tasks, each one performed by a person with specialized skills in that area.

Two changes are occurring now to advance this historic process of specialization. First, reduction of tariffs and growth in economies of scale in certain types of products are combining to give many firms a larger global market for their output. Second, knowledge-based industries are becoming increasingly important, especially in high-income countries such as the United States and Canada. When a product costs a lot to develop but not much to manufacture, the vastness of a global market makes it easier for a firm to recover its development costs. The combined revolution in computer technology and telecommunications has made possible this high degree of specialization in knowledge as a productive input to economic activity. These technological changes also facilitate the international trade of knowledge-based goods and services.

Advances in computer technology and telecommunications also have eased the international movement of financial transactions. Companies now can move funds between countries instantaneously at very low cost. This easy movement of money has made the relative cost of financing capital, rather than the direct input costs in manufacturing, an important factor in determining where a firm chooses to locate its operations. Andrew Karolyi compares this availability of lower-cost financing to a powerful narcotic that drives corporate executives to consider global options.[2]

Technology Shock

Globalization is aided by freer trade. Tariffs . . . are falling or have already been eliminated. For a relatively small country like Canada, access to a large market is of paramount importance. It helps to boost productivity because plants can be built at the most efficient scale. Knowledge-based products, which are typified by high costs of development, but very low costs of production, benefit as well. By expanding the market available, the potential revenue stream for these products is much greater. Further innovation, which is at the heart of technological progress, is thus promoted.

These changes are already sweeping through the world economy. High technology and highly knowledge-intensive goods are making a much larger contribution to international trade growth than low technology and goods that require less knowledge to produce. This is a double-edged sword for Canada. We enjoy a comparative advantage in natural resources, but international trade in these commodities is generally growing much more slowly than in high-tech goods.

From Robert Fairholm, "Technology Shock," *The Financial Post 2000* (October 11, 1997), 5. Material reprinted with the express permission of the National Post Company, a CanWest Partnership.

Large Corporations Are Driving Globalization

The main institution that makes globalization happen is the corporation. Whether in manufacturing, agribusiness, finance, marketing, or advertising, it is large corporations that have the capacity to locate branch plants or offices wherever they wish. Some have become so large that the value of their annual output exceeds the Gross Domestic Product of some entire countries.

It is not necessary, though, to be a large corporation in order to participate actively in the global market. *The Economist* describes how small farmers in southern India have become active participants in the global market for pepper. A market large enough to absorb the pepper these Indian farmers produce requires most of the world. To compete, the farmers have to play by the rules set by large corporations. They have even set up a market in pepper futures to reduce some of the risks of fluctuating prices.

Whereas both large and small producers can grasp the new opportunities presented by globalization, it is the large corporations that are ideally placed to take advantage of advancing technology. They have the expertise, financial resources, and experience to benefit from the globalization process.

A Taste of Adventure

Until you talk to them about the world market, Iddicki's residents seem much like farmers anywhere else in the developing world—scraping a living at the margins of the market economy. Thomas, one of the several hundred thousand smallholders who grow Kerala's pepper, is a good example. A humble man of the earth, he speaks softly and still wears his dhothi, a traditional loincloth, when he tills his soil. But with a little prompting he will give you an analysis of the pepper market sophisticated enough to make a Chicago commodities trader blush: current prices, the direction of the futures market, the costs versus the benefits of holding stocks. A local spice dealer explains over a feast of fiery snapper and spiced tapioca at his spacious bungalow that "there is full price-discovery in this market." The farmers who sell their crops to him (for resale at the big market in Jewtown, which has replaced Calicut as the hub of Kerala's pepper trade) do so with the latest New York and Rotterdam prices in hand. One particularly sharp farmer, he moans, is cutting out the middlemen altogether and shipping his stocks directly to Europe.

From "A Taste of Adventure," *The Economist* (December 19, 1998), 51. The Economist Newspaper Ltd. All rights reserved. Reprinted with permission. Further reproduction prohibited. www.economist.com.

Some of the Effects of Globalization

This rapidly expanding globalization process is profoundly affecting each of us. David Korten observes that:

Corporations have emerged as the dominant governance institutions on the planet, with the largest among them reaching into virtually every country of the world and exceeding most governments in size and power. Increasingly, it is the corporate interest more than human interest that defines the policy agendas of states and international bodies, although this reality and its implications have gone largely unnoticed and unaddressed.[3]

This is especially so in medium-sized and smaller countries, including Canada. The immense size of corporations gives them tremendous economic power, including the ability to close plants in one country and move operations elsewhere. This power is so great that governments are held hostage, forced to come up with huge subsidies to keep the corporations at home in their countries.

George Soros argues that globalization affects the way morality is formed in our societies.[4] Corporate activities, especially in the labor market, tend to destroy rather than build community. This erodes the traditional process of forming morality on the basis of a sense of belonging to a community.

As corporations move their production from country to country in search of lower labor costs, the high-wage labor

Ottawa to Fund Development of IBM's E-Commerce Software

The federal government is providing $33-million to IBM Canada Ltd. to develop E-commerce software and is justifying support as a means to keeping high-tech jobs in the country. . . .

Ottawa expects the TPC grants to be repaid from royalties on products that achieve commercial success, although it gets nothing if the project flops. . . .

Federal officials have said the government support was crucial to allowing IBM Canada to maintain its global mandate with the parent IBM Corporation to develop the E-commerce software.

"This could have gone elsewhere," a federal source said. . . .

Earlier this spring, IBM threatened to move 1,500 research and development jobs, including its E-commerce project, out of the country.

From Shawn McCarthy and Simon Tuck, "Ottawa to Fund Development of IBM's E-Commerce Software," *The Globe and Mail* (July 6, 1999). Reprinted with permission from *The Globe and Mail*.

force must compete against people who are earning lower wages, working where health and safety standards are weaker, and tolerating less secure employment conditions. Local economies suffer severe losses as companies that can see no farther than the issue of wages shop around the world for new locations where human labor is cheap and plentiful. Volkswagen's production of the new Beetle in Mexico illustrates this process. In Germany, Volkswagen employees work a twenty-eight-hour week; in Mexico a forty-two-hour week. The average wage in the Mexico plant is $13.50 per day.[5]

The Globe and Mail reports that 350 Canadian companies now operate in Mexico.[6] Most of them have done so to take advantage of lower wages and easy, tariff-free access to the U.S. market.

Finally, globalization is reducing stability in the market. This hungry search for lower wages is causing a persistent excess supply of output at the global level in industries such as car manufacturing. This has one potential benefit—these large producers are subject once more to the discipline of competition. But it also will prove to be destabilizing as a number of these firms are forced into bankruptcy or are taken over by stronger corporations.

Can National Institutions Control International Activity?

Globalization Challenges the Authority of Nation-States

The process of globalization is challenging the ability of nations to properly govern their people. Governments find it increasingly difficult to exercise control over corporations that know no borders. As stated by *The Economist*, "modern computer and telecommunications make capital controls impossible to enforce; networked multinationals are creating a borderless world, forcing governments to compete for investment."[7]

Corporations active in two or more countries have to deal with local differences in such areas as laws, customs, employment practices, consumer tastes and environmental standards. The ideal corporation wants to satisfy all of its suppliers, customers, employees, and shareholders. In the global context this corporation is like a chameleon, which changes color to blend into whatever environment it finds itself in. One illustration of adapting to local conditions is that of the Coca Cola plant in Guangdong Province in China. In addition to making Coke and Sprite, it churns out 11 million cases annually of local fruit drinks such as carbonated coconut juice and tea-based drinks.[8]

As Rodney Wilson observes, the ideal corporation does not exist in practice. Corporate managers are primarily responsible to their shareholders, so the corporation tends to reflect the laws, values, and methods of the home country. This makes the operation of the corporation especially threatening in the other countries, which have goals, laws, values, and methods quite different from those of the home country. Nonetheless, corporations frequently find that their win-win profit strategies lead to criticism at home as well as in foreign host countries. Some examples, according to Wilson, are a willingness to pay bribes to influence decisions—illegal for U.S. and Canadian corporations but not necessarily for European corporations—and avoiding stricter pollution controls and employee benefits regulations.

Operation abroad opens up the possibility that the local people where the plants are located will learn from the corporation and eventually form competing firms. William Greider interprets this result as a real benefit.[9] It spreads industrialization beyond the borders of the current industrialized countries to at least the middle-income countries of the world. But new firms established by local people also represent competition. They increase the vulnerability of the multinational in this global market. To counter this competition corporations are forming partnerships with their potential competitors in middle-income countries. This allows them to guide such competitors and make arrangements to share markets.[10]

Benefits of Globalization Tend to Flow to the Wealthy Elite

In low-income countries the presence of multinational corporations typically benefits primarily the rich elite. Korten provides a summary of the negative side effects for the truly poor people of the world.

> Rapid economic growth in low-income countries brings modern airports, television, express highways, and air-conditioned shopping malls with sophisticated consumer electronics and fashion labels for the fortunate few. It rarely improves living conditions for the many. This kind of growth requires gearing the economy toward exports to earn the foreign exchange to buy the things that wealthy people desire. Thus, the lands of the poor are appropriated for export crops. The former tillers of these lands then find themselves subsisting in urban slums on starvation wages paid by sweatshops producing for export. Families are broken up, the social fabric is strained to the breaking point, and violence becomes endemic. Those whom growth has favored then still need more foreign exchange to import arms to protect themselves from the rage of the excluded.[11]

Governments have a limited ability to respond to the actions of corporations. If a government imposes conditions on capital, the multinational corporations will threaten to move theirs elsewhere. There is a temptation for governments to offer tax breaks, looser labor conditions, and lax enforcement of environmental laws to attract multinational corporations.

This doesn't mean that all overseas production occurs in sweatshops. Toy manufacturing at the Early Light factories in China, described in *The Economist*, is more typical of low-wage-cost production in low- and middle-income countries.

The Role of Transfer Pricing in the Movement of Profits

The ability of governments to require multinational corporations to pay for the major benefits they receive from such national programs as defense, police protection, the court system, fire protection, education, and urban amenities is weak. These corporations engage in what is called transfer pricing to avoid paying taxes for significant benefits they may receive in each country in which they operate.

Transfer pricing refers to the price they charge themselves for parts, output, and services they send from one branch of the firm to another located in some other country. This price is manipulated so that the branches in a higher-tax country show no profits; corporate profits are then declared where taxes are lowest.

Take, for example, an oil company that operates in both Venezuela and Canada. It pumps oil from the ground in Venezuela, then ships it to Canada where it is refined and sold through its service stations located in Eastern Canada. The firm operates a branch on a Caribbean island where a handful of employees deal only with financial matters. The multinational corporation sells the Venezuelan oil to its island branch at a price so low that the Venezuela branch has

Where the Furbies Come From

With 20,000 workers spread over two factory sites, Early Light looks like a Silicon Valley industrial campus. . . . The factory floors are marvels of high-volume manufacturing, with computer-controlled laser-cutting machines and huge rooms of workers assembling printed circuit boards to the din of "Buzz Lightyear!" as hundreds of toys are tested to infinity and beyond. Around them are dormitories with cafeterias, karaoke rooms, libraries and basketball courts.

A walk through just one of Early Light's buildings takes you past Matchbox cars, Small Soldiers, Bug's Life figurines. Tonka trucks and all the biggest brand names in the business: Hasbro, Mattel, Playskool, Fisher-Price and Bandai. These (mostly) American giants may design and market most of the world's toys, but when it comes to making them they all head for China, where unheralded manufacturers such as Early Light do all the hard work. Children may want to believe that Santa's helpers are Nordic elves. In fact they use chopsticks.

no profits and hence pays no taxes. The island branch then sells the oil to the Canadian branch at a price so high that the Canadian firm cannot make a profit and thus pays no taxes in Canada. All of the profits on this oil business are declared in its island branch in a country that happens to have a zero tax rate on corporate profits.

This is particularly problematic for smaller countries such as Canada, many of whose multinational corporations are headquartered in the United States. Generally corporations are subject to some form of taxation in their home country. Even so, when President Clinton first ran for office he advocated a 15 percent tax on all foreign corporations operating in the United States. The underlying assumption was that these corporations must be engaged in transfer pricing, and 15 percent was an estimate of the taxes they were avoiding in the United States.

Corporate Strategies to Limit the Powers of Government

Many governments are under increasing pressure from their electorates to do something about the multinational corporations operating in their midst. For most low- and middle-income countries the primary option is to accept that these branches will continue to operate and provide some benefits but without paying a fair share for the services they draw from the host country. The exception is the country that has resources so valuable or a market so important that the multinational corporation is willing to pay a decent price for the privilege of operating there.

As countries with such bargaining power exercise their strength, the large corporations are joining forces to fight back. An example was the recent attempt by the major industrial countries to negotiate a Multilateral Agreement on Investment (MAI). Its purpose was to create an international charter of rights for multinational corporations that would forbid member countries from treating them differently from their own business firms. As a means of enforcement, the multinational firms would be able to sue the host country government if they felt they were being singled out for less favorable treatment.

Such a charter of rights governing all forms of international investment would have shifted the balance of power significantly in favor of the large corporations. The MAI was also unique in that it was an initiative undertaken by the major industrial countries outside of the relevant international body, the World Trade Organization, whose rules make the process of negotiations slow and cumbersome because they give the low- and middle-income countries at least a little voice in the process. The corporations involved in the MAI effort wanted quicker action to produce an agreement that could be more or less imposed on the less industrialized countries of the world.

The proposed MAI had a precedent in the North American Free Trade Agreement (NAFTA), which aimed, among other things, to protect U.S. and Canadian corporations from discriminatory practices in Mexico. Ironically, two of the first three challenges that arose out of this agreement were successful actions by U.S. corporations against Canada. This experience contributed to significant opposition to the MAI within Canada. Ordinary citizens in the United States did not appear to be aware of these negotiations and hence were unconcerned.

> Governments seem wholly incapable of responding, and public frustration is turning to rage. It is more than a failure of government bureaucracies, however. It is a crisis of governance born of convergence of ideological, political, and technological forces behind a process of economic globalization that is shifting power away from governments responsible for the public good and toward a handful of corporations and financial institutions driven by a single imperative—the quest for short-term financial gain. This has concentrated massive economic and political power in the hands of an elite few whose absolute share of the products of a declining pool of natural wealth continues to increase at a substantial rate—thus reassuring them that the system is working perfectly well.
>
> David C. Korten, *When Corporations Rule the World* (1995), 12.

The MAI's fast-track approach to protecting large corporations failed. Canada wanted to maintain at least some control over the influx of culture-related industries such as publishing and television. Similarly, France was concerned about maintaining its film industry, which is important to its culture. Other countries wanted other exceptions. As the process of arguing for exceptions gained momentum, the large corporations began to fear they might end up with many new restrictions on international investment rather than a desired charter of freedoms and rights. So they withdrew their support and the governments involved in the negotiations lost interest.

This does not mean the large corporations have given up their quest for enforceable international provisions to protect them against individual governments. Rather, they must now pursue this objective through the World Trade Organization. So stay tuned on this issue.

The NAFTA, meanwhile, represents a new kind of intergovernmental partnership that provides more control over multinational corporations than any one country could have individually.

Under NAFTA goods and services can move relatively freely across the mutual boundaries of Canada, the United States, and Mexico, though each country can still set its own tariffs on imports from the rest of the world. A much stronger alliance is the European Economic Community. That partnership allows for free trade among member countries, sets a common tariff for all members against outside countries, allows for resources such as labor to move among member countries as well, and now is moving toward a common monetary and fiscal policy. The introduction of the euro as a common currency for the member countries is a major step toward a common monetary policy.

The NAFTA, which is driven by the United States, primarily increases the economic space within which multinational corporations are free to operate. As noted by the *Globe and Mail*, the European Community, in contrast, seeks to define common social and political goals for all of its member countries. It then uses its vast economic power to pressure large corporations to abide by the common goals, aspirations, and methods of the European Community members.

Individual countries cannot control the behavior of large corporations, and although the European Community can do more than individual countries, it acts like merely one larger state operating against powerful multinational corporations. Still, many economists, who remain firm in their belief in a market that is always tending toward equilibrium, are confident that global competition will limit the power of any one corporation.

What if NAFTA Ruled the Waves?

In many ways, Britain is more suited to joining NAFTA than deepening its ties to the EU. NAFTA and the EU represent two very different visions of globalization. NAFTA is about free trade, period. It's something that a majority of the British people, including the strong Euroskeptic contingent, can understand and support; their 19th-century forebears virtually invented the practice of free trade.

The EU, by contrast, is largely about building something that can prevent a rerun of the First and Second World Wars. Created by the leaders of a continent cursed with more history and nationalisms than geography, it is an attempt to create an overarching structure able to subsume national rivalries into a co-operative, continent-wide project. That structure was at first largely economic, but a new political wing is under construction.

From "What if NAFTA Ruled the Waves?" *The Globe and Mail* (August 4, 1998). Reprinted with permission from *The Globe and Mail.*

George Soros, who has benefited immensely from the global corporate system, does not agree. He concludes that a system in which the pursuit of money overrides social considerations is deeply flawed. The problem arises in part because the development of global society has not kept pace with the development of the global economy.[12]

Soros favors some form of international control. He sees a serious imbalance when political and social life are governed at a national level while the capitalist economic system operates unfettered at the international level. He argues that the heart of the matter is the financial component, the part of the larger market in which corporations can easily move money across international boundaries. He challenges the whole economics profession by arguing that financial markets are essentially immune to those forces that we normally count on to return the market to some form of equilibrium. Unless controlled in some way, these financial markets can utterly destroy certain economies, and if enough countries' economies are destroyed at one time, the whole capitalist system could be at risk. Some recent examples of countries where this has happened are Mexico, Russia, Brazil, Argentina, Japan, and several Southeast Asian countries.

Soros advocates the formation of an international organization that has the responsibility to control financial markets. Alternatively, the major countries would have to agree to act together to impose common restrictions on the free movement of international capital.

The Role of International Institutions

Up until World War II, every international war was followed by a severe depression. This was the result of countries shifting production from military to domestic use, international trade relations being reestablished, and soldiers returning and needing jobs. After World War II there was a real fear that the Great Depression of the 1930s would resume. In anticipation of this, representatives of various countries met in Bretton Woods, New Hampshire, in 1943 to create two world institutions designed to reduce the severity of the expected depression. These two sister institutions are the International Monetary Fund (IMF) and the International Bank for Reconstruction and Development, known more popularly as the World Bank.

The International Monetary Fund (IMF)

From the mid-1800s to World War I, international trade and finance was governed by the gold standard. It worked quite well, keeping international finances in order during a period when the world was relatively stable. The gold standard was suspended during World War I and reestablished immediately afterward. But the relative trade and financial strength of the member countries had changed so much during the war that the gold standard no longer served as well as it had in the past. As the Great Depression set in, one country after another abandoned it, creating a financial vacuum for the remainder of the Depression and during World War II.

The IMF was created to fill this vacuum. It had some of the same elements of the gold standard but was designed to be much more flexible. Under the gold standard each country set the value of its currency according to the international price of gold. A country could repay trade deficits and international debt by sending gold or by paying with its own currency, which could be changed into gold at a fixed price. Within the IMF, the United States set the value of its currency to gold, and every other member country had to set the value of its currency to the U.S. dollar. This gave the United States immense power, as every other country had to adjust its own economy to maintain this foreign exchange ratio while the United States sat back and enjoyed watching them struggle to do so.

The voting power of IMF member countries is defined by the amount each pays into IMF reserves. As a result, the United States has some 20 percent of the votes. It and the European Community together carry enough votes to block any changes in IMF responsibilities or operations. Because of this lopsided voting structure, many see the IMF as just another tool of the major industrialized countries.

Besides helping to stabilize the foreign exchange system,

the IMF helps countries with their balance of payments. If a country persistently imports more goods and services than it exports, its international payments are out of balance. To pay for these excess imports the country can borrow the currency it requires with a three-year loan from the IMF. The IMF is able to make such loans from deposits that each member country placed in the IMF at the time of joining.

A country can borrow up to the equivalent of the amount it deposited originally in the IMF at any time to meet a balance of payments problem. If it requires a larger loan, it has to submit to changes the IMF recommends so that the country can overcome the balance of payments problem during the three-year period of the loan. Thus the IMF can act like a disciplining parent: "I will lend you this extra money if you agree to meet the following changes in your spending habits."

The IMF's right to impose conditions was expanded significantly during the debt crisis of the 1980s. The countries that were owed money, such as the United States and Canada, typically forced debtor countries to agree to IMF conditions before their debt could be rescheduled. At the time the IMF had limited experience in funding economic development. Its staff tended to view every problem as a balance of payments problem. Solutions based on this narrow view have caused considerable harm, along with a little good, in heavily indebted countries that had other severe economic problems.

Over time the IMF has sought to protect its empire by becoming more flexible in allowing countries to change the value of their currency relative to that of the U.S. dollar. In the early 1970s the member countries agreed to expand the IMF's resources by allowing the creation of Special Drawing Rights (SDRs) as a form of international currency. The value of an SDR is based on an average of that of sixteen major currencies. The amount created is periodically distributed to member countries according to the size of their respective deposits. The United States receives 20 percent; the poorest countries receive virtually nothing.

The IMF is at the forefront of the promotion of globalization. Without accepting any responsibility for the sad state of numerous economies in Africa, the IMF blames the individual governments for failing to participate fully in the globalization process. As a result, the high-income countries that are leading the globalization process are marginalizing Africa further.

The World Bank

Initially the sole purpose of the World Bank, the IMF's sister institution, was to fund the reconstruction of Europe after World War II. Delegates meeting at Bretton Woods had to admit that John Maynard Keynes was correct when he predicted in 1919 that the peace imposed on Germany following World War I would cause another war. There was no way Germany could pay for its own reconstruction plus reparations to the European powers that had defeated it. Therefore, after World War II the international community invested significantly in the reconstruction of all of Europe, not just the countries of the victorious Allies. The World Bank was the major means for channeling investment funds to Europe for this purpose.

The World Bank's actions in Europe were so successful that the international community allowed it to remain in existence with a new mandate. In the 1950s and the 1960s many colonies in Asia and Africa were gaining independence from their European masters. The World Bank would use the same approach it had used in Europe to help these newly independent countries develop. This new mandate was accepted because, according to the economic theory of the 1950s, lack of capital was the primary reason why countries were undeveloped. In taking on this new mandate, the

International Bank for Reconstruction and Development of Europe became, indeed, a world bank.

The World Bank has made some significant errors over the years, but in the end its work will likely be interpreted in favorable terms. It has transferred significant financial capital to many parts of the world, has funded large infrastructure projects that no one else could afford, and has kept the confidence of the international community by maintaining an excellent repayment record for the loans extended. The World Bank also has become an important source of data for other organizations working in development. In-country representatives in the low- and middle-income countries frequently provide important insight into what is happening there.

The World Bank got off to a bad start, however, because the development process turned out to be much more complex than just pouring in more financial capital. It failed miserably in trying to develop agriculture in Africa because, as the World Bank admits, its staff and consultants did not understand peasant farmers and couldn't help them work toward development. Not surprisingly, some of the large infrastructure projects created significant environmental problems or failed to live up to their planned level of output.

When it comes to controlling or channeling the process of globalization, the World Bank has little to offer. This is simply not part of its mandate. If anything, it facilitates globalization by pursuing large infrastructure projects and by encouraging all countries to be more open and to rely more on international trade.

The World Trade Organization (WTO)

A third international institution that arose after World War II was the General Agreement on Tariffs and Trade (GATT). This institution was replaced during the 1990s with the World Trade Organization. A significant problem during the Great Depression was that each country tried to restrict imports as a way to deal with its own unemployment problem. When nobody imports, international trade dries up. Without the possibility of exports, more unemployment was created than was resolved by the restriction of imports. Therefore, the major trading countries were determined to make sure the trade-restricting actions used during the Great Depression would not be repeated. GATT was the means to this end.

The first task was to reduce the significant tariffs and other trade barriers that existed. Under GATT, any country that offered lower tariffs or other preferential treatment to one country then had to extend the same to all other countries within the GATT. This meant a country no longer had to negotiate with every nation with which it had trading relations. Rather, it could negotiate with its major trading partner, and all other members of GATT would abide by the same terms. Once an agreement was reached, GATT also provided a way to settle disputes that such agreements generated. Over the years, GATT has reduced significantly both tariffs and other trade restrictions.

One anomaly of GATT was U.S. insistence that it exclude the agriculture sector from the provisions of the agreement. The United States was the world's primary exporter of agricultural goods at the time, and over the years this exemption allowed it to export its agricultural products at prices below what it charged its own consumers.

The United States also began to use food as a political weapon, forcing other countries to bend to its foreign policy demands as a condition for receiving food. This so angered the European countries and Japan that they resolved to never again depend on the United States for essential food. They heavily subsidized their own agriculture production, and now the high-income countries together pay approximately $1 billion every day in subsidies to their farmers. This ploy was so successful that Europe and Japan have overcome their food deficit, and together with the United States they are exporting their surpluses at a fraction of the cost of producing the food. As a result, exempting agriculture from the provisions of GATT is no longer in the interest of the United States.

During the Uruguay round of GATT negotiations in the late 1980s and the first part of the 1990s, the United States sought not only to bring agriculture into the GATT but also to widen the GATT net to include the international trade of services. In addition, multinational corporations were creating pressure for a common set of rules that would apply to all member countries of GATT to protect their investments in those countries. The original mandate was seen as inadequate to cover all aspects of this agenda, so the World Trade Organization has been created to replace GATT. Another significant change under the WTO is a much stronger and more efficient mechanism for dealing with disputes between member countries and for enforcing its decisions. The Doha round of negations initiated in 2001 has sought to address issues left unresolved at the end of the Uruguay round.

WTO's increased power to deal with disputes is evident in the banana dispute between the United States and the European Union. Europe's import system gives preference to bananas produced in the former British and French colonies in Africa, the Caribbean, and certain islands in the Pacific. The United States protested this "discrimination." The United States does not export bananas but has used first

> Commerce either persuades a society to relax its laws and social obligations or it exits to another society. As production moves elsewhere, a second great political task emerges: persuading the developing territories themselves to adopt new rules, laws to protect the free flow of commerce and, above all, to protect the property rights of capital.
>
> William Greider, *One World Ready or Not* (1997), 28.

GATT and now the WTO on behalf of its corporations, such as Chiquita Brands, that produce bananas in Latin America. GATT ruled against the restrictions, but the European Union ignored these rulings. A similar negative ruling by the World Trade Organization cannot be ignored because the WTO has an enforcement mechanism.

Transforming the World Trade Organization to Serve the People

The international community could choose to use the WTO as a means to exercise control over multinational corporations. The corporations are taking advantage of the freedom to move capital and skilled labor across international boundaries. If all resources were free to flow across international boundaries, then all labor, including unskilled labor, would move to where the market was and there would be no need to move goods and services across international boundaries. We have international trade in goods and services precisely because natural resources and most labor, except for highly skilled labor, cannot move internationally. Therefore, corporations move capital and skilled labor to where unskilled labor costs the least and resources are abundant. There they produce goods for the major markets in North America, Europe, and the more developed parts of Asia.

In addition, we allow corporations based in one country to own both natural resources and capital in other countries. The international trade these corporations then carry out is designed to maximize the return on the capital and natural resources they own. The way goods are produced and the benefits generated for the exporting countries would likely be quite different if the citizens of those countries always exercised their ownership rights over the labor employed and the natural resources used to produce goods and services within their own borders.

The WTO could deal with this by focusing only on trade between countries rather than serving to protect corporations involved in such trade. Then it would not trouble itself with complaints from the United States on behalf of corporations exporting bananas from Latin America. If multinational corporations were always subject to local laws, countries would be able to protect themselves against some of the more harmful effects of corporate activities. Specifically, the WTO would have to grant each country the right to define whether foreign corporations can own capital in that country, and if they permit such ownership, how those capital goods are to be used in the production of goods and services.

To keep countries from competing with each other to attract multinationals, the WTO might set out a code of conduct that would apply to all corporations in all of its member countries. For example, it could require a corporation to have the same workplace standards and environmental practices wherever it operates. Ideally such a code would also stop transfer pricing by requiring corporations to pay a common income tax rate in all countries according to the value added by the corporation's activities in that country.

The United Nations could be the source of such a code of conduct. For example, the World Health Organization has played a role in monitoring corporations that had agreed to a UN code of conduct for promoting infant formula. In general, though, the United Nations is not likely to have a strong enforcement capacity since the five largest countries have the right to veto legislation that they find unsuitable.

The Place of Local Initiatives in Globalization

The data on the effect of globalization are mixed. For 3 billion people the ratio of trade to GDP and per capita income are both up. This is cited as proof that globalization benefits low-income countries. These numbers are shaped primarily by China and, to a lesser extent, India. For another 2 billion people globalization has not had this impact. This includes most of Africa and a number of Muslim countries.

Defenders of globalization dismiss this negative result by arguing that these countries have turned their backs on what globalization had to offer. More balanced views note the negative impact of lower oil and cocoa prices plus the devastating effect of September 11 on tourism.[14]

Is Dropping Out an Option?

From the perspective of the poor people of the world, even those in the countries that are seen to be benefitting from globalization, the process is basically a failure, says David Korten. But the phenomenon of globalization is so massive that it is difficult to know what to do. How can we encourage solutions that build community? Korten recommends that communities opt out of the system and reclaim direct ownership of the resources required to ensure that basic human needs will be met.

Korten's gloomy assessment of globalization is one interpretation. An alternative viewpoint argues that the poverty still evident is the product of government interference in the private economy's activity to create new wealth. I believe that Korten's is the more credible of these two competing views, but that does not prove the other view wrong. Some evidence can be presented on both sides.

Taken together, these manifestations of institutional failure constitute a global threefold human crisis of deepening poverty, social disintegration, and environmental destruction. Most elements of the crisis share an important characteristic: solutions require local action—household by household and community by community. This action can be taken only when local resources are in local hands. The most pressing unmet needs of the world's poor are for food security, adequate shelter, clothing, health care, and education—the lack of which defines true deprivation. With rare exception, the basic resources and capacity to meet these needs are already found in nearly every country—if those who control the resources would make meeting basic needs their priority. The natural inclination of local people is usually to give those needs priority. If, however, control lies elsewhere, different priorities usually come into play.

David Korten, *When Corporations Rule the World* (1995), 21-22.

A problem with urging communities to opt out of globalization is the "fleshpots of Egypt" syndrome. Once one has tasted the lifestyle offered by the free-market economy it is hard to give it up, even for the prospect of a superior promised land. Most people won't voluntarily choose a lower material standard of living than what they enjoy now. In general, the only people who will choose to opt out of the existing system are those who are so poor they have nothing to lose.

The Need to Define the Purpose of Globalization

If we choose to coexist with gobalization, we still need to address the fundamental question that plagues our economic system: Where are we going? Greider is correct, we are being driven.[15] The current spurt of technological advances has given the emerging global market another push forward, much like what happened during the industrial revolution. But we have no ready way to direct or channel this revolution. Even the powerful multinational corporations lack the means to do this.

We have created this situation by allowing our technological advances to outpace our social development. According to Soros, our dependence on the market has allowed economic values to squeeze out social values. The latter, however, are essential to sustain society and to sustain human life.[16]

The challenge before us is twofold: to develop our social capacity to form values that build community and sustain society, and then to find ways to allow such values to shape the purpose and direction of globalization. At a United Nations conference on globalization and citizenship, a distinction was made between a "captured market economy" created by globalization from above and a "social market economy" as the outcome of globalization from below.[17] It is the latter that we need to strive for with our social actions at the community level.

This doesn't mean we can avoid the impact of actions of others far away. Globalization is here to stay. The speakers at the United Nations conference argued that being global citizens will require progress in "greater democratization; improved co-ordination and financial reform of the United Nations system; greater accountability of international financial and trade institutions; increased social and environmental responsibility on the part of transnational corporations; new global sources of finance for international aid; and effective international legal structures."[18]

The Importance of Community Control in Defining Employment

The ability to address these issues democratically will depend on the maintenance of community control over how people's labor is employed and how natural resources are sustained as they are being used by our system. Limits on the unequal distribution of wealth and income will be necessary so all persons can contribute to the building of community and have a voice in shaping the goals of our economic, social, and political systems.

Greider states the employment challenge before us bluntly. Corporate leaders care less about community and well-being than about low-cost labor. They profit from a denial of freedom, especially for their own employees in overseas operations.[19] The profitability of the system depends on finding settings where the right to work, as set out in chapter 6, is least evident.

There are two basic issues here: workplace standards and wage levels.

The extension of specialization to a global scale means that the production of goods and services traded internationally will leave North America for lower-labor-cost areas such as Asia and Latin America. Within North America, the remaining low-wage jobs will involve goods and services that are produced and consumed locally.

Applying the conditions set out in chapter 6 to the global operations of corporations will require addressing wages, working conditions, and the nature of the employment relationship itself. Abuses in all three areas are cited in an article in *The Economist* that credits the Asia Monitor Resource Center in Hong Kong with being an effective watchdog of business firms in Asia.[20] The center's reports facilitate ethical shopping in the higher-income countries. One of the advantages of globalization is the increased competition that makes it easier for consumers to boycott firms that ignore basic workplace standards.

In his discussion of workplace standards Philip Rosenzweig lists three options available to multinational corporations: (1) merely meet local standards of the host country; (2) maintain a common set of standards in all countries; or (3) create some combination of the first two.[21] He calls for setting common standards in all countries in which a corporation operates but using the local wage rate in any one country.

Some corporations try to get around their responsibilities to employees in other countries by contracting out production rather than producing the goods themselves. Rosenzweig finds this unacceptable.[22] He proposes that a firm's responsibility for workplace standards should increase with the amount of business contracted out. This is especially the case if the subcontractor is located in a country where workplace standards and enforcement capabilities are low.

Guidelines for Responsible Social and Environmental Actions

An example of a company that combines a concern for social progress with environmental stewardship is Placer Dome, a mining company that has set out guidelines for all of its subsidiary operations:

- Placer Dome, wherever it operates, will adhere to high standards of ethics, transparency, and fundamental freedoms in the conduct of our activities.
- Every Placer Dome project and operation will provide for the effective involvement of communities in decisions which affect them; treat them as equals; respect their cultures, customs, and values; and take into account their needs, concerns, and aspirations in making our decisions.
- At every stage from exploration to mine closure, we will recognize and respect the importance of the land and traditional knowledge to local indigenous or aboriginal communities and be sensitive to their cultural distinctiveness.
- We will work with governments and communities to contribute to improvements in medical services, educational opportunities, social conditions, and governance in the areas of our operations.
- Our mines will collaborate with communities and governments to plan for mine closure and the sustainability of social improvements.
- We will support a fair distribution of economic benefits from mining to local communities and the national economy.[23]

Our global citizenship would be advanced significantly if we could mobilize local action that would lead to all multinational corporations adopting comparable guidelines and requiring their auditors to hold them accountable to abide by them.

Giving a Voice to the People in Low- and Middle-Income Countries

One form of local action is to strive for the governance of multinational corporate activity by international institutions. The success of the leaders from a number of low- and middle-income countries in blocking agreement at the WTO meetings in Seattle has shown the people from these countries the benefits of combining in strength within global institutions.[24]

George Soros argues for the creation of some form of international institution, possibly attached to the IMF, to ensure stability in international financial markets, but since voting power in the IMF rests primarily with the high-income countries, we question whether that would serve all societies well.

I find a proposal by Jeffrey Sachs more convincing.[25] He advocates establishing a group of sixteen specific countries, which would represent the vast majority of humanity. This group of sixteen would have an explicit mandate to design rules and institutions that would make globalization work for all people.

While these are being created, we can alleviate the financial instability by instituting something like the Tobin tax. This would place a low tax rate, for example, 0.25 percent, on the value of all international flows of short-term capital. If this slight increase in the cost of transferring capital managed to reduce such flows, we would have a more stable international financial system. If it failed to deter capital flows, then significant tax revenues would be collected and could become a new source of international funding for development aid.

In summary, the current level of technology means people from afar can seriously affect our lives and actions here and now. We cannot reverse that. Our challenge is to recognize the extent to which our economic system uses global access and global forces to benefit the elite who already live in high-income countries. In the next chapter we'll discuss how our economic system affects people in low- and middle-income countries of the world.

The forces operating to dilute,
assimilate, and destroy cultural
communities are so great that the
future of many of them is uncertain.
Authentic cultural diversity,
expressing various modes of being
and of social organization with
integrity and vitality, is doomed
unless the positive value of such
diversity is recognized. Development
planners at every level must
incorporate the active defense of
cultural diversity into their
decisions about resource use. Such
active development must not be
treated as a mere externality of the
cost-benefit equation.
—*Denis Goulet*

11

The Victims of
Our Global Reach

Development is a vast subject. I do not claim to address all of its various dimensions in this chapter; rather, I focus here on how North American markets, in their drive to obtain a global reach, are affecting the societies of low- and middle-income countries.

Defining Development

To place this discussion in context we need to define development. Denis Goulet is one of a growing number of specialists who see development as more than simply a matter of possessing and consuming an increasing quantity of goods and services.[1] He uses the phrase *to be more* to capture this additional dimension of development. Subsequently, he links this concept with the values of optimal life sustenance, esteem, and freedom.

Similarly, K. K. S. Dadzie emphasizes the means of achieving development as well as the possible ends or goals of development.

> Development is the unfolding of people's individual and social imagination in defining goals and inventing ways to approach them. Development is the continuing process of the liberation of peoples and societies. There is develop-

ment when they are able to assert their autonomy and, in self-reliance, to carry out activities of interest to them. To develop is to be or to become. Not only to have.[2]

I see development as a set of abilities. The locus for these abilities is a society, and it may or may not coincide with a set of existing national boundaries. For a society to be more, or to become more, requires at least three abilities:

- the ability to define the problems that confront the society and hold it back;
- the ability to come up with appropriate solutions for overcoming these limitations; and
- the ability to create institutions that will help the society implement these solutions.

The emergence and use of these abilities should enable a society to achieve development.

Our Economic System Tends to Exclude Marginal Societies

The Ability to Buy in the Market

None of this happens in a neutral environment. An influential player in the development drama is contemporary capitalism and its growing global reach. Unfortunately, not everyone is able to participate in capitalist markets. Members of any society with plenty of income are welcome, but those with lower incomes are largely excluded because they have a limited capacity to buy.

Africa, labeled "The Hopeless Continent" by *The Economist*, is the contemporary example of the latter.[3] Forty-five percent of Africans live in poverty. Real economic growth of 7 percent annually would be required to cut this poverty in half in fifteen years.

Most people in the United States and Canada are admitted as participants in capitalist markets, but some 15 to 20 percent of these countries' populations would be marginal participants at best. In a typical low-income country the proportions are reversed. The rich elite, possibly fifteen to 20 percent of the population, are full participants. They enjoy a lifestyle similar to or in excess of that of the average North American. In a middle-income country with an emerging middle class, perhaps a third to a half of the people are participants in the global markets. Your participation in the global market is established if you have an e-mail address or ready access to the Internet.

Going Up the Down Escalator

Excluded parties, whether whole societies or individual households, are not free to decide to leave their old way of life and become active players in global markets. To understand their situation better, imagine that you are located on the first floor of a major department store. You must get to the second floor to participate in global markets, but the only way to do that is to go up the escalator that is coming down from the second floor.

You might say, "That's easy. I'll sprint up the down escalator." If so, you're thinking like a typical healthy North American. If you are part of the excluded poor, you might not have the energy to sprint all the way up that escalator coming down. If you are a young woman, you're likely pregnant. This may be your second pregnancy, and your first child may have died within a year of birth. Also, you may have one or more of several debilitating diseases associated with poverty: tuberculosis, dysentery, schistosomiasis, malaria, or HIV/AIDS. Only one of these would rob you of vital energy.

Even if you personally have the health and energy to sprint up to the second floor you'd likely choose not to do so on your own. What if you should stumble and fall? For us in North America, the worst that would happen if we couldn't bolster our business or keep our job in our effort to get to the second floor is that we may need to declare bankruptcy and possibly go on welfare. Poor people in low-income countries face consequences that are much worse: failure to make it to the second floor can mean death for one or more members of the household. They cannot count on unemployment insurance, health insurance, or welfare. Their survival depends on their relationships to their kin: friends and extended family.

To ensure that kin will be there in time of need, no one sprints alone. People move up the escalator together, helping each other as needed. Time and resources are expended as premiums on this unique social insurance policy that is the helping hands of kin. These premiums include taking time to chat a little, to inquire about another's health and the well-being of family members. They include preparation of feasts for such life-cycle events as births, weddings, and funerals. The community also comes together to celebrate annual events such as thanksgiving for another harvest.

To the Western mind these cultural practices appear to stand in the way of development. The people seem to lack entrepreneurial drive. They waste time in lengthy greetings and frequent celebrations. They consume precious capital by making the celebrations more elaborate than they can afford. What the Western mind doesn't always grasp is that one aspect of being poor is a low tolerance for risk. Working together, celebrating together, and moving together minimizes risk. Paying high social assurance premiums means helping hands will be there if one stumbles and falls on the way up the down escalator.

Grease Makes the World Go Around

The Ruling Elite Serves Corporate Interests *Discourage Unions*

So, what if poor people, moving together, are making good progress up that down escalator? An additional problem they face is that their ruling elite on the second floor can control the speed of the escalator. To keep the poor people in their marginal status they merely grease the elevator to increase its speed.

Who are the people who make up this ruling elite? They are the politicians in power and the upper-level civil servants who help formulate government policies and enforce regulations. They are business leaders, both local and multinational, who control firms large enough to operate above the control mechanism of effective competition. They may also be labor union leaders who agree to policies that provide high-paying jobs for a few but deny effective employment for the majority.

The ruling elite does not act alone in deciding the speed of the escalator. As active participants in global markets, we provide incentives for the ruling elite to choose a speed that benefits us as well. We do some of this through our countries' foreign policy, which decides who receives foreign aid and for what purpose. Here military aid is a special problem. We exert

> Bribery was simply a case of the free market at work simplifying the decision-making process.
>
> —Garrison Keillor, Wobegon Boy (1997)

even more influence, however, by demanding that the many multinational corporations bring us the goods and resources of low- and middle-income countries at affordable prices.

As Diane Francis notes, doing business in low- and middle-income countries requires a customer as well as a seller. Corporations do what it takes to find markets for their products and to gain access to the resources of these countries. They may contribute to political campaigns, wine and dine influential decision makers, appoint key politicians to the company's board of directors, or pay outright bribes.

Not all members of ruling elites are corrupt. Some countries are so poor that there are few decision-making powers worth buying. Other countries have committed leaders who have served tirelessly without enriching themselves, though these are the notable exceptions rather than the rule.

Building Social Capital to Hold Our Leaders Accountable

A key issue in this world of grease is the presence of social capital. Governments can play a vital role in bringing people together to address the problems that confront them. Whether these problems are approached through public or private initiatives is not the primary issue. What counts more is the participation of the people in building the institutions and developing the programs required to tackle the problems that hold them back. A World Bank study of rural villages in Tanzania shows that villages with a strong social-capital base

It's hardly surprising business is worried.... Many countries are dealing with serious corruption charges against their politicians.

The American business community is leading the charge because it is constrained under its laws from handing out bribes.

Meanwhile, Europeans and Asians can deduct bribes for tax purposes without consequence. And most do.

Americans and Canadians bribe too, but these payments are hidden or euphemistically described as "commissions" to middlemen.

The World Bank's Wolfensohn made an excellent point when he noted that it is not fair to simply blame poor countries for corruption. "You need two to corrupt," he pointed out.

"It is as much a moral issue for the corrupted as it is for those who corrupt."
...

Grease makes the world go around, but that's no reason to allow it to continue.

The problem with allowing corruption to continue is that the public sector is not forced to work in the best interests of voters or their societies—which is supposed to be its responsibility.

Excerpts from Diane Francis, "Not Fair to Lay the Blame for Corruption on Developing Nations," *The Financial Post* (February 8, 1997), 21. Material reprinted with the express permission of the National Post Company, a CanWest Partnership.

have higher per capita income on average than villages that do not demonstrate similar levels of participation by the people.[4] The presence of social capital also reduces the likelihood that government leaders will be bought by outsiders.

Does Social Capital Matter?

A recent study of villages in rural Tanzania found that households in villages with high levels of social capital (defined in terms of the degree of participation in village-level social organization) have higher adjusted incomes per capita than do households in villages with low levels of social capital. When other non-social capital determinants are controlled for, there also appears to be a strong correlation between a village's well-being and its level of social capital. This result points to important spillover effects at the village level arising from individual participation in local associations and groups. Although no general conclusions could be drawn about the impact of social capital on government performance, the study points to a number of important linkages, including a positive association between social capital and the quality of local schooling.

From World Bank, *World Development Report* 1997: *The State in a Changing World* (New York: Oxford University Press, 1997), 115. Copyright 1997 by the International Bank for Reconstruction and Development/The World Bank. Used by permission of Oxford University Press, Inc.

Shifting the Burden to the Powerless

As if the actions of multinational corporations and low-income countries' ruling elites and the policies of high-income countries were not enough, the marginal players in global markets also face the power of international agencies. These include the World Bank, the International Monetary Fund (IMF) and the World Trade Organization (WTO), all of which are dominated by the high-income countries.

Solving the International Debt Crisis at the Expense of Poor People

A good example of how high-income countries dominate is the way the international debt crisis of the 1980s was handled. Actions designed to protect the big players in the global markets can unfairly burden poor people.

The debt crises arose because banks had a lot of money

to lend and were eagerly looking for customers. During an eleven-year period debt increased fivefold, to more than U.S.$500 billion. Private banks' share of this debt soared from 35 percent (of $100 billion) to 50 percent (of $500 billion).

In late 1981 the monetary reserves of banks plummeted as a result of the restrictive monetary policies of three major countries: Great Britain, the United States, and Canada. Because of their actions, unemployment rose and the price of oil and gold fell. With their reserves depleted, banks had to reduce lending, and the price of loans, the interest rate, jumped dramatically. Poland and Mexico did not have enough foreign exchange to pay the higher interest rates plus repay the loans as they fell due. A number of other countries soon faced similar problems.

The U.S. government, the IMF, and the World Bank moved quickly in a divide-and-conquer strategy to prevent the countries with significant international debt from forming a debtor's cartel. If these countries had formed a common front they could have threatened to default on their debt all at the same time. To prevent this, key individual countries were offered special deals that effectively postponed the repayment of their debt but did not address the underlying causes of the larger crisis.

Had the major debtor countries all defaulted on their debt at the same time, a number of North American banks would have faced a severe crisis, possibly even bankruptcy. Even though there was little likelihood of an imminent collapse of our banking systems, fears rose, for bankers are powerful and effective lobbyists. As a result, during the 1980s much North American and international attention was focused on reducing the vulnerability of Western banks. The voices of the poor people in low- and middle-income countries were not heard in the deliberations that shaped these financial developments.

How the Burden of the Debt Crisis Was Shifted to the Poor

When a debt crisis arises in a low-income country, the first symptom is a shortage of foreign currency: there is not enough currency available to purchase imports and still meet payments of interest and principal on money borrowed from outside the country. A crisis can be caused by a combination of factors: an increase in interest rates, a bad harvest of an export crop, a decrease in the prices received for exports, and an increase in prices paid for imports.

The likely reaction of such a country is to restrict imports and try to increase exports. The downside of restricting imports is that there will be a shortage of things like spare parts and other goods needed for production. Over time as things cannot be repaired, more and more shortages will occur and unemployment will increase. Also, if foreign currency is not available, food and medicine for lower-income groups cannot be imported. The temptation to bribe officials to obtain an allocation of foreign exchange will increase. Parallel markets for both foreign currency and imported goods will emerge.

And what happens when a country tries to increase exports? Typically it will turn to agriculture because the resources that can be transferred most readily from local to export production are labor and land. It takes time to boost other kinds of production, but increased agricultural output for export becomes available after one growing season.

Such a transfer of resources affects the people directly as less food is produced for local consumption. In some cases, sharecroppers and tenant farmers are the immediate losers as their land is taken from them to grow more export crops. In other cases, land reform may be delayed. If the large farms now used to grow export crops had been subdivided and sold to the landless, they could have been used by small farmers to grow food. In Kenya during the mid-1980s, a government official stated that selected large farms would not be subdivided for the landless because Kenya could not afford to lose the foreign exchange these farms generated.

The Role of Structural Adjustment Programs

If increasing exports and reducing imports isn't enough to solve the debt crisis, the country's next step is to appeal to lending agencies for a rescheduling of loans. Then commercial banks will attempt to force the country to borrow from the IMF. This requirement extends the IMF's power to impose strict conditions on a country, conditions the commercial banks favor. The IMF typically requires a government

- to cut back its spending, especially on social programs;
- to reduce or eliminate any protection workers may have against inflation;
- to allow food prices to rise to free-market levels; and
- to devalue its currency relative to the currency of other countries.

The intent of the IMF is to make imports more expensive and exports cheaper, to provide farmers with greater incentives to produce, and to transfer income to the wealthy, who presumably will invest and hence make the economy grow.

Whether this intended result actually happens varies from country to country. In all cases, however, IMF conditions place the primary burden for solving the debt crisis on low-income consumers, employees, and small farmers. They become the immediate victims of the debt crisis.

The Right to Choose

The marginal participants in global markets have limited control over their livelihood. Their economic environment dominates their livelihood, and at best they are always reacting to that changing environment. In that case, how we achieve development is as important as the development itself. If development involves attaining and exercising a set of abilities, then the people involved in the development process deserve the right to make choices.

Access to Science and Technology

One choice for marginal participants is to break free from a very limited physical and economic environment. Given the science and technology available to them, they simply will not be able to boost output fast enough to keep up with the growing demand for foreign currency. Part of the problem is that their role in global markets is mainly to export primary commodities, the price for which is controlled elsewhere. So they have lost most of the control over both production and marketing decisions. Reducing the vulnerability of such people will involve their having access to science and technology that is utilized elsewhere and the ability to put such technology to work and to use the markets for their own benefit rather than merely reacting to markets as they change.

In consequence the economies of the developing countries are disarticulated: they lack organic linkage, rooted in an indigenous science and technology, between the growth and structure of domestic production and the growth and pattern of their domestic demand. The principal economic activity other than subsistence agriculture is dominated by exports of primary commodities for which the control of production as well as of market decisions lies at their destinations abroad.

From K. K. S. Dadzie, "Economic Development" *Scientific American* (September 1980). Copyright © 1980 by Scientific American, Inc. All rights reserved.

The Freedom to Choose Their Own Leaders

A second choice is to break free from a ruling elite that enriches itself by catering to the demands of the major corporate players in the global markets. From the former Soviet Union and other developing countries we have learned the importance of a stable, competitive market that provides the price signals needed to guide the use of resources in an efficient manner. Stability also requires avoiding such disruptions as high inflation, high unemployment, and social and political turmoil.

The World Bank has commissioned studies that show that when market stability is combined with promotion of free trade, it will generate much stronger growth from the foreign aid received. If a society chooses to follow the consumption patterns of the high-income countries, it typically will choose to become more integrated into the global markets. It will aspire to become a miniversion of the high-income countries in whose hands its future lies. Both the World Bank and the IMF would encourage such a choice.

Dennis Goulet, however, suggests a more revolutionary approach: a society should aim for self-reliance and carve out its own social, political, and economic goals. As Goulet notes, such a choice is not without risk.

> If one adopts a frontal attack on mass poverty and unemployment as one's basic strategy, a strong bias exists in favor of less integration with international markets and greater local inventiveness to correct factor distortions inherent in technology imported from rich countries. In every case, limits exist beyond which neither efficiency or equity can be fully ignored. Because reality constantly imposes compromises, no country plan is fully consistent with its basic options. Moreover, unexpected events (abrupt rises in import prices or disastrous floods) can suddenly force relatively self-reliant nations into more "integration" with the outside than they had planned. Nonetheless, any nation's decision-makers must ultimately attach primary importance to integration or to self-reliance. In large measure, the degree to which they blend the two depends on the overarching incentive systems at work in their societies.[5]

During the period of struggle for world dominance between the United States and the Soviet Union, countries wanting independence from global markets became more integrated into the economies of the Soviet Union and Eastern European countries. Cuba is a case in point. Other examples include Nicaragua during the 1980s, Chile under the rule of Salvador Allende, and Tanzania during the rule of Julius Nyerere.

These countries represented a threat to multinational corporations and global markets far beyond their numerical and military strength. What if they actually did improve the overall well-being of their people without relying on either multinational corporations or participation in global markets? That was a challenge the multinational corporations could not face. Hence Tanzania was cut off for a time from most U.S. development assistance as well as development loans from the IMF and the World Bank. For four decades Cuba has been subjected to an international boycott. Nicaragua fell victim to the U.S.-funded contra war. Chile's Allende was overthrown via coordinated action between multinational corporations and U.S. foreign-policy makers. Given the enormous economic and military power of the high-income countries, this second choice, to go it alone, becomes a very difficult option.

The Freedom to Maintain and Practice a Culture

A third choice involves the place of a society's culture in the development process. If development is defined as becoming more like the high-income countries, Goulet

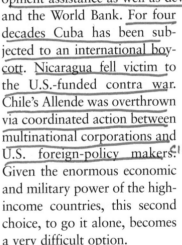

Rethinking Development

Traditional values frequently harbor a latent dynamism which can be activated to bring about developmental change in ways that cause minimal harm to the identity and integrity of the populations concerned. Sound development ought to be grounded in traditional and indigenous values since ultimately both economic and social development are means to a larger end, the fostering of human development. Integral human development, however, rests on a secure sense of identity and cultural integrity, and on a system of meanings to which one can give enthusiastic allegiance. These values are so vital that economic and institutional modernization need to be judged in the light of their contribution to these values. Material improvement should not, and need not, be obtained at the price of a general impoverishment of spirit. This conviction lies behind the search for change strategies which take the traditional values of living communities as the foundation upon which to build humane forms of development.

Denis Goulet, *Development Ethics* (1995), 141.

argues, a society's culture will be seen primarily as an obstacle to development. If societies are actually allowed to choose the process and goals of development, they will, according to Goulet, build on their existing culture rather than deny it or destroy it. He says that all cultures have at least a latent form of dynamism. Good development builds on this dynamism to transform culture in such a way that a society can work toward the kind of development it wants.

The Right to Participate in Development Decision Making

If we agree that the right to choose is a basic value, there can be no question that the opportunity to participate in decision making must be extended to societies undergoing development. Goulet believes such participation is essential. To him, the chief issues are the nature and quality of such participation, and implementing it is no simple challenge.

Let's imagine we are development practitioners going on a trip in a new, air conditioned Land Rover. On our way we encounter people who are obviously poor and need food, health care, education, and family planning assistance. Being both kindhearted and naive, we offer to take them along on our trip. We are sure there must be a better place for them somewhere along the road on which we are traveling.

As we travel together we tell them about the wonders

Does Participation Improve Project Performance?

Using data from 121 diverse rural water supply projects in forty-nine countries in Africa, Asia and Latin America, a recent study tested the relationship between participation and project performance. Participation was measured on a continuum ranging from simple information sharing through in-depth consultation with beneficiaries to shared decisionmaking. The authors found a strong correlation between high levels of beneficiary participation, especially in decisionmaking, and project success. Of the forty-nine projects with low levels of participation, only 8 percent were successful. But of the forty-two projects with high levels of beneficiary participation, 64 percent were successes.

of this place called Development. If they could get to it they would find land that is productive, farming techniques that will produce abundance, facilities that will provide good health care, education that will liberate them, and jobs so they can be productively employed. In addition to telling them all about Development, we draw maps and explain very carefully how they can get there.

After we have traveled awhile together, we stop and invite our guests to disembark. Our term of service is now up, our funding has run out, and the geographical area is no longer the center of media attention. With the assistance we have provided so far, they should be able to find their way to Development on their own.

But most never get there! Why? They were never asked whether they wanted to go there in the first place. While we were traveling together, we tried our best to explain how great Development is, and we tried to equip them with what they needed to continue on their own. But they weren't listening. They were fascinated with our Land Rover, and they were prepared to go anywhere provided they could travel in it. Once it became clear that we would be taking our vehicle with us, deep disappointment set in. From experience, given their limited resources, they knew that what we called Development was merely a mirage.

The Practice of Development Requires Patience

A lesson to be learned from the past experiences of our development agencies—for example, OXFAM, Mennonite Central Committee (MCC), Mennonite Economic Development Associates (MEDA), Canadian Foodgrains Bank, and Canadian Catholic Organization for Development and Peace (CCODP)—is that how we get to development is just as important as arriving there. When we are in a hurry to get there, it is tempting to make an instant analysis of the problem and of what it is the people must want. Having decided what needs to be done, we are well-equipped to do it. We have the training, technology, resources, and business skills to accomplish anything. As a result, we are usually successful at whatever we decide to do for people.

When we leave, some of the people doubtless are better off than they were when we found them. But they typically do not continue doing for themselves what we were doing for them and with them. For that to happen as well, we need to learn patience. With patience, we would take time to learn where it is they would like to go and then determine together with them the various ways to get there. Once they had identified the options, it would be important for them to choose the route they would like to follow. Then they would be more likely to want to continue on their way after we left. Meanwhile, it would be important that we not distract them with the dazzling vehicles we would use if we were making the same trip.

Patience, like wisdom, is a scarce commodity. It is not something that can be taught in college. Nor is it covered in the orientation sessions of non-governmental development organizations. It is, however, a precious possession of poor people. No doubt they would gladly share it with us if we would tarry a little.

Fair Trade as a Means to Realizing Development

Unequal Sharing of the Benefits of International Trade

An important way that low- and middle-income countries are linked to North America is via international trade. Economic theory can demonstrate that all countries involved benefit from such an international exchange of goods and services. Two of these benefits are economic growth and access to goods that a country cannot produce locally.

The prices at which these goods and services are exchanged internationally, however, shape how such benefits are divided among the trading partners. These prices, after adjustment for the exchange rate, are known as the terms of trade between two countries. Let's say the increase in economic growth from engaging in international trade is 1 billion dollars. If the terms of trade channel 60 percent of this money to the high-income countries and 40 percent to the low-income countries, then the trade contributes to the growing income gap between these two sets of countries.

In North America, with a focus on the level of poverty within a country, we broadcast that trade has caused economic growth in low-income countries equal to $400 million or 40 percent of the total. Within the latter countries the focus is on the growing income gap between the high- and low-income countries. It is this difference in perception that creates the impression that development-related debates within the United Nations never lead anywhere.

Economists generally do not worry about this seeming unfairness in the way the terms of trade divide the benefits of international trade. After all, the cause is that the lower-income countries are hungrier for the output of the higher-income countries than vice versa. Some products are exceptions, such as oil, tourism, and nutmeg. For most countries, though, many economists believe that the terms of trade merely reflect the tremendous satisfaction the people must be getting from importing goods and services from the high-income countries.

A second factor in determining the terms of trade is the unequal power in the trading process. Typically a few large multinational corporations buy from a large number of small producers in the low-income countries. The size and power of these multinational firms lets them dictate the terms. Some countries have tried to counter this unequal power by creating a marketing board as a monopoly exporter of a primary commodity. The success of such efforts has been mixed at best.

Groups of well-meaning people within North America have set up alternative marketing links for goods made in lower-income countries. Bridgehead Trading and Ten Thousand Villages are two examples. Their actions have given particular artisans and producers more direct access to North American markets with a consequent increase in income. But the overall efforts have been too limited to affect the terms of trade between the countries involved. Multinational corporations are very efficient at accessing production overseas and bringing it to the North American market, provided the volumes are high. The coffee illustration at the beginning of this book is a good example.

The Limited Potential of Commodity Agreements

Existing international trading mechanisms based on global markets will not ensure that trade among countries is fair. Collusion among exporters, as in the case of the Organization for Petroleum Exporting Countries (OPEC), is one possible approach that may work for certain commodities. An alternative, multilateral commodity agreements, has pushed prices up for members when the countries involved managed to restrict production enough to limit the overall supply of the commodity on the market. But such efforts frequently break down. For example, when Vietnam entered the market as a major supplier of coffee at the same time Brazil was recovering from a string of poor harvests, it caused a glut in the market in 2001. As a result, coffee prices declined significantly.[6]

Attempts at supply control have had success in stabilizing some commodity prices, but they have not served over time to increase prices and the share of benefits from international trade that flows to producers in the lower-income countries. And price stabilization is important because countries dependent on a few commodity exports are the most vulnerable to adverse trading conditions caused by fluctuating international prices.

Foreign Aid as an Offset to Unfair Trade

Foreign aid has been seen as a possible way to address continuing inequities in international trade. According to Craig Burnside and David Dollar, foreign aid should be reserved for those countries that implement policies designed to promote growth in income.[7] They admit that past aid, distributed on the basis of political criteria, has not served this purpose. Their simulation exercise shows that if all aid had been invested in the subset of countries with "sound policies," the growth rate in these countries would have increased by one-third. When aid is invested in a form that generates at least a 30 percent increase in income growth, it can also produce greater fairness and reduce per capita income gaps in the recipient countries.

Before we get carried away with "good" foreign aid as the solution let's keep in mind that the high-income countries, pushing for freer trade, have trade restrictions against the potential exports of low- and middle-income countries the value of which is estimated to exceed the value of foreign aid flowing to these lower-income countries.

A related problem is that of extensive agricultural subsidies in donor countries. The issue is not whether farmers in high-income countries should receive income support. Rather, it is doing so in a way that is linked to how much the farmers produce,

In past years, farm subsidies have been criticized for widening the gap between rich and poor. Since Sept. 11, such subsidies have generated an even sharper controversy: they work directly against the U.S. effort to combat global poverty as part of a broader campaign against terrorism.

Roger Thurow and Scott Kilman, "How a Cotton Glut Bred by U.S. Hurts Poor African Tillers," *The Asian Wall Street Journal* (June 27, 2002).

The biggest favor the rich could do the poor would be to give less aid—to their own farmers. Rich countries protect their farmers with subsidies, high tariffs, import quotas and a tangle of other barriers masquerading as health and safety standards. This makes it hard for farmers in poor countries to sell their produce in rich countries.

The Economist, "Farm Aid: The Kindest Cut," *International Herald Tribune* (June 15, 2002), 8.

which distorts international markets and reduces significantly the income of farmers in low- and middle-income countries.

The Costs and Benefits of Foreign Investment

In addition to receiving foreign aid, low-income countries can encourage large corporations to invest in their economies. Economists like to argue that this gives the low-income countries access to skilled labor, technology, and capital. This flow of capital usually also shifts ownership of the other resources involved within the country receiving the foreign investment. For example, a foreign company buying out a Canadian forestry company gains the capital the Canadian firm had plus its cutting rights within Canada's forests. Therefore, a discussion of fair exchange must look not only at the benefits flowing from foreign investment but also at who controls production decisions and who gets the profits.

In summary, free-market activity promotes efficient allocation of resources within and among societies. Such efficiencies lead to higher material standards of living. If these arrangements are entered into voluntarily by all societies involved, it can be demonstrated that all participants will benefit from such trade. But there is no guarantee that this will lead to greater fairness. Investment and trading patterns as currently practiced are widening the gap in material standards of living among societies.[8]

The distribution of income and wealth, and thus economic power, shape how benefits of international trade and economic growth are shared. A more fair trading system will require more equal participation in decisions about what should be produced, how it should be produced, and how it should be distributed.

Peace as a Priority

The freedom to choose and to participate requires the presence of appropriate political institutions. It also requires political, economic, and social stability. In short, it requires peace, both as a state of being and as a means to encourage change and development.

War and Civil Unrest as Primary Causes of Hunger

As the struggles of the continent of Africa have shown, one cannot separate development initiatives from the struggle for peace. The two are strongly linked. There is now general agreement that the leading cause of hunger and starvation is civil unrest. During the 1980s it was Ethiopia, Sudan, Chad, Angola, Mozambique, Uganda, and Somalia. More recently it has been Rwanda, Burundi, Somalia, Liberia, Sierra Leone, Afghanistan, and now Iraq. In all cases, people have suffered severe food shortages because of armed conflict. Rain may end a drought but it will not end this suffering.

The struggle for appropriate political institutions in Nigeria cost Ken Saro-Wiwa his life. His poem, "The True

The True Prison

It is not the leaking roof
Nor the singing mosquitoes
In the damp, wretched cell
It is not the clank of the key
As the warden locks you in
It is not the measly rations
Unfit for beast or man
Nor yet the emptiness of day
Dipping into the blankness of night
It is not
It is not
It is not

It is the lies that have been drummed
Into your ears for a generation
It is the security agent running amok
Executing callous calamitous orders
In exchange for a wretched meal a day

The magistrate writing into her book
A punishment she knows is undeserved
The moral decrepitude
The mental ineptitude
The meat of dictators
Cowardice masking as obedience
Lurking in our denigrated souls
It is fear dampening trousers
That we dare not wash
It is this
It is this
It is this
Dear friend, turns our free world
Into dreary prison

Ken Saro-Wiwa, "The True Prison" (1993), as printed in *The Financial Post* (November 8, 1997). Material reprinted with the express permission of the National Post Company, a CanWest Partnership.

Prison," captures the essence of what it means to suppress change and development militarily. Those who exercise such suppression fail to take personal responsibility for their role in denying others the right to choose and realize a better way of life.

As Amartya Sen observes, famines are rare in democratic societies where responsible institutions hold political leaders accountable for their actions between elections.[9] For the hungry of warring countries to achieve food security will require an end to civil unrest and alternative means of political decision making.

The Spread of Weapons by Countries with Vested Interests

We may be comforted to interpret these various forms of civil unrest as local wars with local causes. The World Bank recognizes that external funding has to some extent aided the continuation the civil war in Liberia and admits the need for outside actions to end the conditions that facilitate the war, but it still blames the conflict primarily on local economic forces. Similar conclusions will no doubt be made regarding Mozambique, Angola, Congo, and Sierra Leone.

The Economic Underpinnings of Conflict

Initially, the war in Liberia was fought largely for social and political motives, with control over the central government as the central objective. Foreign support helped finance the launching of the war. Gradually control over Liberia's rich natural resources and other assets, in addition to being a means of ensuring funding for the war, has become an end in itself for the fighting factions. . . .

To restore peace, any intervention will have to include actions that make the "surplus" accruing to the fighting organizations zero or negative, while simultaneously eliminating individual fighters' income from looting, or raising the associated risk. Such actions range from economic sanctions on the export of timber and rubber to international agreements that increase the cost of arms. In addition, combatants' incentives to continue the war must be removed through a combination of carefully planned demobilization and enforcement of criminal laws.

From World Bank, *World Development Report* 1997: *The State in a Changing World* (New York: Oxford University Press, 1997), 160. Copyright 1997 by the International Bank for Reconstruction and Development/The World Bank. Used by permission of Oxford University Press, Inc.

Nonetheless, the primary determinants of armed conflict in Africa are rooted first in the colonial past and then in the global interests of the United States and the former Soviet Union. People of both countries believed that they were in a struggle for the hearts and minds of the people in the lower-income countries. The two superpowers made only limited provision for the people involved to choose their own way.

The superpower not in control in a particular low-income country typically chose to arm the opposition in the hope of achieving political change there. The result was more armed conflict and serious environmental deterioration. Eventually the refugees and starving people were featured prominently on our television screens.

The United Nations Development Programme documents the severe adverse effects of civil unrest on human development. Disease and death rates increase by up to twenty times. In conflict zones more than 100 million people are chronically malnourished. In part, these problems arise because of the large number of refugees and displaced persons uprooted by the conflict. UN data show a clear link between armed conflict within a country and a low human development

Conflict

Since the Second World War the number of conflicts in the world has increased more than fivefold, more than 90% of them internal. Bombs, bullets and landmines might be thought the greatest risks in conflict, but many more people die from indirect causes—such as the disruption of food or water supplies or the destruction of health services. In today's conflict zones more than 100 million people are chronically malnourished. In the Horn of Africa in the early 1990s, mortality and disease rates were more than 20 times as high as normal. This takes a terrible toll on children. While under-five mortality is 120 deaths per thousand live births in South Asia and 175 in Sub-Saharan Africa, it is more than 250 in Afghanistan, Angola, Mozambique and Sierra Leone.

The connection between conflict and human development runs both ways. Years of internal warfare undermine standards of human development. And long periods of neglect of human development, especially for particular racial or ethnic groups, can eventually provoke violent conflicts.

From United Nations Development Programme, *Human Development Report* 1996 (New York: Oxford University Press), 25-26. Copyright 1996 by the United Nations Development Programme. Used by permission of Oxford University Press, Inc.

index, and causes and effects can go in both directions: with continued low levels of human development, ethnic and racial tensions tend to increase and civil unrest is more likely.

The Need for a Ministry to Reduce Conflict and Promote Peace

The breakup of the Soviet Union has reduced the use of armaments as a means of international competition. The World Bank reports that average military expenditures fell from 4 percent of global GDP in 1990 to 2.4 percent in 1995.[10]

A ministry of peace designed to reduce the worldwide proliferation of arms would have a significant impact. At the height of the superpower competition such a ministry, if successful, would have eliminated at least 60 percent of the armaments brought into low-income countries. Also, it would have drastically cut the rate at which debt increased in these countries.

A ministry of peace would enable government officials in low-income countries to become more relaxed in dealing with their own people, and there would be less need for them to look over their shoulder, fearing the next military coup. Also, without large supplies of armaments, opposing groups would have to seek political rather than military solutions to their differences.

A limited military need not mean a lack of internal security. Spending on an effective police force is qualitatively different from training and supplying a military force. As Ernie Regehr observes, police seek to bring parties to a court system that is a nonviolent forum for dealing with disputes. The military, in contrast, is designed to resolve the issues it confronts through the use of force.[11]

A Peace Dividend as the Source of Resources for Development

An effective ministry of peace would enable all societies to reap a peace dividend that would include greater security and increased investor confidence.

In the longer term these societies could also draw from the major industrialized countries an increased supply of machines, technology, and other inputs required for development. Unfortunately, given the way the Soviet Union's economy was structured and the way the U.S. economy continues to be structured, shifting from producing the means of war to producing the means of development will not happen quickly or easily. Some of the largest corporations might well face bankruptcy if suddenly forced to compete in the open market producing nonmilitary goods. This would cause considerable unemployment, especially among highly trained scientists and engineers.

In the meantime, the people affected by civil unrest continue to suffer. It is easier for both governments and non-governmental organizations to raise money to provide relief for the victims of civil unrest than it is to raise money to eliminate the root causes of strife. Leaders in government and in the churches prefer to travel the road of least resistance. A ray of hope became evident at the 1999 World Trade Conference in Seattle. There a group of leaders from low- and middle-income countries rejected the normal practice of delivering a favorable vote in exchange for receiving more foreign aid. They saw it as in their joint interest to vote down the proposed changes to the WTO. Hopefully their courage is a sign of a brighter future.

The group of seventy-seven countries, not aligned to either the United States or the former Soviet Union, met in Havana in 2000. They sought to extend this ray of hope by calling for a New Global Human Order. As part of this New Order they proposed that the countries from the global south be given the right to "participate on an equal footing" with the countries from the global north on all decisions that affect the countries of the south.[12]

The church and its representatives continue to pour forth pronouncements on economic life. ... Materialism is condemned, charity is urged, stewardship is praised, the dignity of work is celebrated, God is thanked for blessings received and petitioned for blessings hoped for. But all of this noise makes no difference. The economy as a whole proceeds exactly as if none of these preachments had ever been made; and individual believers do function and must function within the economy just like everyone else, each pursuing his or her own interests. No longer can anyone give "a genuinely Christian character" to his or her economic life.

—*Nicholas Wolterstorff*

12

Where Do We Go from Here?

The capitalist system is like a massive eighteen-wheel truck barreling through history. It has an excessively powerful motor driven by the sum of all human selfishness. It has no brakes. The steering mechanism is clearly faulty. As a passenger on this truck, are you inclined to ask where we are going? Are you worried about arriving there safely?

An Economic System Without Direction or Purpose

What Are We Striving For?

Being driven by an economic system with faulty steering should alarm us about our future. One-third of the world's adults who are willing and able to work are reported to be unemployed. While per capita consumption soared by 45 percent over the last two decades, many people's quality of life has declined. Some 42 percent of North American employees say they feel "used up" by the end of the day. In the United States, the 1 percent of the people with the highest income earn approximately as much as the 40 percent with the lowest income.[1] This, along with many delightful material things, is what progress has brought us.

And we had to work for it. In the United States a married couple works on average 247 hours a year more in 1996 than they did in 1989. The proportion of workers with employer-paid health insurance has fallen by more than

7 percent over the past two decades. Even when the economy was booming, only two-thirds of displaced workers found another job within a year, and when they did find work, their average income was 13 percent lower than it had been in the previous job.[2]

Society has not defined progress. We are working longer and rushing onward without deciding where we want to go. As a society we lack a basis for deciding what research should be pursued vigorously, and we do not have a means to evaluate which technology should be implemented. We have tried to avoid the issue by elevating progress to a matter of faith.

> It is intriguing to note that this motif of progress has indeed presented itself frequently as faith, and that as a result it has often been described in terms of the inspiring dynamics of an authentic faith. The word faith . . . refers to the propelling, all-embracing visions which direct persons in everything they feel, think and do. Insofar as an opinion or conviction becomes a matter of faith in this sense, its influence will inescapably be noticeable in the architecture of society.[3]

This blind faith is empty because the progress we believe in seems to be utterly lacking in human values. Shona McKay suggests that we have chosen to go nowhere in particular in a great hurry. But do you recall making such a choice? Did any politician ever make it part of a platform that you could decide to accept or reject?

The Age of Anxiety

As the clock runs down on the 20th century, we all feel adrift in a world of disruptive change. Isn't the problem that we've lost our bearings on our values?

At the same time as corporations, seemingly out of necessity, proceed at a millennial clip, there is emerging a growing doubt about the wisdom of an economic order and, by extension, a society that chooses to operate at breakneck speed. As the century gasps its last, the questions must be: Where are we going in such a hurry? Why, and at what cost?

From Shona McKay, "The Age of Anxiety," *The Financial Post Magazine* (January 1999), 16. Material reprinted with the express permission of the National Post Company, a CanWest Partnership.

The Fallacy That Consumers Control the System

Economists want to claim that you did make such a choice by expressing yourself as a consumer in the market. We consumers are portrayed as interacting with producers to obtain exactly what is best for us. It follows, according to economists, that society has chosen the best of all possible worlds.

This reasoning exhibits several fallacies. First, it assumes consumers are still in control and that each one of us makes free choices independent of any influence by suppliers. We know that this is not the case: large corporations cannot afford for consumers to be completely free to choose. We also know some choices are simply thrust upon us. An example is Canada's effort to join the United States in trying to force all countries to allow the importation of genetically engineered food regardless of whether the consumers in those countries want such food. When national governments join hands with giant chemical companies to lobby for the "right" of producers to define the world's trading rules, how free are consumers to choose what they will consume?

A second fallacy arises because economists exclude from their analysis anyone who has no income to spend. The homeless, for example, didn't get to choose.

Even if all consumers could participate and were free to choose, the third fallacy would still remain. Economists'

> **Ottawa to Fight for Global Biotech Rules**
>
> Federal Agriculture Minister Lyle Vanclief is planning to fight for strict international rules that would force countries to accept safe genetically modified foods, even if their consumers do not want them.
>
> "The world wants a clear set of rules in reference to biotechnology, whether you're a supporter of biotechnology or not," Mr. Vanclief said. . . .
>
> The platform, which will be made public this month, recommends that Canada join the United States in pushing hard for a new set of scientific rules for genetically modified foods under the World Trade Organization.
>
> From Heather Scoffield, "Ottawa to Fight for Global Biotech Rules," *Globe and Mail* (August 5, 1999). Reprinted with permission from The Globe and Mail.

notion of individual choice ignores the reality that who we are as persons is deeply rooted in our being part of a community. Economists assume that people buy and sell in the market in a manner that leaves them unaffected. Samuel Bowles and Herbert Gintis claim quite the contrary; they say that the act of exchanging with others in the market has changed us into what we have become. Our society is the product of our economic system. Individuals rush madly for self-gratification because we have allowed economists to claim that human needs can be separated from human wants so that each one of us can define our self-interest without any reference to others. We should not be surprised to see that this destroys rather than builds community.

Allowing Society's Values to Direct the Economy

We like to think we have the best the world has to offer. After all, for several years running the United Nations has designated Canada as number one in the world on the basis of the Human Development Index. The United States is not

Traders make trades, but trades also make traders. Though the fact is unrecognized by economists, exchanging goods in markets is not altogether unlike exchanging greetings, kisses, or blows. Goods and services are indeed allocated through market exchange, but the exchanging parties are themselves transformed or reproduced in the process. The becoming-by-acting model treats exchange as an interaction between subjects shaping human development. Indeed, there is a strong analogy between exchange and language in that both represent forms of social interaction that shape who we are and who we might become.

Samuel Bowles and Herbert Gintis, "The Economy Produces People" (1991), 227.

Indeed many poor societies have long understood what developed countries are just beginning to discover, namely that the meaning attached to life and death are ultimately more important than mere material abundance or technological control over nature. It has been said that we put our pride in technical achievements, probably because they are less arduous than social betterment and spiritual improvement, and because they entail no heart-searching, no laborious choices, as do social ends based on human values.

From "Development Ethics," the February 1996 issue of *Development Express*, a publication of the International Development Centre at the Canadian International Development Agency (Ottawa).

far behind. North America is the preferred destination for the world's refugees. But we lack something that many poorer societies possess: their limited material standard of living forces them to make hard choices about social ends and human values that we prefer to avoid.

I concur with Bowles and Gintis that in order to gain a sense of direction as a society, a purpose for being, we must decide together what we want to become. Then we should fashion an economic system that will allow us to reach that goal.

Drawing on the sacred values outlined in chapter 3, we should expect that a primary outcome of our institutions and systems should be to maintain the human dignity of all people. Further, our systems should contribute to an environment within which communities of people can flourish. Third, they should provide us all with a sense of purpose by encouraging creativity, skill, and diligence. Our contribution to community should be evaluated in more than merely financial terms.

This need not mean getting rid of self-interest altogether. Rodney Wilson draws on Umer Chapra's Muslim teachings to clarify this matter. The appropriate corrective balance to exercising self-interest is being accountable to God. This accountability emphasizes our relationships to others rather than measuring progress by the material

The stress on the "right motivation" provides an important clue. Self-interest has its role, and is, according to Chapra, not necessarily bad. This is only one driving force, however; humans are also social beings. There is a contradiction here. Capitalism is about self-motivation, but it cannot accommodate social conscience. Socialism can, but it destroys self-motivation. Some other way is needed. For Chapra it is the accountability before an all-powerful being from which nothing can be hidden. Rational man is concerned not just with the physical world and the material, but the hereafter. The economic challenge is ultimately a test. It is the human response which matters, not the material outcome. Viewed from this perspective it is not at all clear that the developed countries are in fact developed in human terms, or that the so-called less developed or developing countries are underdeveloped.

Rodney Wilson, *Economics, Ethics, and Religion* (1997), 142.

things we possess and consume. It gives purpose to our individual lives and direction to our society. The question we still must confront is whether our economic system allows us to be accountable to God. If it does not, how might it be changed?

Our Environment as the Ultimate Check

Our economic system has too much power and has no brakes. So how will its trip end? One possibility is that it will run out of fuel when the majority of consumers say that they have enough. With no need for more, economic growth could slow to the rate of growth of the population. This seems unlikely. Corporations, for which growth is a narcotic, won't let it happen. With massive advertising budgets and control of the media, they have immense power to shape and drive our wants—and they don't hesitate to use it.

The New Limits Being Set by Our Natural Landscape

A more likely brake will be our natural environment. As more and more of our nonrenewable resources run out, our eighteen-wheeler will face an uphill road that keeps getting steeper. Eventually even the most powerful engine won't be enough.

I am not predicting that we are about to run out of resources. Totally exhausting particular resources is not an immediate possibility. Rather, the dwindling of supplies will hamper our growth. For example, certain supplies of a resource, say oil in Texas, Alberta, or Libya, were once relatively cheap to exploit. But M. King Hubbert, a Shell geologist, predicted in 1956 that oil production in the United States would peak during the 1970s and then begin to decline. His prediction proved to be correct.[4]

Now that these easy sources of oil are beginning to run out, we have to turn to more expensive sources, such as oil in northern Canada and shale deposits in the western United States. Those supplies become available only at a much higher cost per barrel than what we are now paying. Having to turn to such expensive sources will limit our growth.

Our economic system will respond to this increasingly steep hill with rising prices—inflation. It happened once in the 1970s when we reached the limits to growth in oil supplies. Then higher prices forced us to explore new ways to heat our houses and drive our cars. Many turned to alternative sources of energy, and the crisis motivated a search for new energy-saving technologies. The crisis also caused the oil-rich Middle Eastern countries to pump more oil. All of these effects together brought the price down again. It won't be as easy the next time.

Entrusting Central Bankers with the Power to Limit Growth

In anticipation of inflation, Western governments have been persuaded to free their central banks from political control and make them solely responsible for controlling inflation. *The Economist* notes, for example, that the new central bank for the European Union is described as having been given the goal of "price stability."[5]

While the editors at *The Economist* have traditionally worried more about inflation than unemployment, by the end of the 1990s they were asking whether central bankers were taking their responsibility too seriously.[6] They noted that the European Central Bank defines price stability as inflation of less than 2 percent a year and observed that no major country had been able to meet that target during the 1990s. The average rate of inflation was 3.3 percent. The Bank of Canada had held Canada's inflation rate below 2 percent for some years during the 1990s but at the cost of slower economic growth and more unemployment than the United States. In short, there is a danger that the tight

monetary policies of our central banks will purchase inflation rates below historic levels by limiting economic
growth.

If central banks successfully keep in check the inflation
caused by rising natural resource prices, we will face the
prospect of growing unemployment. Already an estimated
one-third of the world's labor force is unemployed, and with
high unemployment comes social unrest.

In the 1930s we responded to severe unemployment and
social unrest by turning to government to modify the
extremes of capitalist system.

> After World War II, at different speeds in different
> countries, capitalism became a somewhat more benign
> economic system in the advanced countries. The Great
> Depression convinced people that capitalism was an
> essentially unstable system subject to economic cycles and
> that for this reason governments should extend a helping
> hand to industries and the general population during peri-
> ods of decline. And the war demonstrated that greater
> government control actually made the national economy
> thrive.[7]

Is more government the most creative means to slow
down our runaway system? Or can we come together within our societies to define what we would like to become and
then redesign our system to achieve that end?

In chapter 3 I called for an economic system that recognizes the integrity, fullness, and sacredness of the created
order and helps human beings carry out their shared responsibility for maintaining life. Our system should help us balance our relentless pursuit of abundance with our responsibility to ensure the sustenance of life on this planet. It should
promote fairness rather than bowing to the interests of a
privileged few who can dictate what is produced, how it is
produced, and how it is distributed.

The Case for a New Driver

Capital Has Served Its Purpose

My focus thus far has been on the eighteen-wheeler that is our economic system. Even if we could add a proper set of brakes and repair the steering, we would still need to replace the driver. In the eighteenth and nineteenth centuries, capital was the key resource in short supply, and it governed what and how much we produced. At that time, designating the capitalist as the driver of our economic system was appropriate. But things have changed. Now the governing factor that limits continued "progress" is our environment—the gifts of nature. As our material standard of living rises, the natural landscape deteriorates, the threat of local wars grows, and species become extinct.

The Case for Ecolpreneurship

To change our mad pursuit of "progress," we will require a new driver for our economic system, a driver that will use the gifts of nature in such a way that nonrenewable resources are conserved and the environment is sustained.

We still want a driver that will experiment, innovate, and risk new approaches. We want one with all the characteristics of an entrepreneur, except that of being motivated primarily by high rates of return on capital. We want a driver that will conserve and sustain the natural landscape rather than merely maximizing the value of output from a particular unit of capital.

Because God gives us responsibility for ongoing creation, we are responsible for the earth. Whether we have the might to change the earth can be debated. God's charge to us to tend creation like a garden does not give us the right to dominate the natural world. I concur with David Suzuki's observation that we must rediscover our place in nature, that we must work with nature and form an alliance with it.[8]

With natural resources becoming the factor that limits where we might want to go as a society, we need an approach that will minimize the use of nonrenewable resources, strive to maintain biodiversity, and promote the continued renewal of our natural landscape. We need more than just environmentalism that seeks to take us back to some former natural state. We need ecological entrepreneurship that will combine innovation with ecology. We propose to call our new driver ecolpreneurship.

An Incentive System to Guide the Ecolpreneurs

Not only do we need to name a new driver to replace the capitalist, we also need ways to motivate people to become ecolpreneurs. We need an incentive comparable to a return on capital that ecolpreneurs can claim as their reward for tilling and caring for the garden as God intended.

Monsanto illustrates what conserving and sustaining the environment will look like if the current incentive system is not replaced. Its goal is to use expected food shortages in the future as a means to maximize its return on invested capital, especially the investment in research.

Monsanto's prediction about future food requirements may be correct. Its research will contribute to the solution by increasing food

Food By Design

Because genetically modified crops produce more food per acre, with less input of labor, fuel and fertilizer, Monsanto's senior executives like to emphasize the company's commitment to sustainable development. Sounding like an environmental extremist from the 1980s, Hendrik Verfaillie, head of the agricultural division, recently told a Toronto conference that the company has estimated demand for food will increase by a factor of three over the next 50 years; at current rates of production, this will require an additional 15 million square miles of land devoted to agriculture. "If that were the case, we would have to burn down the rain forest. We would have to eliminate all the wetlands and tax the environment in a way that would be totally unacceptable. Another possibility is to increase productivity by a factor of three. And one way to do that is through biotechnology."

From David Lees, "Food by Design," *The Financial Post Magazine* (October 1998), 24. Material reprinted with the express permission of the National Post Company, a CanWest Partnership.

output per hectare of farmland. It will also contribute to the problem because it seeks to maximize its return on capital, which is no longer the scarce resource. What the future requires is the drive and innovation of a Monsanto, but motivated by a passion to renew and conserve our natural landscape.

Well before we run out of food there will be major upheavals caused by the unemployed and the landless who cannot afford to buy the existing, still adequate, supplies of food. If Monsanto's motivation was purely to increase food supplies while sustaining all agricultural land, its research would seek to develop land and water conserving technology that is accessible to all. Our economic system does not encourage such action. It still requires a maximum return on the money invested in research. Monsanto responds to that incentive with seed that has to be bought annually from its licensed producers. This eliminates the poorest farmers, who cannot afford to buy both the seed and the related inputs to make it produce well. It also ignores the poorest families, who depend on crops like millet, sorghum, and cassava. Because the market for these foods of the poor is not growing, firms driven purely by a return on capital will not bother to devote research resources to increase the yield of these crops.

The owners of capital and the managers they hire use the revenue they gain from maximizing returns to compete with lower-income farmers for the limited land resources available. Annie Bergeron

> **The Political Economy of Golf in East Asia**
>
> The green and "natural" qualities of golf resorts promoted under this scheme are often deceptive. They are achieved only at the price of three to four tonnes of herbicides, pesticides, fertilizers, coloring agents and other highly carcinogenic chemicals, which subsequently drain off into rivers, ponds and reservoirs. Water consumption is also a bitter issue as drought conditions are prevalent in most of Southeast Asia. Each golf course needs at least 3,000 cubic metres of water a day, leaving local farmers with no means to irrigate their crops.
>
> From Annie Bergeron, "From Landscape to Linkscape," *APRRC Newsletter* 7, no. 2 (May 1998), 7.

illustrates this well with her discussion of golf course development in Southeast Asia. Each course requires 160 to 320 hectares (400 to 800 acres), versus 64 hectares (160 acres) in Europe because a course requires various luxury housing and shopping facilities to make it complete. The growing popularity of golf is seen as one of the causes of increasing landlessness in the area.

Finally, biotechnology research that is driven by maximization of returns on capital tends to be too impatient to wait and take responsibility for possible long-term effects. When such effects occur on a large scale, the corporation's shares drop to zero, it declares bankruptcy, and the managers and scientists move on to another firm. Their personal liability for their decisions and research tends to be limited by corporate law. Our legal system does not provide a way to compensate those who end up suffering from such errors.

If all else fails, immortality can always be assured by spectacular error.

–John Kenneth Galbraith

Designing an alternative incentive system for food and medical research will be a challenge. After all, the old way of maximizing return on capital is so easy to see and measure. Its effects are immediate and real: more money flowing into our bank accounts.

Non-monetary incentives for human action need to be explored further by social scientists. Each of us must learn to understand and appreciate how our daily existence is enriched by all of the species of plants and animals that make up our natural landscape. Then we will pay more heed to preserving the habitat each species requires.

Earlier in this book I promoted some form of a Sabbath as a way to gain such an appreciation. That would help restore the balance between what constitutes enough for our well-being and the capacity of our environment to keep meeting our daily needs.

A Renewed Incentive System Based on Society's Values

How could the market be used to motivate ecolpreneurs? Economists and accountants might consider entering a value for the stocks of natural resources as if they were a form of capital. The use of such natural capital would then show up as a cost of production. Rates of return take into account the use of natural capital, rewarding those who use less, those who restore and maintain our natural landscape, and those who develop technologies that extend our supply of nonrenewable resources.

If the market could be modified to serve such a new, environmentally friendly economic system, we would still need to guard against unequal distribution of income and wealth. The possibility of peace among societies depends on reversing environmental destruction and achieving a more equitable distribution of income and wealth. Communities where people can flourish with dignity must be inclusive, allowing everyone to participate. We need to work toward a shared political discourse that enables all participants to shape and attain community aims. Given globalization, our economic system should enable other societies to develop their respective potentials. It should help us to develop relationships to other societies by promoting peace through a fair exchange of resources, goods, and services.

Environment, Development and Security

The Brundtland Report popularized the notion that environmental considerations need to be factored into the development/security equation. The link between environment, development and security is based on the hypothesis that environmental threats—mostly environmental degradation and resource depletion—contribute to the emergence of violent conflicts. Many analysts would now agree that the nexus where underdevelopment, environmental degradation and overpopulation meet, constitutes a boiling point that can result in civil wars and interstate conflict.

From Jean-Francois Rioux and Robin Hay, "Development, Peace, and Security: The Possibilities and Limits of Convergence," *Development Express* 6 (1996), 5.

Can We Get There from Here?

Let's imagine that we have repaired the truck and have a new driver. Will that allow us to travel toward a destination that embodies our deepest values and is sustainable over time? Is it really possible to get there from where we are now?

Rediscovering Economic Activity as a Means to an End

I want to end with an optimistic yes. True, it will not be easy. The road ahead will be difficult, perhaps downright painful. But if we set our minds firmly on a common destination and if we have the will to persist, we can turn our overhauled truck in the right direction and keep it going.

An appropriate starting point is to see economic activity as a means to an end. We have fallen into the trap of believing that economic development is a desirable end in itself and that people are an important means to achieving it. In fact, the reverse is true. The well-being of people is the end, and economic development is merely a means to that end.

Developing this theme, Bowles and Gintis argue for a fundamental shift in power relations. Specifically, they say that democracy must be extended to include the large business firms, and the power to decide how resources will be used must be shifted to the people living in the communities where those resources are located. They must be able to control both the labor resources they embody and the gifts of nature that form their immediate natural landscape.

These necessary changes to our economic system will

We are thus led to propose a vision of a new economic order . . . in which dignity and community are achieved by fostering the growth of democratically controlled firms and economically powerful communities. These institutions, we suggest, can provide the solidarity and meaning required to offset the anonymity of the abstract individual, the power that wealth conveys, and the power of both the state and the global corporation in modern capitalism.

Samuel Bowles and Herbert Gintis, "The Economy Produces People" (1991), 222.

be difficult because the corporate leaders and the politicians who represent their interests will not give up their power voluntarily. It will also be difficult to achieve control over the media, which corporate advertisers dominate. The Internet is somewhat of an exception, but without vigilance it will succumb to the same fate as the rest of the media.

Enabling the People to Decide

The beginning of a shift in power back to communities of people will be dialogue, first among people within each community and then among communities. This dialogue must draw on the many values and beliefs that shape our actions. The seven basic values I presented in chapter 3 are rooted in a particular faith tradition. In a dialogue across different faiths and with people who are nonreligious, other values will come to the fore. Naturally, there will be some peaks of self-interest. But there also will be considerable overlap between such peaks. Our dialogue must seek to distill from these areas of overlap a set of values we all hold in common.

Historically churches have served to model alternatives that are both possible and socially desirable. For example, churches were a driving force that eventually gave rise to the establishment of hospitals, universities, and the welfare system. They could also be the driving force to encourage their members to experiment with new institutions that build community, enhance human dignity, and develop new approaches to sustaining our environment.

These dialogues and experiments will shape our culture as well as our economic system. Our culture is all those things that bind us together in some way as a people: our means of livelihood; our language, cuisine, games, and social customs; how we interpret our history; and the way we pass wisdom from generation to generation. The list goes on. Not all of these elements have to be changed simultaneously. History has shown that changing a few elements can reshape the whole culture.

Social change can occur without cultures being destroyed and people being left in a huge vacuum. It is important to build on those change elements that exist in every culture to enable all people to develop further. Experience with this process of development has demonstrated again and again that changes will succeed if they are owned by the people involved. Allen Sauder, drawing on his extensive experience in the development field, identifies this as a key success factor.

When Business Helps the Poor

While it is wonderful to see projects grow and evolve, it is still sometimes difficult to connect one's daily work with these "successes." All projects are the result of many persons' ideas and efforts. Most also are subject to the fortunes or misfortunes of happening at the right or wrong time and place in the macro political and economic context. However, almost invariably, I have been struck by the importance of putting management and eventual ownership in the hands of local staff and national institutions. Those projects which have remained in the hands of outsiders from North America, however well-meaning, have too often languished.

From Allen Sauder, "When Business Helps the Poor," *The Marketplace* (November-December, 1998), 7.

Re-examining Our Laws and Institutions

Ownership of resource use at the community level will require major shifts in how the law defines property. In posing the question Whose Property? Roy Vogt develops the theme that property rights are not static.[9] They change over time as society changes. As capitalism evolved, the property rights of shareholders increased at the expense of those of employees. Moreover, the emphasis on individual rights increased the rights of private-sector firms and reduced the power of governments. In my discussion of consumers, I noted how large firms redefined the rights of producers at consumers' expense. I also noted that large firms have taken advantage of a property-rights vacuum for the various parts of the environment that are held in common and have harmfully exploited the gifts of nature.

Starting with the lopsided imbalance of property rights between owners of capital and the employees of firms, we draw from Vogt's book two ways to restore balance and fairness. One approach is that of the state of Pennsylvania, where a majority of the citizens used their government to redefine property rights in an attempt to soften the power of large firms. The second example is the European approach of granting employees influence through "works councils and membership on boards of directors."[10] These two examples illustrate differing ways to reverse the erosion of workers' property rights. They can serve as ideas for reshaping our economic system so that development serves people.

> ### Protection During Hostile Take-overs
>
> In April 1990, the Pennsylvania legislature . . . passed a law protecting local industry against some abuses that frequently accompany hostile take-overs from outside. One of the law's provisions guaranteed severance pay for workers dislocated by a take-over and the continuance of existing labour contracts once a hostile take-over bid had begun. Another provision encouraged directors of corporations weighing take-over bids to consider not only the shareholders' interests but also those of employees, suppliers, and the company's surrounding community.
>
> Roy Vogt, Whose Property? (1999), 143.

Alternative Ways to Fund Our Institutions

In chapter 5, I called for alternative ways to fund our media. As a starting point, I suggested that advertising expenses designed to create wants no longer be a tax-deductible business expense. If firms want to manipulate us to serve their interests, we should not have to subsidize their doing so with our taxes. We may, however, be willing to help new firms and new products break into the market. We could achieve this by setting a time period, say six months or a year, during which firms could deduct their advertising costs for tax purposes.

Thought must also be given to the future of education. The emphasis on individual rights is moving us away from community-based schools to a system in which students pay the full cost of education and schools are forced to compete with each other for students. If this is allowed to run its course, the notion of equal opportunity will be crushed.

Recognizing this, Bruce Ackerman and Ann Alstott have put forward a radical proposal according to which each high school graduate would be given a grant of $80,000.[11] The graduates could use it to purchase an education or could invest it as they see fit. The grants would be paid for with a 2 percent tax on wealth. Does this bold plan have merit? Or would we prefer to return to an earlier balance between public and private property rights with most of the cost of education borne by the communities that own and manage the public schools?

One value our current economic system brings to this debate is efficiency. This is a significant value, given public resistance to taxation. Should that be our primary consideration? We need to develop efficient alternatives for delivering social services that also meet other goals that flow from our common values.

Various academic disciplines will also need a new focus. Economists, for example, can no longer hide behind the glib assumption that consumers make independent decisions about what is best for them. The cartoonist Chance Browne pokes fun at our theory: Hi and Lois are joining a queue at a toy store during the Christmas rush. The people in front of them explain: "We're standing in line for the hot toy of the season." Lois asks: "What is it?" The response of two supposedly well-informed, truly independent consumers is: "No clue! All we know is that our kids will want it."[12] Economic theory must recognize that social settings shape demand. What we choose to buy and consume, in turn, shapes our future needs and wants.

Similarly, the accounting profession needs to shift from an approach based solely on capital to an alternative accounting method that considers the gifts of nature as the new scarce constraint. Our accounting traditions and practices can help shape a reward system that coaxes out ecolpreneurs who will direct their creative energies toward conserving the gifts of nature for the well-being of all.

Within the science disciplines the challenge will be whether to keep following the market incentives based on maximizing profit or to redirect research according to the new reality in which the environment has replaced capital as the key resource. Similarly, members of the legal profession will need to decide whether to stay where the money is, with politicians and the owners of capital, or to lead the way in redefining property rights in a more wholesome way.

Sharing Our Wealth with Others

While natural resources are becoming the key limiting factor, one area where capital is still in short supply is in the low-income countries. We concur with an editorial in *The*

The Aid Imperative

Thirty years ago, retired Canadian prime minister Lester Pearson headed a commission for the World Bank to investigate foreign aid. It concluded that "the widening gap between the developed and the developing countries has become the central problem of our times."

During those times, the ratio of living standards among the world's richest countries and the world's poorest countries was more than 40 to one. We can say safely, however, that nobody paid much heed to Lester Pearson. Today, the same ratio is more than 70 to one. It is difficult to argue with the United Nations Development report for 1999, which stated that such inequalities "have reached grotesque proportions." . . .

The recent decision of the G7 countries for accelerated debt-forgiveness is a modest first step along that road, important to the extent that it acknowledges the moral obligations of the First World and the limits on national sovereignty that solutions to global problems demand.

The only response that cannot be condoned is the one that greeted Mr. Pearson's plea 30 years ago and has become deeply entrenched in our policy. Self-interest should tell us that. Worsening poverty in much of the world is the root causes of the wars, terrorism and ecological catastrophes that affect us all. . . .

We can no longer delude ourselves, as Mr. Pearson said so long ago, "that the poverty and deprivation of the great majority of mankind can be ignored without tragic consequences for all."

"The Aid Imperative," an editorial in *The Globe and Mail* (July 15, 1999). Reprinted with permission from *The Globe and Mail.*

Globe and Mail that aid continues to be pivotal in maintaining relationships between rich and poor countries. The vast spending on military resources to protect ourselves can be reduced only if we alleviate widespread poverty and deprivation. We also agree that accelerated debt forgiveness is a modest first step in acknowledging our moral obligation to the people in low-income countries.

Mobilizing for a Renewal of Our Economic System

Becoming Informed as a Place to Start

The danger with specifying things that need to change is that you, the reader, will become overwhelmed with the magnitude of our task. It is important to realize that no one person is responsible for our current problems or for their solutions. Rather, we need to understand the larger economic and political system to see how each of us is being used to benefit a select few who own one of the means of production, capital.

Well-informed citizens can carry on the dialogue needed to redefine what progress should mean on the basis of agreed-upon core values. Given a will to see change, small groups of informed and dedicated members of communities can coax out and motivate the ecolpreneurs we need for a better, more sustainable future.

In defining the sacred values set out in chapter 3, my reference group and I declared from the outset that we are part of a particular faith tradition. For us, a logical starting point is the church, the community that nourishes and encourages our religious beliefs and practices. As Robert Simons observes, churches will need to reach out and work on this larger economic and political agenda with others who do not necessarily share their faith orientation.[13] A real test of our commitment to working for the well-being of society will be our openness to join with others who also fear the violent, non-sustainable future we face if capitalism continues to propel us onward with faulty steering and no brakes.

Creating a Vision for a Better Future

Simons goes on to provide concrete direction on how we can proceed:

> Faced with the obstacles encountered in working for a more equitable society, structural change requires critique, vision, strategy and organization. It is important, then, to turn from a method and program of critique to vision in order to suggest the type of future worth struggling for. . . . While doing this, however, the system also has to remain aware of the ultimate purpose of economic organization: liberation from domination by scarcity and provision with the conditions necessary to a fully human existence—that is, one in which the higher ends of the human family and creativity are possible.[14]

What is your vision for the future? Can others identify with it? If not, do they have a perspective you need to hear? What points of commonality can you find? Could you work together on a strategy and organize to implement that strategy? If we can find enough in common with one another, our many little strategies and organizations, working together, can become a powerful force to transform our stubborn status quo.

The costs of challenging the current power structure may be high. Let us clarify and demonstrate a vision for a better future, then continually invite others to join us on the journey.

Large corporations that are dependent on powerless employees and compliant consumers are vulnerable to unified communities of people who want a better future for their children, a future in which they can freely express their creativity and build communities that cherish human dignity and fairness.

Along the way we can prepare our children to live for and with globalization in a way that draws on the wealth that people of other cultures have to offer, rather than exploiting them as a source of cheap resources and a market for output. Let us strive for an improved economic system that makes fairer trade possible. May our vision lead us to a way of life in which our pursuit of abundance is balanced by our responsibility to ensure the sustenance of life on this planet.

Notes

Chapter 1: Driven by the Market

1. The economics literature does not give much attention to defining or describing the market. It is assumed that because we participate in the market we know what it is. Elementary textbooks explain how markets operate primarily by developing the concepts of demand and supply. James Halteman's *The Clashing Worlds of Economics and Faith* (Scottdale, Pa.: Herald Press, 1995), makes only passing reference to the market, in chapters 2 and 8. Robert Heilbroner and Lester Thurow devote four chapters of *Economics Explained* (New York: Touchstone, 1998), chapters 10 to 13, to the topic. Advanced literature in economics analyzes in detail specific markets such as the labor market, the money market, the foreign-exchange market, and the stock market, as well as specific industries within the larger market.

2. "The Spiciest Futures of All," *The Economist* (September 20, 1997), 83.

Chapter 2: The Capitalist Market

1. "How to Live with Falling Prices," *The Economist* (June 12, 1999), 57-58.

2. The primary source for understanding the free enterprise system is Adam Smith, *An Inquiry into the Nature and Causes of the Wealth of Nations* (New York: The Modern Library, 1937). Other books that explain the system and locate its origins within their historic context include George Soule, *Ideas of the Great Economists* (New York: Mentor Books, 1965), and Robert L. Heilbroner, *The Worldly Philosophers: The Lives, Times, and Ideas of the Great Economic Thinkers*, 5th edition (New York: Simon and Schuster, 1980).

3. The literature of comparative economic systems provides a comparison of capitalism with other economic systems. With the decline of the Soviet Union, many countries that had practiced communist-style socialism are turning to a more market-oriented system.

This process is discussed in the literature of transitional economies.

4. Smith, *Wealth of Nations*, 670.

5. "Nestlé: A Dedicated Enemy of Fashion," *The Economist* (August 31, 2002).

Chapter 3: Sacred Values and the Worship of Abundance

1. Bob Goudzwaard, *Capitalism and Progress: A Diagnosis of Western Society* (Grand Rapids, Mich.: Eerdmans, 1979), 16.

2. Ibid., 21.

3. This need not imply that economists are unconcerned about moral issues. Rodney Wilson argues John Stuart Mill "stressed economic outcomes. . . . His interest was in how much was produced, rather than the ethics of how goods were produced, and on satisfaction in consumption." Karl Marx was certainly concerned about moral issues. Wilson argues that some liberation theologians used "a Marxist framework for the analysis of capitalism as a system, but they have not supported the adoption of Marxist policies, given the essentially materialistic nature of Marxism, which has economic rather than spiritual objectives." Rodney Wilson, *Economics, Ethics, and Religion: Jewish, Christian, and Muslim Economic Thought* (New York: New York University Press, 1997), 10 and 113.

4. "Road to Riches," *The Economist* (December 31, 1999).

5. John Boli, "The Economic Absorption of the Sacred," in Robert Wuthnow, ed., *Rethinking Materialism: Perspectives on the Spiritual Dimension of Economic Behavior* (Grand Rapids, Mich.: Eerdmans, 1995), 98.

6. Wilson concludes that elements common to Jewish, Christian, and Muslim religions are "honesty, justice in economic transactions and a concern for the dignity of the poor." Wilson, *Economics, Ethics, and Religion*, 213.

7. Robert G. Simons, *Competing Gospels: Public Theology and Economic Theory* (Alexandria, N.S.W., Australia: E. J. Dwyer, 1995), 72.

8. *Merriam-Webster Dictionary of English Usage*, in *Infopedia* 2.0, CD-ROM (Softkey Multimedia Inc., 1996).

9. Paul, the author of the first letter to the Corinthians, expresses this idea in this way: "'All things are lawful,' but not all things are beneficial. 'All things are lawful,' but not all things build up. Do not seek your own advantage, but that of the other" (1 Corinthians 10: 23-24).

10. From Juli Loesch, "Human Work for Human Beings," *The Other Side* (August 1979). Reprinted with permission. For subscriptions or for more information call 1-800-700-9280 or visit www.theotherside.org.

11. For an expanded discussion of the content of this sacred value see Robert Fogel, *The Fourth Great Awakening and the Future of*

Egalitarianism (Chicago: University of Chicago Press, 2000).
12. "Health Care in Poor Countries," *The Economist* (August 17, 2002), 20.

Chapter 4: Born to Shop
1. Paul L. Wachtel, *The Poverty of Affluence* (Philadelphia: New Society Publishers, 1989), 157.
2. Juliet B. Schor, *The Overworked American: The Unexpected Decline of Leisure* (New York: Basic Books, 1991), 1-2.
3. From a report on Robert Gordon's study *Two Centuries of Economic Growth* in "Economic Focus: Chasing the Leader," *The Economist* (February 8, 2003), 70.
4. "Healthy Calories," *The Economist* (August 2, 1997), 68-69.
5. Bob Goudzwaard, *Economic Stewardship Versus Capitalist Religion* (Toronto: Institute for Christian Studies, 1972), 68.
6. Eva Weidman, "Consuming Easy If We Don't Think," *Winnipeg Free Press* (January 25, 1998).
7. Mark Vincent, *A Christian View of Money* (Scottdale, Pa.: Herald Press, 1997), 26. Used with permission from Herald Press.
8. Several sources that suggest practical alternatives to current consumer behavior are David Schrock-Shenk, ed., *Basic Trek: Venture into a World of Enough* (Scottdale, Pa.: Herald Press, 2002); Richard J. Foster, *Freedom of Simplicity* (San Francisco: Harper & Row), 1981; Gerald W. Schlabach, *And Who Is My Neighbor: Poverty, Privilege, and the Gospel of Christ* (Scottdale, Pa.: Herald Press, 1990); and Mark Vincent, *A Christian View of Money: Celebrating God's Generosity* (Scottdale, Pa.: Herald Press, 1997).

Chapter 5: The Visible Hand and the Bottom Line
1. Sean Silcoff, "Black Gold," *Canadian Business* (October 30, 1998), 94.
2. Scott Taylor, "Bravo to Another Really Big Show," *Winnipeg Free Press* (January 26, 1998).
3. Americans have been known to pay several thousand dollars for a box of real Havanas. "Cuban Cigars: Let the Good Times Roll," *The Economist* (May 2, 1998).
4. "The Decline and Fall of General Motors," *The Economist* (October 10, 1998), 63.
5. Peter Drucker, "Will the Corporation Survive?" *The Economist* (November 3, 2001).
6. Shawna Steinberg, "Have Allowance, Will Transform Economy, *Canadian Business* (March 13, 1998), 65-66.
7. Elizabeth Renzetti, "Little Girls: Signed, Sealed, Delivered to the Label Marketers," *The Globe and Mail* (September 9, 1999).
8. As cited by Rodney Wilson, *Economics, Ethics and Religion:*

Jewish, Christian and Muslim Economic Thought (New York: New York University Press, 1997), 21.

9. "Big Shots," *The Economist* (May 9, 1998).

10. William Pfaff, "Economic Development," *New Yorker* (December 25, 1978), 46.

11. Bob Goudzwaard, *Capitalism and Progress: A Diagnosis of Western Society* (Grand Rapids, Mich.: Eerdmans, 1979), 29.

12. Max Clarkson as quoted by Sara Jean Green in an obituary in his honor: "U of T Visionary Champion of Ethics," *The Globe and Mail* (June 17, 1998).

13. Wilson, *Economics, Ethics, and Religion*, 176-77.

14. Scott Adams, "Dilbert," *Winnipeg Free Press* (March 3, 1998).

15. "Guilty as Charged," *The Economist* (October 31, 2001).

16. "The Diamond Business," *The Economist* (December 20, 1997), 113.

17. "Who's Wearing the Trousers?" *The Economist* (September 8, 2001), 27-28.

18. Louis Emmerij, "The Paradox of Competition," *UNRISD News* 16 (spring-summer 1997), 1.

19. "Dangerous and Overpriced," *The Economist* (August 10, 2002), 54.

20. Sarona Global Investment Fund, a program of Mennonite Economic Development Associates (MEDA), is a social investment fund with an aggressive focus on ventures that strengthen the economic prospects of the poor in low-income countries: www.sarona-fund.com. Mennonite Mutual Aid screens companies in its financial services using a set of core values to evaluate how a company performs in terms of its responsibilities to society and advice. You can read their stewardship investing guidelines at www.mma-online.org/corporate/investing_guidelines or call 1-800-348-7468 for more information. Other North American resources include Ethical Investing: www.ethicalinvesting.com; Ethical Funds: www.ethicalfunds.com; and Meritas is Canada's newest socially responsible mutual fund company, a joint venture of the Mennonite Savings and Credit Union (Ontario) Limited, the Mennonite Foundation of Canada and Mennonite Mutual Aid: www.meritas.ca.

Chapter 6: The Right to Work

1. Bob Goudzwaard, *Capitalism and Progress: A Diagnosis of Western Society* (Grand Rapids, Mich.: Eerdmans, 1979), 68.

2. "Monkey Business," *The Economist* (December 13, 1997), 57.

3. Goudzward, *Capitalism and Progress*, 31.

4. Tom Kochan and Willis Nordlund, *Reconciling Labor Standards and Economic Goals: An Historical Perspective*

(Washington: U.S. Department of Labor, Bureau of International Labor Affairs, 1989), 8.

5. Richard Chaykowski, "Not Going Quietly," *The Financial Post 2000* (November 1, 1997), 8 and 12.

6. "The High Price of Labour Strife," *The Globe and Mail* (July 15, 1998). It must be noted that in September 2002 General Motors and Canadian Auto Workers successfully negotiated a three-year labor contract.

7. "Caterpillar's Comeback," *The Economist* (June 20, 1998), 7.

8. In his helpful survey article on work, "No End in Sight," *The Financial Post 2000* (November 1, 1997), 4-6, Gordon Betcherman recommends the following as suggested reading:

Jeremy Rifkin, *The End of Work: The Decline of the Global Labor Force and the Dawn of the Post-Market Era* (New York: G. P. Putman's Sons, 1995).

William Bridges, *JobShift: How to Prosper in a Workplace Without Jobs* (Toronto: Addison Wesley, 1994).

Gordon Betcherman and Graham Lowe, *The Future of Work in Canada* (Ottawa: Canadian Policy Research Networks, 1997).

Robert Reich, *The Work of Nations: Preparing Ourselves for Twenty-First-Century Capitalism* (New York: Knopf, 1991).

Chris Freeman and Luc Soete, *Work for All or Mass Unemployment: Computerised Technical Change into the Twenty-First Century* (London: Pinter, 1994).

9. Kochan and Nordlund, *Reconciling Labor Standards.*

10. For information on this firm see T. E. Friesen, *A History of DW Friesen: A Unique Company*, 1907-1993 (Altona, Man.: DW Friesen, 1993); and Janis Thiessen, "'Working with Friesens': Labour Within a Mennonite Business, 1933-1995." Mimeo. University of Manitoba, Winnipeg, 1995).

11. Thiessen, "'Working with Friesens,'" 24.

12. Gordon Sinclair Jr., "Manitoba's South in Full Bloom" and "Secret to Success Lies in Greatness," *The Winnipeg Free Press* (March 30 and April 2, 1997).

13. Bill Tieleman, "Executive Pay Backlash," *Financial Post* (January 4, 1999), C4.

14. Juliet B. Schor, *The Overworked American: The Unexpected Decline of Liesure* (New York: Basic Books, 1991), 155.

15. Eric Pfanner, "France's Short Work Week a Mixed Blessing," *International Herald Tribune* (June 15, 2002); and "Economic Focus: Labours Lost," *The Economist* (June 15, 2002): 78.

16. Bruno Frey, *Not Just for the Money: An Economic Theory of Personal Motivation* (Cheltenham: Edward Elgar Publishing, 1997), ix.

17. Kathryn Leger, "As Subtle as a Blowtorch," *The Financial Post* (August 22-24, 1998), 10.

18. Gayle MacDonald, "Penniless and Proud of It," *The Globe and Mail* (April 15, 2000).

Chapter 7: Creation Sighs and Throbs in Pain

1. Richard Welford, "Corporate Environmental Management Means Business as Usual," *UNRISD News* 17 (autumn-winter 1997), 5.

2. As cited by Chris Wood in "Our Dying Seas," *Maclean's* (October 5, 1998), 50.

3. "California v. Detroit: Green Davis," *The Economist*, (July 27, 2002), 29.

4. Thomas M. Power, *Lost Landscapes and Failed Economies: The Search for a Value of Place* (Washington, D.C.: Island Press), 1.

5. Herman E. Daly, *Beyond Growth: The Economics of Sustainable Development* (Boston, Beacon Press, 1996), 37.

6. Joseph MacInnis, "Breaking the Bonds," *Maclean's* (October 5, 1998), 58.

7. Andrew Nikiforuk, "When Water Kills," *Maclean's* (June 12, 2000), 18-21.

8. Jane Taber, "Natives Face Upstream Battle over Salmon Rights," *The Ottawa Citizen* (November 28, 1998).

9. G. Cornelis van Kooten, *Land Resource Economics and Sustainable Development: Economic Policies and the Common Good* (Vancouver: UBC Press, 1993), 7.

10. "How Many Planets? A Survey of the Global Environment," *The Economist* (July 6, 2002), 16.

11. For additional discussion of the failure of market prices to guide us to optimal rates of resource use over time see Daly, *Beyond Growth*, 32.

12. Ibid., 78.

13. "Money to Burn?" *The Economist* (December 6, 1997).

14. Bruno S. Frey, *Not Just for the Money: An Economic Theory of Personal Motivation* (Cheltenham: Edward Elgar Publishing, 1997), 65.

15. "How Many Planets?" 14.

16. "The Aging of China," *The Economist* (November 21, 1998).

17. "How Many Planets?" 15.

18. Welford, "Corporate Environmental Management Means Business as Usual," 5.

19. MacInnes, "Breaking the Bonds," 59.

20. The thesis of the city as a malignancy was advanced as a topic for debate in a panel at the 1998 American Anthropological Society meeting. Andy Lamey, "Humanity Seen as a Cancer on Earth," *National Post*, (December 2, 1998).

21. van Kooten, *Land Resource Economics*, 179.

22. "Punch," guest cartoon in the *National Post* (December 1, 1998).

23. Welford, *Corporate Environmental Management*, 6.

24. As cited in "How Many Planets?" 3.

25. A. C. Grayling, book review of *The Sixth Extinction*, by Richard Leakey and Roger Lewin, *The Financial Post* (March 10, 1996), 25.

Chapter 8: The Role of Government

1. World Bank, *World Development Report 1997* (New York: Oxford University Press, 1997), 4. See also Table 1.1 in the report.

2. Peter Kuitenbrouwer, "Driven to Distraction," *The Financial Post* (August 9, 1997), W2.

3. "The Electric Revolution," *The Economist* (August 5, 2000), 19.

4. "The Great Food Debate," *The Economist* (August 31, 2002), 23.

5. David Zussman, "Government's New Style," *The Financial Post 2000* (October 18, 1997), 4-6.

6. Shawn McCarthy, "Federal Government Remains Relevant, Finance Minister Says," *The Globe and Mail* (August 7, 1998).

7. For example, see "The Wages of War," *The Economist* (September 22, 2001), 62.

8. A quotation drawn from *Merriam-Webster Dictionary of Quotations* in *Infopedia* 2.0, CD-ROM for Windows (Softkey Multimedia, 1996).

9. Justin Yifu Lin and Jeffrey B. Nugent, "Institutions and Economic Development," in J. Behrman and T. N. Srinivasan, eds., *Handbook of Development Economics* (Amsterdam: Elsevier Science, 1995), 3:2304, 2307. The issue of institutions and the market is also discussed by Samuel Bowles in "Endogenous Preferences: The Cultural Consequences of Markets and Other Economic Institutions," *Journal of Economic Literature* 36, no. 1 (1998).

10. Robert G. Simons, *Competing Gospels: Public Theology and Economic Theory* (Alexandria, Australia: E. J. Dwyer, 1995), 70-71.

Chapter 9: Penalizing the Achiever, Rewarding the Parasite?

1. As cited by Robert G. Simons, *Competing Gospels: Public Theology and Economic Theory* (Alexandria, Australia: E. J. Dwyer, 1995), 33-34.

2. Peter Bauer, "Ecclesiastical Economics: Envy Legitimized?" Paper presented at a seminar sponsored by the Fraser Institute on Theology, Third World Development, and Economic Justice, Regina, Sask., December 1983.

3. "Growth Is Good," *The Economist* (May 27, 2000), 82.

4. Michael Novak as quoted by Norman Podhoretz in "The New

Defenders of Capitalism," Ethics and Public Policy Reprint, Ethics and Public Policy Center, Washington, D.C. (December 1981), 101.

5. Hugh Segal, "The Issue Is Not Whether Wealth Is Good or Evil, but How It's Used," *The Financial Post* (September 6, 1997), 30.

6. *Webster's New World Dictionary of the American Language* (Cleveland: The World Publishing Company, 1964).

7. Margaret Randall, *The Price You Pay: The Hidden Cost of Women's Relationship to Money* (London: Routledge, 1996), 37.

8. Rodney Wilson, *Economics, Ethics, and Religion: Jewish, Christian, and Muslim Economic Thought* (New York: New York University Press, 1997), 65.

9. Ibid., 162.

10. Ibid., 77.

11. As cited by Simons, *Competing Gospels*, 96.

12. Randall, *Price You Pay*, 43-44.

13. Amartya Sen, *Inequality Reexamined* (Oxford: Clarendon, 1992), 19-20.

14. Ibid., 69.

15. Michael Novak as quoted by Podhoretz in "New Defenders," 75.

16. Sen, *Inequality Reexamined*, 81-82.

17. "Sense of Community Feared Lost in Canada." A Canadian Press report on an interview with Julia Bass, *Winnipeg Free Press* (December 10, 1997).

18. John Dalla Costa, "At Home and Homeless," *The Financial Post Magazine* (March 1998), 35. The quotation from this article that opens this chapter is reprinted with the express permission of the National Post Company, a CanWest Partnership.

19. "A Little Learning," *The Economist* (December 13, 1997), 72.

20. Jesus M. Cruz, "Business Practices and Anabaptist Spirituality," *Conciliation Quarterly* 17, no. 1 (winter 1998), 5.

21. Herman E. Daly, *Beyond Growth: The Economics of Sustainable Development* (Boston: Beacon Press, 1996), 210.

Chapter 10: Our Place in the Global Market

1. Vijay Govindarajan and Anil Gupta, "Setting a Course for the New Global Landscape," *The Financial Post* (September 26, 1997), 6-7.

2. Andrew Karolyi, "Perpetual Motion Machine," *The Financial Post 2000* (November 29, 1997), 5.

3. David Korten, *When Corporations Rule the World* (West Hartford, Conn.: Kumarian, 1995), 54.

4. George Soros, *The Crisis of Global Capitalism: Open Society Endangered* (New York: Public Affairs, 1998), 91-92.

5. Joel Millman, "Mexico's Car Production Gaining Speed," *The Globe and Mail* (June 30, 1998).

6. Barrie McKenna, "More Firms Flock to Mexico," *The Globe and Mail* (July 8, 1998).

7. "Unfinished Battle," *The Economist* (April 10, 1999), 77.

8. Financial Post, "Coke Knows How to Make Things Go Better in China," *The Financial Post* (March 28, 1998), 20.

9. William Greider, *One World, Ready or Not: The Manic Logic of Global Capitalism* (New York: Simon and Schuster, 1998), 123.

10. Ibid.

11. Korten, *When Corporations Rule*, 42.

12. George Soros, *Crisis of Global Capitalism*, 102.

13. Ibid., xvi.

14. "Globalisation: Is It at Risk?" *The Economist* (February 2, 2002), 66.

15. Greider, *One World*, 26.

16. Ibid., 46.

17. United Nations Research Institute for Social Development, "Globalization and Citizenship," *UNRISD News* 15 (autumn 1996-winter 1997), 2.

18. Ibid.

19. Greider, *One World*, 388.

20. "Sweatshop Wars," *The Economist* (February 27, 1999).

21. Philip Rosenzweig, "How Should Multinationals Set Global Workplace Standards?" *The Financial Post* (November 21, 1997), 8.

22. Ibid., 18.

23. John M. Willson, "Corporate Responsibility in the Global Marketplace," *The North-South Newsletter* 2, no. 2 (1998): 6.

24. "Developing Countries Challenge the Rich," *The Globe and Mail* (April 15, 2000).

25. A statement by Jeffrey Sachs as reported in "Global Capitalism: Making It Work," *The Economist* (September 12, 1998), 23-24.

Chapter 11: The Victims of Our Global Reach

1. Denis Goulet, *Development Ethics: A Guide to Theory and Practice* (New York: Apex, 1995), 6-7.

2. K. K. S. Dadzie, "Economic Development," *Scientific America* (September 1980), 3-9. Copyright © 1980 by Scientific American, Inc. All rights reserved.

3. "Africa," *The Economist* (May 13, 2000).

4. World Bank, *World Development Report 1997: The State in a Changing World* (New York: Oxford University Press, 1997), 115.

5. Goulet, *Development Ethics*, 75-76.

6. "Drowning in Cheap Coffee," *The Economist* (September 29, 2001), 43.

7. Craig Burnside and David Dollar, "Aid Spurs Growth—in a

Sound Policy Environment," *Finance and Development* (December 1997), 6-7.

8. Robert Wade, "Winners and Losers," *The Economist* (April 28, 2001), 74.

9. Amartya Sen cited in United Nations Development Programme, *Human Development Report* 1996 (New York, Oxford University Press, 1996), 58.

10. World Bank, *World Development Report* 1997, 140.

11. Ernie Regehr, as cited by Ted Koontz, MCC *Peace Office Newsletter* (October 1997), 5.

12. "Developing Countries Challenge the Rich," a report of the meeting of the Group of 77, made up of 133 low- and middle-income countries, in *The Globe and Mail* (April 15, 2000).

Chapter 12: Where Do We Go From Here?

1. Data were drawn from Charles Handy, *The Hungry Spirit*, as reported by Shona McKay in "The Age of Anxiety," *The Financial Post Magazine* (January 1999), 18.

2. Judith Maxwell, "Don't Be Seduced by the U.S. Boom," *The Globe and Mail* (August 30, 1999).

3. Bob Goudzwaard, *Capitalism and Progress: A Diagnosis of Western Society* (Grand Rapids, Mich.: Eerdmans, 1979), xxii.

4. "Sunset for the Oil Business?" *The Economist* (November 3, 2001), 81.

5. "Europe's New Currency," *The Economist* (January 2, 1999).

6. "The New Danger," *The Economist* (February 20, 1999).

7. Gregory Baum, "An Ethical Critique of Capitalism: Contributions of Modern Catholic Social Teaching," in Michael Zweig, ed., *Religion and Economic Justice* (Philadelphia: Temple University Press, 1991), 86.

8. David Suzuki, *The Sacred Balance: Rediscovering Our Place in Nature* (Vancouver: GreyStone Books, 2002).

9. Roy Vogt, *Whose Property? The Deepening Conflict Between Private Property and Democracy in Canada* (Toronto: University of Toronto Press, 1999).

10. Ibid., 172.

11. "Staked Out," a book review of Bruce Ackerman and Ann Alstott, *The Stakeholder Society*, in *The Economist* (May 15, 1999), 9.

12. Chance Browne, "Hi and Lois," *Winnipeg Free Press* (December 17, 1999).

13. Robert G. Simons, *Competing Gospels: Public Theology and Economic Theory* (Alexandria, Australia: E. J. Dwyer, 1995), xiv.

14. Ibid., 153.

Bibliography

Adams, Scott. "Dilbert." *Winnipeg Free Press* (March 3, 1998).
_____. *The Dilbert Principle: A Cubicle's-Eye View of Bosses, Meetings, Management Fads and Other Workplace Afflictions.* New York: Harper Business, 1996.

"Africa." *The Economist* (May 13, 2000), 22.

"The Aging of China." *The Economist* (November 21, 1998), 21.

"The Aid Imperative." *The Globe and Mail* (July 15, 1999).

Bagnell, Kenneth. "Segal Laments Lost Conservatism." *The Financial Post* (November 15, 1997).

Bauer, Peter. "Ecclesiastical Economics: Envy Legitimized?" Paper presented at a seminar sponsored by the Fraser Institute on Theology, Third World Development, and Economic Justice. Regina, Sask., December 1983.

Baum, Gregory. "An Ethical Critique of Capitalism: Contributions of Modern Catholic Social Teaching," in Michael Zweig, ed., *Religion and Economic Justice,* 78-94. Philadelphia: Temple University Press, 1991.

Bergeron, Annie. "From Landscape to Linkscape: The Political Economy of Golf in East Asia." *APRRC Newsletter* 7, no, 2 (1998), 5-7.

Betcherman, Gordon. "No End in Sight." *The Financial Post 2000* (November 1, 1997), 4-6.

Betcherman, Gordon, and Graham Lowe. *The Future of Work in Canada.* Ottawa: Canadian Policy Research Networks, 1997.

Bierce, Ambrose. *The Devil's Dictionary: Merriam-Webster*

Dictionary of Quotations. In *Infopedia* 2.0, CD-ROM for Windows (Softkey Multimedia, 1996).

"Big Shots." *The Economist* (May 9, 1998), 63.

Blank, Rebecca M. *Do Justice: Linking Christian Faith and Modern Economic Life.* Cleveland: United Church Press, 1992.

Boli, John. "The Economic Absorption of the Sacred." In Robert Wuthnow, ed., *Rethinking Materialism: Perspectives on the Spiritual Dimension of Economic Behavior,* 93-115. Grand Rapids, Mich.: Eerdmans, 1995.

Bowles, Samuel. "Endogenous Preferences: The Cultural Consequences of Markets and Other Economic Institutions." *Journal of Economic Literature* 36, no. 1 (1998), 75-111.

Bowles, Samuel, and Herbert Gintis. "The Economy Produces People: An Introduction to Post-Liberal Democracy." In Michael Zweig, ed., *Religion and Economic Justice,* 221-44. Philadelphia: Temple University Press, 1991.

Bridges, William. *JobShift: How to Prosper in a Workplace Without Jobs.* Toronto: Addison Wesley, 1994.

Browne, Chance. "Hi and Lois." *Winnipeg Free Press* (December 17, 1999).

Brubaker, Pamela. "Economic Justice for Whom?" In Michael Zweig, ed., *Religion and Economic Justice,* 95-127. Philadelphia: Temple University Press, 1991.

Burnside, Craig, and David Dollar. "Aid Spurs Growth—in a Sound Policy Environment." *Finance and Development* (December 1997), 4-7.

"California v. Detroit: Green Davis." *The Economist* (July 27, 2002), 29.

Canadian International Development Agency. "Development Ethics." *Development Express* (February 1996).

"Caterpillar's Comeback." *The Economist* (June 20, 1998), 7.

Centra Gas. "Notice of Rate Change: How Much and Why?" A Centra Gas statement enclosed with its natural gas bills to Manitoba customers (December 1, 1999).

Charlebois, Cameron. "A New View of Volunteerism." *Winnipeg Free Press* (December 5, 2000).

Chaykowski, Richard. "Not Going Quietly." *The Financial Post 2000* (November 1, 1997), 8, 12-13.

Chwialkowska, Luiza. "Earnings Not Limited by Income of Father." *National Post* (November 6, 1998).

"Coke Knows How to Make Things Go Better in China." *The Financial Post* (March 28, 1998), 20.

Cork, David, and Susan Livingstone. *The Pig and the Python: How to Prosper from the Aging Baby Boom.* Toronto: Stoddart, 1996.

Crook, Clive. "Globalisation and Its Critics." *The Economist* (September 29, 2001), 3-28.

Cruz, Jesus M. "Business Practices and Anabaptist Spirituality." *Conciliation Quarterly* 17, no. 1 (winter 1998), 5.

"Cuban Cigars: Let the Good Times Roll." *The Economist* (May 2, 1998), 59-60.

Dadzie, K. K. S. "Economic Development." *Scientific American* (September 1980), 3-9.

Dalla Costa, John. "At Home and Homeless." *The Financial Post Magazine* (March 1998), 33-36.

Daly, Herman E. *Beyond Growth: The Economics of Sustainable Development.* Boston: Beacon Press, 1996.

Daly, Herman E., and John B. Cobb Jr. *For the Common Good: Redirecting the Economy Toward Community, the Environment, and a Sustainable Future.* Boston: Beacon Press, 1989.

"Dangerous and Overpriced." *The Economist* (August 10, 2002), 54.

"The Decline and Fall of General Motors." *The Economist* (October 10, 1998), 63-69.

DeMont, John. "Carol Ann." *Maclean's* (December 21, 1998), 75.

"Developing Countries Challenge the Rich." *The Globe and Mail* (April 15, 2000).

De Villiers, Marq. *Water.* Toronto: Stoddart, 1999.

"The Diamond Business." *The Economist* (December 20, 1997), 113-15.

"Drowning in Cheap Coffee." *The Economist* (September 29, 2001), 43-44.

Drucker, Peter. "The Next Society." *The Economist* (November 3, 2001), 3-20.

_____. "Will the Corporation Survive?" *The Economist* (November 3, 2001), 15-16.

"Economic Focus: Chasing the Leader." *The Economist* (February 8, 2003), 70.

"Economics Focus: Labours Lost." *The Economist* (June 15, 2002), 78.

"The Electric Revolution." *The Economist* (August 5, 2000), 19-20.

Ellwood, Wayne. "No Commercial Advertising." *New Internationalist*, n.d.

Emmerij, Louis. "The Paradox of Competition." *UNRISD News* 16 (spring-summer 1997), 1-2.

"Europe's New Currency." *The Economist* (January 2, 1999), 19-22.

Fairholm, Robert. "Technology Shock." *The Financial Post 2000* (October 11, 1997), 4-7.

"Farm Aid: The Kindest Cut." *International Herald Tribune* (June 15, 2002), 8.

Fidelman, Charlie. "No One Wants Toxic House, Except Family That Lives There." *National Post* (December 3, 1998).

Finlay, J. Richard. "Civic Decline an Unnecessary Cost of Capitalism's Success." *The Financial Post* (June 27-29, 1998), 23.

Fogel, Peter. *The Fourth Great Awakening and the Future of Egalitarianism.* Chicago: Chicago University Press, 2000.

Foster, Richard J. *Freedom of Simplicity.* San Francisco: Harper & Row, 1981.

Francis, Diane. "Not Fair to Lay the Blame for Corruption on Developing Nations." *The Financial Post* (February 8, 1997), 21.

Freeman, Chris, and Luc Soete. *Work for All or Mass Unemployment: Computerised Technical Change into the Twenty-First Century.* London: Pinter, 1994.

Frey, Bruno S. *Not Just for the Money: An Economic Theory of Personal Motivation.* Cheltenham: Edward Elgar Publishing, 1997.

Friesen, T. E. *A History of DW Friesen: A Unique Company*, 1907-1993. Altona, Man.: DW Friesen, 1993.

Gannon, Thomas M., ed. *The Catholic Challenge to the American Economy: Reflections on the U.S. Bishops' Pastoral Letter on Catholic Social Teaching and the U.S. Economy.* New York: Macmillan, 1987.

Gardner, Marilyn. "Finding 'A Lifetime of Work to Do.'" *Edmonton Journal* (May 28, 2000).

"Global Capitalism: Making It Work." *The Economist* (September 12, 1998), 23-24.

"Globalisation: Is It at Risk?" *The Economist* (February 2, 2002), 65-68.

Gooding, Wayne. "The Dilemma of Business Ethics." *The Financial Post Magazine* (December 1998), 10.

_____. "What Do You Want from Your Media?" *The Financial Post Magazine* (October 1997), 10.

Gorky, Maksim. *The Lower Depths, and Other Plays.* New Haven: Yale University Press, 1959.

Goudzwaard, Bob. *Capitalism and Progress: A Diagnosis of Western Society.* Grand Rapids, Mich.: Eerdmans, 1979.

_____. *Economic Stewardship Versus Capitalist Religion.* Toronto: Institute for Christian Studies, 1972.

Goulet, Denis. *Development Ethics: A Guide to Theory and Practice.* New York: Apex, 1995.

Govindarajan, Vijay, and Anil Gupta. "Setting a Course for the New Global Landscape." *The Financial Post* (September 26, 1997), 6-7.

Granberg-Michaelson, Wesley. "Renewing the Whole Creation." *Sojourners* (February-March 1990), 10-14.

Grayling, A. C. Book review of *The Sixth Extinction*, by Richard Leakey and Roger Lewin. *The Financial Post* (March 10, 1996), 25.

"The Great Food Debate." *The Economist* (August 31, 2002), 23-24.

Green, Sara Jean. "U of T Visionary Champion of Ethics." Obituary for Max Clarkson in *The Globe and Mail* (June 17, 1998).

Greider, William. *One World, Ready or Not: The Manic Logic of Global Capitalism*. New York: Simon and Schuster, 1998.

"Growth is Good." *The Economist* (May 27, 2000), 82.

"Guilty as Charged." *The Economist* (October 13, 2001), 68.

Gutiérrez, Gustavo. *On Job: God-Talk and the Suffering of the Innocent*. Maryknoll, N.Y.: Orbis, 1988.

Halteman, James. *The Clashing Worlds of Economics and Faith*. Scottdale, Pa.: Herald Press, 1995.

Harder, James M., et al. "Release the Poor People from the Bondage of Debt: Mennonite Economists Support Jubilee 2000." *The Marketplace* (July-August, 2000), 16-19.

Hawken, Paul, Amory Lovins, and L. Hunter Lovins. *Natural Capitalism: Creating the Next Industrial Revolution*. Boston: Little, Brown, 1999.

"Health Care in Poor Countries." *The Economist* (August 17, 2002), 20-22.

"Healthy Calories." *The Economist* (August 2, 1997), 68-69.

Heilbroner, Robert L. *The Nature and Logic of Capitalism*. New York: W. W. Norton & Company, 1985.

_____. *The Worldly Philosophers: The Lives, Times, and Ideas of the Great Economic Thinkers*, 5th edition. New York: Simon and Schuster, 1980.

Heilbroner, Robert L., and Lester Thurow. *Economics Explained: Everything You Need to Know About How the Economy Works and Where It's Going*. New York: Touchstone, 1998.

"The High Price of Labour Strife." *The Globe and Mail* (July 15, 1998).

"How Many Planets? A Survey of the Global Environment." *The Economist* (July 6, 2002).

"How to Live with Falling Prices." *The Economist* (June 12, 1999), 57-58.

Jegen, Mary Evelyn. "An Encounter with God." *Sojourners* (February-March, 1990), 15-17.

Jerome-Forget, Monique. "Taking a Closer Look at Personal Motivation." *The Financial Post* (August 16, 1997), 23.

Karolyi, Andrew. "Perpetual Motion Machine." *The Financial Post 2000* (November 29, 1997), 4-6.

Keillor, Garrison. *Wobegon Boy.* New York: Viking Penguin, 1997.

Kelly, Marjorie. "Questioning the Purpose of Capitalism." *Business Ethics* (January/February 1996), 13.

Kochan, Tom, and Willis Nordlund. *Reconciling Labor Standards and Economic Goals: An Historical Perspective.* Washington, D.C.: U.S. Department of Labor, Bureau of International Labor Affairs, 1989.

Koontz, Ted. "The Peacekeeper Debate in Perspective." *MCC Peace Office Newsletter* (May-October 1997), 2-5.

Korten, David C. *When Corporations Rule the World.* West Hartford, Conn.: Kumarian, 1995.

Kuitenbrouwer, Peter. "Driven to Distraction." *The Financial Post* (August 9, 1997), W2.

_____. "Filling the World's Basket." *The Financial Post* (October 11, 1997), 9.

Kunde, Diane. "Climbing Corporate Ladder Loses Its Appeal for Some." *The Ottawa Citizen* (June 20, 1998).

Lamey, Andy. "Humanity Seen as a Cancer on Earth." *National Post* (December 2, 1998).

Lees, David. "Food by Design." *The Financial Post Magazine* (October 1998), 24-32.

Leger, Kathryn. "As Subtle as a Blowtorch." *The Financial Post* (August 22-24, 1998), 10.

"A Lemon Law for Software?" *The Economist* (March 16, 2002), 3.

"Lexington: In Praise of the Unspeakable." *The Economist* (July 20, 2002), 28.

Lin, Justin Yifu, and Jeffrey B. Nugent. "Institutions and Economic Development." In J. Behrman and T. N. Srinivasan, eds., *Handbook of Development Economics*, 3:2301-70. Amsterdam: Elsevier Science, 1995.

"A Little Learning." *The Economist* (December 13, 1997), 72.

Loesch, Juli. "Human Work for Human Beings." *The Other Side* (August 1979), 46-48.

Loy, David R. "The Religion of the Market." *Journal of American Academy of Religion* 65, no. 2 (summer 1997), 275-90.

Lutz, Charles P., ed. *God, Goods, and the Common Good: Eleven Perspectives on Economic Justice in Dialog with the Roman Catholic Bishops' Pastoral Letter.* Minneapolis: Augsburg, 1987.

MacDonald, Gayle. "Penniless and Proud of It." *The Globe and Mail* (April 15, 2000).

MacInnes, Joseph. "Breaking the Bonds." *Maclean's* (October 5, 1998), 58-59.

"A Man of Flint." *The Economist* (June 20, 1998), 79.

Maxwell, Judith. "Don't Be Seduced by the U.S. Boom." *The Globe and Mail* (August 30, 1999).

McArthur, Keith. "Kraft Boycott Is Urged to Punish Philip Morris." *The Globe and Mail* (May 30, 2000).

McCallum, John. "New Managers, Same Old Skills." *The Financial Post 2000* (November 22, 1997), 4-6.

McCarthy, Shawn. "Federal Government Remains Relevant, Finance Minister Says." *The Globe and Mail* (August 7, 1998).

McCarthy, Shawn, and Simon Tuck. "Ottawa to Fund Development of IBM's E-Commerce Software." *The Globe and Mail* (July 6, 1999).

McKay, Shona. "The Age of Anxiety." *The Financial Post Magazine* (January 1999), 16-22.

McKenna, Barrie. "More Firms Flock to Mexico." *The Globe and Mail* (July 8, 1998).

McKinnon, Ian. "Agricultural Commodity Prices Fall Off a Cliff." *The Financial Post* (December 12, 1998), C1.

Meeks, M. Douglas. *God the Economist: The Doctrine of God and Political Economy.* Minneapolis: Fortress, 1989.

Merriam-Webster Dictionary of English Usage. In *Infopedia* 2.0. CD-ROM for Windows (Softkey Multimedia, 1996).

Merriam-Webster Dictionary of Quotations. In *Infopedia* 2.0. CD-ROM for Windows (Softkey Multimedia, 1996).

Millman, Joel. "Mexico's Car Production Gaining Speed." *The Globe and Mail* (June 30, 1998).

"Money to Burn?" *The Economist* (December 6, 1997), 86.

"Monkey Business." *The Economist* (December 13, 1997), 57.

Nairne, Doug. "Credit Card Busiest Day." *Winnipeg Free Press* (December 24, 1997).

National Conference of Catholic Bishops. *Economic Justice for All: Pastoral Letter on Catholic Social Teaching and the U.S. Economy.* Washington, D.C.: National Conference of Catholic Bishops, 1986.

"Nestlé: A Dedicated Enemy of Fashion." *The Economist* (August 31, 2002), 47-48.

"The New Danger." *The Economist* (February 20, 1999), 15-16.

Nikiforuk, Andrew. "Putting a Price Tag on the Planet." *Canadian Business* (August 1997), 83.

_____. "When Water Kills." *Maclean's* (June 12, 2000), 18-21.

"Out of Sight, Out of Mind." *The Economist* (May 20, 2000), 27-29.

Parkinson, Roger. "Notes from the Publisher." *The Globe and Mail* (June 22, 1998).

Pfaff, William. "Economic Development." *The New Yorker* (December 25, 1978), 44-47.

Pfanner, Eric. "France's Short Work Week a Mixed Blessing." *International Herald Tribune* (June 15, 2002).

Podhoretz, Norman. "The New Defenders of Capitalism." *Ethics and Public Policy Reprint*, 96-106. Ethics and Public Policy Center, Washington, D.C., 1981.

Powell, Scott. "Did Foster Miss the Point on Justice?" *The Financial Post* (November 3, 1998), C7.

Power, Thomas Michael. *Lost Landscapes and Failed Economies: The Search for a Value of Place.* Washington, D.C.: Island Press, 1996.

Randall, Margaret. *The Price You Pay: The Hidden Cost of Women's Relationship to Money.* London: Routledge, 1996.

Reich, Robert. *The Work of Nations: Preparing Ourselves for Twenty-First-Century Capitalism.* New York: Knopf, 1991.

Rempel, Henry. "Changes in the Bankruptcy Law." *Mennonite Reporter* (December 21, 1987), 7.

_____. "The 'Cost' of Ethical Investments." *Mennonite Reporter* (September 28, 1987), 7.

_____. "The Fraser Institute on Poverty." *Mennonite Reporter* (June 11, 1984), 7.

_____. "God's Message in an Economic Depression." *Mennonite Reporter* (August 8, 1983), 7.

_____. "The Importance of Peace Ministries." *Mennonite Reporter* (July 29, 1985), 8.

_____. "Justice Is More Than Individual Action." *Mennonite Reporter* (October 3, 1983), 7.

_____. "Our Ministry with Poor People Needs Scrutiny." *Mennonite Reporter* (December 5, 1988), 7.

_____. "Property and Freedom." *Mennonite Reporter* (August 23, 1982), 7.

_____. "A Proposed Security Program." *Mennonite Reporter* (March 17, 1986), 7.

_____. "The Secret of Japan's Success." *Mennonite Reporter* (June 13, 1983), 7.

_____. "When Development Becomes a Mirage." *Mennonite Reporter* (December 23, 1985), 7.

_____. "World Debt Affects Poor." *Mennonite Reporter* (November 12, 1984), 7.

_____. "The World Debt Problem." *Mennonite Reporter* (April 18, 1983), 11.

Renzetti, Elizabeth. "Little Girls: Signed, Sealed, Delivered to the Label Marketers." *The Globe and Mail* (September 9, 1999).

Rifkin, Jeremy. *The End of Work: The Decline of the Global Labor Force and the Dawn of the Post-Market Era.* New York: G. P. Putnam's Sons, 1995.

Rioux, Jean-Francois, and Robin Hay. "Development, Peace, and Security: The Possibilities and Limits of Convergence." *Development Express* 6 (1996), 1-8.

"The Road to Riches." *The Economist* (December 31, 1999), 10-12.

"The Road to 2050: A Survey of the New Geopolitics." *The Economist* (July 31, 1999).

Rosenzweig, Philip. "How Should Multinationals Set Global Workplace Standards?" *The Financial Post: Mastering Global Business* (November 21, 1997), 8, 18.

Saro-Wiwa, Ken. "The True Prison." In *The Financial Post* (November 8, 1997), 28.

Sauder, Allan. "When Business Helps the Poor." *The Marketplace* (November-December 1998), 6-8.

Saul, John Ralston. *Baraka*. Toronto: Vintage Canada, 1983.

Schlabach, Gerald W. *And Who Is My Neighbor? Poverty Privilege, and the Gospel of Christ*. Scottdale, Pa.: Herald Press, 1990.

Schor, Juliet B. *The Overworked American: The Unexpected Decline of Leisure*. New York: Basic Books, 1991.

Schrock-Shenk, David, ed. *Basic Trek: Venture into a World of Enough*. Scottdale, Pa.: Herald Press, 2002.

Scoffield, Heather. "Ottawa to Fight for Global Biotech Rules." *The Globe and Mail* (August 5, 1999).

Segal, Hugh. "The Issue Is Not Whether Wealth Is Good or Evil, but How It's Used." *The Financial Post* (September 6, 1997), 30.

Sen, Amartya. *Inequality Reexamined*. Oxford: Clarendon, 1992.

"Sense of Community Feared Lost in Canada." *Winnipeg Free Press* (December 10, 1997).

Silcoff, Sean. "Black Gold." *Canadian Business* (October 30, 1998), 94-99.

Simons, Robert G. *Competing Gospels: Public Theology and Economic Theory*. Alexandria, N.S.W.: E. J. Dwyer, 1995.

Sinclair, Gordon, Jr. "Manitoba's South in Full Bloom." *The Winnipeg Free Press* (March 30, 1997).

_____. "Secret to Success Lies in Greatness." *The Winnipeg Free Press* (April 2, 1997).

Smith, Adam. *An Inquiry into the Nature and Causes of the Wealth of Nations*. New York: The Modern Library, 1937.

Soros, George. *The Crisis of Global Capitalism: Open Society Endangered*. New York: Public Affairs, 1998.

Soule, George. *Ideas of the Great Economists*. New York: Mentor Books. 1965.

"The Spiciest Futures of All." *The Economist* (September 20, 1997), 83.

"Staked Out." *The Economist*, (May 15, 1999), 9.

Steinberg, Shawna. "Have Allowance Will Transform Economy." *Canadian Business* (March 13, 1998), 59-71.

"Sunset for the Oil Business?" *The Economist* (November 3, 2001), 81-82.

Suzuki, David. *The Sacred Balance: Rediscovering Our Place in Nature*. Vancouver: GreyStone Books, 2002.

"Sweatshop Wars." *The Economist* (February 27, 1999), 62-63.

Taber, Jane. "Natives Face Upstream Battle over Salmon Rights." *The Ottawa Citizen* (November 28, 1998).

"A Taste of Adventure." *The Economist* (December 19, 1998): 51-55.

Taylor, Scott. "Bravo to Another Really Big Show." *Winnipeg Free Press* (January 26, 1998).

Thiessen, Janis. "'Working with Friesens': Labour Within a Mennonite Business, 1933-1995." Mimeo. University of Manitoba, Winnipeg, 1995.

Thurow, Roger, and Scott Kilman. "How a Cotton Glut Bred by U.S. Hurts Poor African Tillers." *The Asian Wall Street Journal* (June 27, 2002).

Tieleman, Bill. "Executive Pay Backlash." *The Financial Post* (January 4, 1999), C4.

"Unfinished Battle." *The Economist* (April 10, 1999), 77.

United Nations Development Programme. *Human Development Report 1996*. New York: Oxford University Press, 1996.

United Nations Research Institute for Social Development. "Globalization and Citizenship." *UNRISD News* 15 (autumn 1996-winter 1997), 1-3.

Van Kooten, G. Cornelis. *Land Resource Economics and Sustainable Development: Economic Policies and the Common Good*. Vancouver: UBC Press, 1993.

Vincent, Mark. *A Christian View of Money: Celebrating God's Generosity*. Scottdale, Pa.: Herald Press, 1997.

Vogt, Roy. *Whose Property? The Deepening Conflict Between Private Property and Democracy in Canada*. Toronto: University of Toronto Press, 1999.

Wachtel, Paul L. *The Poverty of Affluence*. Philadelphia: New Society Publishers, 1989.

Wade, Robert. "Winners and Losers." *The Economist* (April 28, 2001), 72-74.

"The Wages of War." *The Economist* (September 22, 2001), 62.

Wallace, Laura. "Paris Seminar Addresses African Adjustment to the Challenges of Globalization." *IMF Survey* (May 25, 1998), 164-65.

Weidman, Eva. "Consuming Easy If We Don't Think." *Winnipeg Free Press* (January 25, 1998).

Welford, Richard. "Corporate Environmental Management Means Business as Usual." *UNRISD News* 17 (autumn-winter 1997), 5-6.

"What If NAFTA Ruled the Waves?" *The Globe and Mail* (August 4, 1998).

"Where the Furbies Come From." *The Economist* (December 19, 1998): 95-96.

"Who's Wearing the Trousers?" *The Economist* (September 8, 2001), 26-28.

Willson, John M. "Corporate Responsibility in the Global Marketplace." *The North-South Institute Newsletter* 2, no. 2 (1998), 5-6.

Wilson, Rodney. *Economics, Ethics, and Religion: Jewish, Christian, and Muslim Economic Thought*. New York: New York University Press, 1997.

Wolterstorff, Nicholas. "Has the Cloak Become a Cage? Charity, Justice, and Economic Activity." In Robert Wuthnow, ed., *Rethinking Materialism: Perspectives on the Spiritual Dimension of Economic Behavior*, 145-68. Grand Rapids, Mich.: Eerdmans, 1995.

Wood, Chris. "Our Dying Seas." *Maclean's* (October 5, 1998), 50-55.

World Bank. *World Development Report 1997: The State in a Changing World*. New York: Oxford University Press, 1997.

Wuthnow, Robert, ed. *Rethinking Materialism: Perspectives on the Spiritual Dimension of Economic Behavior*. Grand Rapids, Mich.: Eerdmans, 1995.

Zussman, David. "Government's New Style." *The Financial Post 2000* (October 18, 1997), 4-6.

Zweig, Michael, ed. *Religion and Economic Justice.* Philadelphia: Temple University Press, 1991.

About the Author

Henry Rempel, a Senior Scholar in the Department of Economics at the University of Manitoba, served as a professor in that department for over three decades. In addition to teaching economic development, he has led more than twenty missions abroad to evaluate projects for various agencies, including Canadian International Development Agency (CIDA), Mennonite Economic Development Associates (MEDA), and Mennonite Central Committee (MCC).

Community 197   Intro p 202, 204,

  Genin 59
    Ricardo - 210,
Wants/ needs 63 , 70, 186, 200, 2

7 sacred values (65), (141)
                              ↑
7 to choose (78)

Tort (78)

progress 92

growth

solidarity 100

Walmart (100) ubiquitous

unions 116

work (127) - sacred
wars 257.
irreversibility (143), (144), (146)

new theology (150)(84) - evil

Econ dysfunction (153) - church

Sabbath 154,

Public services (157), (161)

Subsidies 160,

1964 - Smoking + Corp - no res. to country
T Ketchum (181) - no society
poverty 192, 201,
fairness 192, 203 , 261, 262,
Something more than $ 193 - society
violence + crime 193, 271, 273
China 148
Corporations (209)(279), - profits
                 dominate
I M F v. poor countries 244,
Socialism - 247,

                    gods growth
                    neutralizes products